LISTEN TO THE SILENCES:

MEXICAN AMERICAN INTERACTION IN THE COMPOSITION CLASSROOM AND COMMUNITY

SECOND LANGUAGE LEARNING SERIES

A Monograph Series Dedicated to Studies in Acquisition and Principled Language Instruction

Robert J. Di Pietro, editor

The Catalan Immersion Program: A European Point of View, Joseph Maria Artigal

A Developmental Psycholinguistic Approach to Second Language Teaching, Traute Taeschner

Reading Development in a Second Language: Theoretical, Empirical, and Classroom Perspectives, Elizabeth B. Bernhardt

Vygotskian Approaches to Second Language Research, James P. Lantolf and Gabriela Appel, editors

Bilingualism and Testing: A Special Case of Bias Guadalupe Valdez and Richard Figueroa

Elizabeth B. Bernhardt, editor

Listen to the Silences: Mexican American Interaction in the Composition Classroom and Community, Kay M. Losey

Input Processing and Grammar Instruction in Second Language Acquisition, Bill VanPatten

LISTEN TO THE SILENCES:

MEXICAN AMERICAN INTERACTION IN THE COMPOSITION CLASSROOM AND COMMUNITY

Kay M. Losey
The University of North Carolina
at Chapel Hill

 Ablex Publishing Corporation
Norwood, New Jersey

The Title *Listen to the Silences* was taken from: A. Rich (1979) *On Lies, Secrets, and Silence: Selected Prose 1966–1978.* New York: W.W. Norton & Co.

Printed in the United States of America

Library of Congress Cataloging-in-Publication Data

Losey, Kay M.
   Listen to the silences: Mexican American interaction in the composition classroom and community/Kay M. Losey
      p. cm.
   Includes bibliographical references   (p.) and index.
   ISBN 1-56750-268-7 (cloth).—ISBN 1-56750-269-5 (paper)
   1. Mexican Americans--Education (Higher)—Social aspects—
California—Case studies. 2. English language—Composition and
exercises—Study and teaching (Higher)—Social aspects-
California—Case studies. 3. Second language acquisition—
California—Case studies. 4. Teacher-student relationships—
California—Case studies. 5. Mexican American college students—
California—Psychology--Case studies. I. Title.
LC2683.6.L67 1996
371.97'6872073—dc20   96-13155
                                                           CIP

Ablex Publishing Corporation
355 Chestnut Street
Norwood, New Jersey 07648

To Hermann and Angelika.

CONTENTS

SERIES EDITOR'S PREFACE

Kay Losey's book, *Listen to the Silences,* contributes important perspectives to the *Second Language Learning Series.* The Losey book reminds readers of complex social dimensions involved in using language. Losey chronicles the lives of Mexican American students as they use literacy in English in instructed settings and in community settings. The book broadens our perspectives on language learning: Losey's subjects came to their classroom with an array of linguistic knowledge; the enormous social pressure both to use and not use that knowledge is an unforgettable theme in the book. I welcome the Losey work to *Second Language Learning.*

—Elizabeth B. Bernhardt
Series Editor

AUTHOR'S PREFACE

The impetus for this work occurred nearly 15 years ago when I was a high school teacher in the East Los Angeles area. Among other duties, I taught writing to a group of mostly bilingual Mexican American students who had failed the district writing proficiency exam. At that point, I joined the ranks of those interested in understanding why overwhelming numbers of such students are failing school, particularly their composition courses, and how educators can prevent this failure.

Researchers in composition and second language pedagogy are coming to recognize that learning occurs through social interaction. To understand the learning process we must study the interaction through which it occurs. With that assumption in mind, I began a two-year classroom ethnography of bilingual Mexican American and monolingual Anglo American students and their monolingual Anglo American teacher in a community college basic writing course. I was interested in learning not only about how communication between Anglo Americans and Mexican Americans occurred in the classroom but also about how it occurred in the community and how it affected the success or failure of these students. The town of Appleton, in which the course was offered and from which most students came, is typical of many small, agriculturally based communities in California. Mexican Americans are the majority there but lack political clout. This historical fact has led to a silencing of Mexican Americans in the community not only politically but also economically, educationally, culturally, and linguistically (see Chapter 3). Because schools are reflective of the larger communities that sponsor them, understanding the sociology of the community was important for interpreting the relationships between the students and teacher in the classroom. Making that "macro–micro" connection was one goal of my study (see Chapter 2).

The structure and content of class discussions and essay assignments also contributed to a silencing of Mexican Americans (Chapters 5 and 6). Patterns of silencing varied, however, depending on the type of interaction (written or oral), the structure of interaction (whole class or tutorial), the gender of the participants, the participants' language proficiency, and the cultural expectations regarding participants' interactions. Mexican American women were generally silenced in whole class discussions, whereas Mexican American men were comparatively "silent" in written interaction. Although there has been much research on how Mexican Americans communicate in the classroom, none of it takes into account gender differences. But gender proved to be important for understanding communication patterns in this classroom, a finding that should lead researchers to reconsider previous studies on the subject. The content of writing assignments and class discussions also made a difference in students' responses. Tasks that did not allow for students to develop their "key themes" or personal interests vis-à-vis the Mexican American community (see Chapter 4) led to silence on the part of both men and women. Social interaction in the classroom had a significant impact on students' progress in college. The teacher based her recommendations concerning which students should proceed to the next level of English on categories determined by students' interaction with her.

The silence that occurred in this classroom should not be interpreted as resistance, although it is fashionable to do so today. The students who were silenced in this classroom *wanted* to interact, and they *tried* to interact. Instead of resisting in the classroom, they were making great sacrifices to gain an education that would allow them to resist Anglo Americans at another level—in the community. But the ongoing silencing in Appleton fed the silencing of Mexican Americans in the classroom. Silencing seemed normal to all participants.

The theoretical perspective and research skills that I brought to this project were developed and refined while I was still a student in the Graduate School of Education at the University of California at Berkeley. I am particularly indebted to my professors, Anne Haas Dyson, Guadalupe Valdés, John U. Ogbu, Glynda Hull, and Sarah Warshauer Freedman. Thanks also to Erika Lindemann, my colleague at the University of North Carolina at Chapel Hill; Elizabeth Bernhardt of Stanford University who is also Series Editor; and Miguel López, my good friend at the University of California at Berkeley, for suggested revisions. Kris Yohe at UNC–CH helped prepare the final manuscript, and Anne Trowbridge at Ablex gave much help during production. A special thank you to my husband, Hermann Kurthen, for his interest in and enthusiasm for my work. In addition, Gordon Fraser, Guillermina Núñez, and Rosa Sánchez R. gave encouragement and support throughout the project.

Without the teacher and the students of English 10 at the Appleton Center, this book would not have been possible. The teacher, Carol, helped me enter the classroom community with ease and gave generously of her time and resources throughout the project. The students, particularly Amado, Federico, Isaura, Juanita, and Mónica, shared their lives and their sometimes painful experiences out of a desire to help future students like themselves. I hope this book will do just that.

—K.M.L.
Durham, NC, September 5, 1996

1

CULTURAL DIFFERENCE, CLASSROOM INTERACTION, AND SILENCE

Talking, a continued dialogue between teachers and students, is an intercultural classroom at its best, while silence is indicative of the most dysfunctional form, which excludes cultural differences.
—Dumont, 1972, p. 348

Silence is the prevailing theme of this book—the silence of Mexican Americans in the classroom and the silence of the Mexican American community.[1] The focus of this discussion is a composition course taught in a community college outreach program and the rural California town in which the outreach program was located. As a point of departure, I present two opposing comments on silence and voice directly from the classroom in question. The first comment was made by a student in the composition course, an 18-year-old native of Mexico who had lived in the United States since she was one year old. Her first language was Spanish.

> Mónica: You know, sometimes I feel like speaking out. Because, you know, I know things that I can say, but then I'm all like, nahh, they don't want to hear it (laughs) . . . 'cause you know, that was one of my fears, speaking out in classes. I've always been bad, until I know the whole class, then I feel free, a little. You know, I don't say anything.

Mónica believed that she ought to talk in class. She considered herself "bad" because she didn't. She wanted to talk, but

---

[1] See pages 6–7 for a discussion of my use of the term "Mexican American."

felt her ideas unworthy of attention from the teacher and her peers. However, Mónica's Anglo American, monolingual English college composition instructor felt differently about silence in the classroom:

> Carol: It's one thing for a student not to speak, it's another for them to be tuned out, or not to care, or to feel it's not relevant. . . . I mean you, you can read so much on their faces. . . . There are the folks who never speak but you know are there. . . . Sometimes when people don't speak it worries me, and sometimes it doesn't worry me at all, just 'cause, you know that they don't, they're among those people who don't speak in class, and they're shy for whatever reason.

Mónica's teacher, Carol, didn't feel it was important for Mónica or other students in her class to talk. She worried about students who didn't talk only if they were obviously inattentive. These quotations reveal differing perspectives on the importance of talk—and silence—in the classroom, perspectives that play an important role in the degree to which students, particularly bilingual students of color, may have opportunities to learn and succeed in the classroom community. These differing perspectives also provide a glimpse into the nature of the higher education experience for Mexican Americans, an experience that has been virtually unexplored from the point of view of the participants.

I wrote this book in response to the lack of information about how adult Mexican American students and their teachers negotiate teaching and learning in a basic writing course. In it I describe the classroom interaction of Mexican American college students such as Mónica in an effort to better understand their academic success or failure. A variety of types of silence characterized the classroom interaction I observed. In this book I explore numerous factors that contributed to the silence. I reveal how the experiences that students like Mónica have had in their communities and educational systems affect their interaction in the classroom. I also show how teachers unwittingly perpetuate silence in the classroom. Mónica's silence was not simply "shyness" without roots. Her teacher may have thought so, and Mónica herself may have come to believe that, but the fact is she lived in a community, attended schools, and was a student in classes such as this one that created a context that accepted and encouraged silent Mexican Americans.

Mónica's community, like many across California and the country, has a striking history of silencing its ethnic minorities—literally and metaphorically. In Mónica's town of Appleton, Mexican Americans have been silenced for hundreds of years on a variety of fronts—political, economic, cultural, and ethnic. They have been denied the right to vote and to political representation, to their property and to fair wages, to celebrate traditional holidays, and to live free of prejudice and bigotry. The teacher, Carol, and her students have spent nearly 20 years in this climate. Living in a community that silences Mexican Americans at every opportunity, and has for generations, creates a context in which the silence of Mexican Americans seems normal—to both Anglo Americans and many Mexican Americans.

In this same community, schools have systematically denied Mexican Americans access to an equal education. Through segregation and severe limitations on bilingual education, students have been denied the opportunity to develop their voices. Moreover, from grade school through community college, Mexican American students interact with teachers and counselors who underestimate their abilities and discourage them from pursuing their aspirations. Like the other factors in the community, these occurrences have been going on for generations and have come to seem normal for many in the community.

Mónica's experience in Carol's class is not unique—either unto herself or among her classmates. Mónica had been silent and had not been expected to talk in other classes before this one, and she probably would have similar experiences again. The same is true of many of her Mexican American classmates. In the classroom, at least the classroom I observed, Mexican American students find interactive patterns established by the teacher and common to classrooms in the United States that interfere with their ability and willingness to express themselves. The structure of interaction around course assignments and whole class discussions limits when Mexican American students can interact so as to effectively silence them. The content of these interactions also affects how students respond. Although they have plenty to say, they are given few opportunities to offer opinions on topics of interest or importance to them. Such constraints lead to silent students.

Many teachers with students like Mónica have little if any understanding of what causes student silence in the classroom. Or, if they do, they hold fast to one of the common explanations of why Mexican Americans are silent in the classroom—because of cultural differences, because of language differences, because of unequal educational experiences, or because of resistance to mainstream cultural hegemony. Others might not think much about the silence at all. To them it is so common and widespread among Mexican Americans that it seems normal. Or teachers may be blind to ethnic/cultural/language differences altogether and consider silence a personal attribute—shyness.

Given the community, educational, and classroom situations that Mexican Americans such as Mónica face daily, it is no surprise that numerous studies document the failure of U.S. schools successfully to educate Mexican Americans, including those at the college level (Brown, Rosen, Hill, & Olivas, 1980; Carter & Segura, 1979; Orum, 1986). When compared to Anglo Americans', Mexican American high school completion, college matriculation, and college retention (or persistence, as it is euphemistically called) is particularly revealing of this failure. In 1990, 80% of whites aged 25 years and older had completed four or more years of college whereas only 44% of Chicanos[2] of the same age had (Aguirre & Martinez, 1993). That year the high school completion rate for Hispanics was only 54.5% but for whites it was 81% (Carter & Wilson, 1993), and the annual high school dropout rate for Hispanics was roughly twice that for whites: 8.4% vs. 4.4% (*National Dropout Statistics*, 1992). Of those few Hispanic students who graduated from high school in 1990, only 53% enrolled in a two- or four-year college the following year, whereas 62% of white high school graduates did (*The Condition of Education*, 1992). Most of the Hispanics who did go to college enrolled at two-year community or junior colleges, where their progress has been limited. In the fall of 1991, 60% of Hispanic undergraduates attended two-year colleges, but only 30% of white undergraduates were at such schools (Aguirre & Martinez, 1993). Only 16.6% of the Hispanic students entering a two-year college in 1989–1990 school year received an AA degree after two years (*Digest of Education Statistics, 1994*, 1994). Of those Hispanic students with an AA, only 15.7% transferred to four-year institutions (Aguirre & Martinez, 1993). In fall, 1991, Hispanics were just 4.4% of enrollments at four-year colleges and universities nationally, but 9.9% of the population (Aguirre & Martinez, 1993). Their progress at four-year institutions has been limited, too. In 1986, Hispanics were 3.6% of the undergraduate population but earned only 2.7% of the BAs. At that time, 56% of white students at NCAA Division I institutions graduated within six years but only 41% of Hispanic students did (Aguirre & Martinez, 1993). Within group comparisons reveal that Mexican American women are the most underrepresented group in higher education in the country. And Mexican American women have a non-completion rate twice that of Mexican American men (Chacón, Cohen, Camarena, Gonzalez & Strover, 1982; Chacón, Cohen, & Strover, 1986).

---

[2] When discussing the works of others, I will use the ethnic and racial terms those authors have used in their research.

Mexican American students who *do* matriculate at institutions of higher education arc over-represented in remedial or basic English courses (Professional Development Program, 1990) and underrepresented in college transfer-level English (Dixon, 1988). Some teachers believe that the reason for the poor retention rate of underrepresented and minority students is "the demand placed on students to write well" (Parmeter, 1990, p. 3). Furthermore, it has been argued that thc basic writing program of at least one prestigious university is a form of gatekeeping or tracking (Hull & Greenleaf, 1990). A publication of the Puente Project, a program designed to improve the transfer rate of Mexican American students through intensive composition instruction, counseling, and mentoring, states that "most Mexican American students drop out of . . . remedial [writing] classes" (Galaviz & McGrath, unpublished manuscript, p. 5). Basic writing courses are a critical juncture in the academic careers of Mexican American college students and therefore important for understanding their academic progress or lack thereof.

The "leakage" of Mexican American students from the "educational pipeline" (de los Santos, 1984, p. 68) is undoubtedly owing in some measure to the unique social, historical, economic, and educational situation of Mexican Americans that has led to a "caste-like" (Ogbu, 1978, p. 26), or "dual-caste" system (Carter & Segura, 1979, p. 15) that continues in many ways today. The failure of schools to educate Mexican American students successfully provides a low-wage labor force necessary for agriculture and other labor-intensive industries. Little is known, however, about how this "leakage" occurs for Mexican American students at the college level.

The classroom interaction between Mexican American adult students, such as Mónica, and their college instructors remains virtually unexamined as a possible source of "leakage." Success and failure are created, in part, in face-to-face interaction during everyday encounters. The nature of interaction in the classroom and the various meanings and understandings that the participants bring to and take from these experiences can have a significant impact on success or failure in school (for reviews of research supporting this position see Cazden, 1988; Mehan, 1979). In other words, "institutional machinery is embedded in social interaction" (Cicourel & Mehan, 1985, p. 20).

In order to examine the role of classroom interaction in the success and failure of Mexican American students, I conducted an analysis of the content and structure of classroom and tutorial interaction that considers a variety of factors that may influence interaction. In this book I: a) describe the various contexts that influence the classroom interaction I observed, including the social, political, and educational situation in which the outreach program is situated; b) describe the educational and social perspectives of the teacher and students that influenced interaction; c) document the interaction in this basic writing classroom, particularly as it varied in structure and content according to differences in ethnicity, gender, and relative authority of the participants; d) document interactions revealing difficulties resulting from languages differences; and e) analyze from the points of view of the participants the processes involved in creating and perpetuating these interactional variations.

This book provides teachers, tutors, administrators, and counselors insight into how adult Mexican American students and their teachers interact, the meanings and purposes of such interaction from the perspectives of both groups, and the success or failure of their interactions. It suggests methods for enhancing the educational experiences of Mexican American students in order to improve their overall success in U.S. schools.

At this point, I would like to discuss my use of the term "Mexican American" to describe in general terms a group whose diversity must be acknowledged and considered. Differences exist within the Mexican American population on the basis of generation (in the United States), nativity (United States or Mexico), residency (urban or rural), occupation, income, education, and language choice (Sánchez, 1983). Some have lived in the United States all of their lives (as have generations before them); others may be immigrants from Mexico. Some come from working class, even migrant families; others are from well-to-do, middle-, and upper middle-class backgrounds.

The language of the home may be Spanish, English, yet another language, or a combination of languages. Some speak English or Spanish in ways that may be considered by others to be nonstandard, either for phonological, syntactical, or lexical reasons. In addition, if two languages are used, it is likely that codeswitching occurs in certain contexts. Some speak Spanish before learning English; some do not speak Spanish at all; others learn the two languages more or less simultaneously. Some are literate in Spanish, some are not; some have attended school in the United States only, others have gone to school in Mexico as well (see Valdés, 1988, for further discussion of these differences).

While some consider themselves Mexican American, others prefer to call themselves Chicano, Latino, *mexicano*, of Mexican descent, Hispanic, or of Spanish descent. Each of these labels suggests a significant difference in how Mexican Americans define themselves and how they wish to be perceived, both by other Mexican Americans and by Anglo Americans, as well. The terms carry not only denotative meanings, such as number of generations in the United States, but also connotations about the social and political orientations of the bearers.

The diversity that exists among the people commonly called "Mexican American" cannot be underestimated. As I mentioned earlier, when describing the research of others, I will use the terms used by the researchers to describe the group or groups studied in an attempt to maintain the integrity of the research findings, although these terms may be less specific than desired. Elsewhere, I will use the term "Mexican American" to refer to persons of Mexican descent living in the United States and those whose ancestors lived in the northern Mexican territories prior to 1848. I have chosen this term largely because of its descriptive nature and relatively apolitical connotation. For similar reasons, I have chosen the term "Anglo American" to denote non-Hispanic whites from the United States.

LANGUAGE LEARNING, SOCIALIZATION, AND CLASSROOM INTERACTION

In this section I explore how the social nature of language learning may lead to variations in interaction across cultural groups, particularly Mexican Americans and women, that ultimately affect school achievement. I also consider the importance of larger social, historical, educational, and linguistic factors in understanding the interaction in the classroom and the role of interaction in the success and failure of Mexican American students. The study of classroom interaction and its role in the success or failure of students assumes that all learning is a fundamentally social process, the result of interaction between two or more individuals. Vygotsky notes that "human learning presupposes a specific social nature" (1978, p. 88). The social process by which learning occurs creates a bridge that spans the learner's "zone of proximal development," such that what one is unable to accomplish alone can be achieved successfully with a more capable peer or adult. Adults, too, learn through social interaction. (See Elsasser & John-Steiner, 1977; Freire, 1970; Lave, 1988; and Wertsch, Minick, & Arns, 1985, for research on the social nature of adult learning.) Because social interaction is the basis for learning, "language poses multiple problems for education . . . it is both curriculum content and learning environment, both the object of knowledge and a medium through which other knowledge is acquired" (Cazden, 1973, p. 137). Through social interaction we humans, to a greater or lesser degree reshape and reinterpret our existing pictures of the world. Some new experiences, some information and ideas, fit comfortably into our view of the world; others require us in a greater or lesser degree to redraw the picture in order to take full account of them. (Barnes, 1990, p. 47)

Likewise, second language learning also occurs through social interaction. McLaughlin (1985) concludes that students have the best chance to learn a second language when they "(a) receive a great deal of oral language input (adjusted to their abilities) from staff and native English-speaking peers, and (b) have an opportunity to use the language in meaningful contexts where they receive feedback from native speakers" (p.162). Similarly, Fillmore (1982) finds "a major problem for language learners involves getting enough exposure to the new language, and getting enough practice speaking it with people who know the language well enough to help them in their efforts to learn" (p. 284). Research and theory on adult second language acquisition and learning suggests that adults, too, need interaction with native speakers to successfully acquire a second language (e.g., Krashen, 1976). In fact, one reason adults are considered notoriously poor second language learners may be a lack of interest or opportunity to interact with native speakers relative to school-age learners (Schumann, 1978).

Because learning occurs through language, success requires more than learning just the content of a particular message; it also involves learning the norms and values of the "speech community" in which it is delivered (Hymes, 1972, p. 54). This process includes learning interaction patterns that differ with varying aspects of a "speech event" (Hymes, 1972, p. 56). Usually these events are comprised of initiations and responses in which initiators ask real questions to which they have no answer but to which respondents do. An exception to this pattern is interaction in the classroom, a point I will discuss in greater detail shortly. The exact "participant structure" of exchanges in a speech event or the "who will talk and when they will talk" (Philips, 1972/1985, p. 373) varies depending on a multitude of factors (Sacks, Schegloff, & Jefferson, 1974).

To interpret the meaning of a speech event one must be a member of, or at least well-acquainted with, the norms and values of the particular linguistic culture of the speaker or his or her speech community. The factors that influence the norms of a particular event include not only the speech community in which it occurs but also the relationships between the speech communities represented by those present. Language attitudes, power, and status are important considerations when attempting to understand the choices made in any speech situation.

An individual may have the ability to communicate effectively in a number of different speech communities as a result of knowledge and experience with the cultural and linguistic norms of these communities. In fact, most individuals are fully functional in several speech communities. For example, students function (to one extent or another) in the speech communities of the school and of the home. In addition, they most assuredly function in several other speech communities, such as those of their peer groups and other formal or informal community and neighborhood organizations. In any given situation the speakers may or may not be members of the same speech community, and some may not be initiated into the subtle rules of language use necessary for understanding a particular event or situation.

Goodenough (1971) notes, "Just as individuals can be multilingual, they can also be multicultural. . . . A person must choose from the several cultures in his repertory the one he regards as most suitable for his purposes on any given occasion" (p. 37). Therefore, according to Goodenough, when we examine the role of culture in social interaction, we are examining the "operating culture" of an individual, "the particular system of standards . . . that he uses to interpret the behavior of others or that guide(s) his own behavior on a given occasion" (p. 41). This system derives from "his experience of their actions and admonitions" (p. 36).

Because more than one language is involved, the norms and values for language use in bilingual communities, such as most Mexican American communities, may seem especially distant from those of monolingual speech communities, leading to increased social distance between these speech communities. Relationships between and attitudes within speech communities become particularly important because membership in various speech communities is a social reality for most bilinguals (as it is for monolinguals) and the language attitudes of both the speaker and listener can influence when and how languages are used. Not only culturally, then, but also linguistically, the relationship is more complex for learners who are bilingual. Linguistic differences compound the challenge (Cummins, 1986; Skutnabb-Kangas, 1981).

Because important social and cognitive knowledge is taught and learned through social interaction, the focus of this classroom research includes more than just the individual student, but also the teacher, the other students, and the classroom environment. I use the term "classroom interaction" to denote not only classroom discourse—the talk of teachers and students in formal learning situations—but also other forms of interaction in the classroom, such as the interaction between teachers and students that occurs through written assignments, student essays, and feedback on papers.

Much is already known about the structure of classroom discourse. One typical interaction pattern known and expected in the speech community of the school during instructional speech events is the Initiation–Response–Evaluation (IRE) exchange (see Cazden, 1988; Mehan, 1979). This pattern is found not only in educational settings, but also in the homes of mainstream, middle-class families (Heath, 1983; Wells, 1985). One result of the pervasiveness of the IRE interaction pattern in educational settings is that the teacher is almost always in control of the topic. Students have limited opportunities to ask questions or to add to the interaction. Therefore, students' needs, interests, and concerns may not be expressed or met in such interactional situations. Additionally, IRE interactions allow for little negotiation of meaning. Although language development is fostered "when one has something important to say and other people are interested in hearing it" (Wells, 1981, p. 107), such an environment does not exist in most classrooms where the IRE pattern predominates. Also limited in IRE classrooms are opportunities for non-native speakers (NNS) to use the target language in "meaningful contexts," a requirement for successful second language learning (McLaughlin, 1985, p. 162). Furthermore, NNS's opportunities for output are severely limited in such situations, reducing their chances to practice expressively the target language. Children (Britton, 1990; Dewey, 1916/1944; Moffett, 1981/1988) and adults (Fingeret, 1989; Knowles, 1973/1978; Soifer, Irwin, Crumrine, Honzaki, Simmons & Young, 1990) alike, whether in first language (L1) or second language (L2) learning situations, need to have their educational goals and interests central to the learning experience if it is to be meaningful to them.

The IRE pattern in classroom discourse also tends to favor some students over others, depending on the interaction patterns of the home. Although the IRE sequence, or a facsimile thereof, may be found in the homes of mainstream middle class students, it is by no means a standard form of communication among other groups, including working class Anglo and rural black families (Heath, 1983), Native Americans (Philips, 1972/1985), ethnic Hawaiians (Jordan, 1985), inner city black youths (Labov, 1972), and, particularly important for this book, bilingual Chicanos (Garcia & Carrasco, 1981). These studies from the cultural mismatch perspective have found that interaction differs not only in terms of questioning, but also in the use of authority structures, methods of social control, and use of narrative.

According to the cultural mismatch theory (and the research that is driven by it), the consequences of differences in home–school interaction patterns are significant for student success in the classroom. In short, such differences are major contributors to the educational failure of many minority students. The cultural mismatch argument contends that students who come to school already familiar with the norms and values of school interaction—that is, primarily mainstream, middle class, Anglo American students—have an advantage over those who do not because they are familiar with the discourse appropriate to the classroom and therefore can concentrate on the content of the teacher's lesson. Students who are unaccustomed to the typical structure of classroom interaction must learn this structure as well as the content of the lesson, a double burden. In addition, students who are not familiar with the interaction of the school may have difficulty, at first, responding as the teacher expects. This difficulty may lead to miscommunication and misunderstanding in the classroom, because teachers often react negatively to students' attempts to interact in a style different from the one they expect and prefer. In fact, interaction styles have been found to be a source of teacher expectations (Brophy & Good, 1974; Hull, Rose, Fraser, & Castellano, 1991).

WHAT WE KNOW ABOUT MEXICAN AMERICAN CLASSROOM INTERACTION

Researchers often connect the academic achievement of Mexican American students like Mónica, described earlier in this chapter, to the interaction patterns of the home. Research from the cultural mismatch perspective on interaction in the homes of Mexican American children has found that for some Mexican Americans there are differences in teaching strategies of the home and school. Some Mexican Americans may be more accustomed to modeling as a form of teaching and may have difficulty adjusting to the IRE inquiry and evaluation method found in most mainstream classrooms. Studies of Mexican American mothers and their children have found that there is not one typical mode of instructional interaction among Mexican Americans.

Interaction has been found to vary depending on the mother's educational level. Generally, the more education, the more closely interaction patterns between Mexican American mothers and their children resemble the IRE interaction style found in traditional, mainstream classrooms. The less education, the more likely mothers are to use modeling as their primary teaching strategy (Laosa 1981, 1982). McGowan and Johnson (1984) found that the number of years the mothers had been in school in the United States had a powerful direct and indirect effect on the classroom and achievement test performances of Mexican American children. They also found that those mothers who had attended more school in the United States also preferred to use English with their children, probably contributing to their children's success.

In school, Mexican American students seem to prefer a collective or cooperative classroom structure over an individualistic, competitive one, and they respond better to opportunities to be responsible than to formal authority structures. Responsibility, the research suggests, is expected in many Mexican American homes but is not in keeping with much interaction in the classroom (Delgado-Gaitan, 1987; Gumbiner, Knight, & Kagan, 1981; Le Compte, 1981). García, Flores, Moll, Prieto, and Zucker (unpublished manuscript) found that Mexican American students were successful in classrooms that had students collaborating on almost all assignments with very little individualized work. These classrooms also had very informal, almost "familial" relationships between teachers and students.

Instruction that resembles ordinary conversation has led to better developed language abilities in Mexican American students than teacher-dominated, IRE instruction. Gutierrez (1992) found that students were able to elaborate on their ideas and use their language skills to a greater extent in classrooms that used a "responsive–collaborative" interactive style. She concluded that the IRE format of recitation instruction limited students to short responses to teacher questions, resulting in little opportunity to develop their language skills or their ideas.

Mexican American students whose teachers draw on their students' interests and experiences when designing assignments also have greater success (Ammon, 1985; Moll, 1988). Trueba (1987) and Díaz, Moll, and Mehan (1986) found that lessons based on findings from a community ethnography led to success for Mexican American students in both mainstream and ESL classrooms. They provided challenging assignments on topics of interest to the students. The lessons were also successful because students were allowed to take part in more class discussions and small group assignments and to develop and provide input on their own assignments.

Students may have been more successful in these programs because they are examples of "culturally responsive pedagogy" (Erickson, 1987). By implementing classroom structures such as cooperative learning, responsive–collaborative instruction, and warm interaction that more closely resemble the teaching of many Mexican American homes, these programs use what is known about the Mexican American culture to improve schooling. Similarly, knowledge about the interests and experiences of Mexican American students allowed teachers to create assignments that led to greater success for their students. The success of these programs is additional proof that movement away from a strict IRE teacher–student interactional style is preferred by some Mexican American children.

Theory and research from the cultural mismatch perspective has provided practitioners with important knowledge regarding possible differences between the structure of interaction in some Mexican American homes and in schools, particularly with regard to teaching strategies. In addition, this work generally has heightened teacher awareness and sensitivity to cultural differences. Nevertheless, the notion that interactional differences and difficulties in the classroom can be traced back directly to the patterns used in the home has been questioned by theorists and researchers and needs to be reconsidered, particularly with reference to the communication patterns of adults. Such an explanation seems plausible for young children, who have been the subjects of most of these studies. But even children have larger spheres of influence over their language choice and communicative style than just the home, and these spheres grow ever wider as they mature. Moreover, classroom factors also contribute to interactional differences. These additional factors suggest the need to question exactly what "cultural mismatch" means when the students are Mexican American adults.

Recently, more researchers of classroom interaction have come to recognize that forces other than those considered "culturally determined" may be involved in what is found in the classroom. They acknowledge that classroom interaction is also the medium by which teachers express their expectations for students and where differential treatment of students, particularly on the basis of race, ethnicity, gender, linguistic competence in English, and socioeconomic class may be observed. Teachers may interact differently with students whom they perceive to be high achievers than with those they see as low achievers, leading to what has been called the "self-fulfilling prophecy" (Rosenthal & Jacobson,

1968; Weinstein, 1986). Perceptions of high and low achievement may be directly or indirectly related to social class, language use, ethnicity, and gender (Brophy & Good, 1974; Coates, 1986; Gearing & Epstein, 1982; Stanworth, 1983; Wells, 1985; Wilcox, 1982). Apparently, as McDermott and Gospodinoff (1981) argue, "Differences in communicative code are secondary to the political relations between different groups in the classroom and in the larger community" (p. 212).

Studies of Mexican American classroom interaction that have moved beyond the cultural mismatch model look not only at students and how they may be different from the teacher, but also at teachers and how they interact with students from a variety of ethnicities. These studies have found that, indeed, Mexican American students may be treated differently than other students in a number of subtle and disturbing ways all serving to distance teacher and student and to limit their interaction.

Calling on Mexican American students less frequently than Anglo American students is one obvious difference researchers have found. Teachers have been found to initiate significantly fewer of the following behaviors with Mexican American students than with Anglo students: (1) praising and encouraging, (2) accepting or using students ideas, and (3) questioning. These behaviors are all either positive or, at least, noncriticizing teacher interactions that are withheld from Mexican American students. As a result, Mexican American students do not benefit from positive teacher attention in equal proportions to Anglo students (U.S. Commission on Civil Rights, 1973).

When teachers *do* call on Mexican American students, the interaction is also qualitatively different from that with Anglo American students. Mexican American students are sometimes interrupted by teachers or, if they show any hesitation in answering, humiliated by teachers who ask Anglo American students to "help" their Mexican American classmates (Parsons, 1965). Moreover, teachers may mispronounce the names of Mexican American students, embarrassing students in the process (Ortiz, 1988). Sometimes teachers even ignore their Mexican American pupils by "forgetting" to call on them when everyone else is given a chance to read aloud or by failing to include them in groups or teams. Teachers have also been found to avoid eye contact, physical closeness, and other types of interaction with their Mexican American students (Ortiz, 1988; Parsons, 1965).

The quality of teacher–student interaction between Mexican American students and their Anglo American teachers is also affected by the segregation of Mexican American pupils resulting from homogeneous ability grouping and bilingual education programs. Parsons (1965) found that homogeneous ability grouping practices across and within classes led to the segregation of Mexican and Anglo students because nearly all Mexican students were placed in lower level groups and all Anglo students in higher level groups. Students were seated according to their reading or math groups, resulting in the Anglo students sitting closer to the Anglo teacher than the Mexican students and leading to more formal interactions between the teacher and the Mexican students. Anglo students could carry on informal conversations with the teacher at her desk without raising their hands, but Mexican students had to raise their hands from the back of the room to talk.

The lack of teacher–student contact in bilingual education programs is more subtle but just as unfair. Mexican American students are often placed in bilingual programs where the normal teacher–student interaction of the classroom is significantly altered (Ortiz, 1977, 1988). Because teachers in bilingual classrooms are often monolingual English, much of the teaching, which is conducted in Spanish, is left to the teacher's aide. In this way, Mexican American students do not receive the same type of interaction or amount of attention from a qualified teacher as students in regular classrooms. Furthermore, because teachers are unable to conduct lessons in Spanish and because of the perceived need to teach "basic skills," these classrooms often use significantly more drill and worksheet-type exercises than mainstream classrooms, again limiting teacher–student interaction.

A comparison of the interaction patterns of bilingual teachers and assistants at an early childhood center serving Mexican American children found significant differences in the teacher and assistant behaviors, both verbally and nonverbally. Verbally, teachers used more praise, acceptance, and encouragement and allowed for more student response than their assistants; the assistants tended to use more "teacher-talk," such as "lecture, telling, and idle-conversation" than the teachers themselves (Townsend & Zamora, 1975, pp. 198–199). Nonverbally, assistants used more negative behaviors to show disagreement with student response than the teachers, such as head shaking and stern looks.

The content of interaction in the classroom can also influence student–teacher interaction. The U.S. Commission on Civil Rights (1973) cites a lack of relevant curriculum, textbooks, and other materials plus teachers untrained to incorporate the experiences of Mexican American children into class discussions as contributing to the feeling in these children that school is alien to them and of little relevance to their lives, beginning a cycle of "lowered interest, decreased participation, poor academic performance and lowered self-esteem" (p. 44).

As a result of the differential treatment described in these studies, Mexican American students interact with their teachers much less than their Anglo American counterparts. The U.S. Commission on Civil Rights (1973) found Mexican American students initiated significantly fewer interactions with their teachers and also responded less often to the teacher. The Commission argues that Mexican American students talked less because of the teachers' relative lack of attention to them. Certainly this explanation accounts for fewer responses, because teachers questioned Mexican American students 21% less often than they did Anglo students. Parsons (1965), too, found that Mexican American students did not interact as much, particularly when teachers asked general questions of the class and the class provided choral responses or shouted out answers. Teachers often explain that they do not call on Mexican American students because of their poor English skills, assuming, evidently, that they might embarrass students or themselves if there were a misunderstanding (Ortiz, 1988). This finding suggests that more that just cultural difference may be occurring in the differential treatment of Mexican American students; language difference may also play a role.

Like the cultural mismatch studies, the differential treatment studies show the relative lack of participation or silence of Mexican American students in U.S. classrooms, but to better understand that silence, they examine the interaction in the classroom rather than the student's cultural background. They find that not only the student's background, but also the teacher, play a significant role in misunderstandings and miscommunication that have traditionally been called "cultural mismatch." They also provide a necessary comparison between the interaction of the teacher with majority versus minority students. Finally, they reveal the interactive, reactive, reflexive nature of classroom life. But they leave certain questions unanswered. For example, if there is differential treatment, is its basis purely ethnic, or is it related to language ability, language choice, or other language-related factors? Many interactional differences described in the research discussed so far might be better understood if language difference were also taken into consideration. There is a need to consider if teachers respond differently to native speakers (NS) and non-native speakers (NNS) of English. Research suggests that this is likely the case.

In research from both the cultural mismatch and differential treatment perspectives, teachers have been found to avoid interaction with their Mexican American students because of the students' "poor English skills." Although not all Mexican Americans are Spanish-speaking, much Mexican American classroom interaction is undoubtedly affected by language difference as well as cultural difference. Research on mother–child instructional interaction suggests the possibility of a mismatch between home and school based on language of instruction as well as the ethnic or cultural mismatch or differential treatment described earlier. Spanish-speaking Mexican American students—whether English- or Spanish-dominant—may be more familiar and comfortable with interaction patterns and paces that differ from those usually found in the classrooms and homes of monolingual English Anglo Americans. These differences could create difficulties for the Spanish-speaking students when they begin to attend school. Exactly how this interaction might differ is unclear, however.

Mothers have been found to pace their IRE sequences differently depending on their language backgrounds (Steward & Steward, 1973). English-speaking Anglo-American mothers provide the largest number of IRE sequences at the fastest pace, followed by Spanish-speaking Mexican-American mothers. Bilingual Mexican-American mothers provide the fewest IRE sequences, taking much longer to complete each sequence because they provide more clarifications and corrections than any other group.

Another study suggests that although the IRE pattern may be found when bilingual Chicano mothers and their English-dominant children take part in instructional interaction in Spanish, when they engage in instruction in English, the typical pattern of interaction is IRIR as if a normal conversation. The "E" turn occurs in Spanish because mothers evaluate their children's use of Spanish vocabulary and pronunciation (García, 1983; García & Carrasco, 1981).

Given these interactional differences in the home, it is not surprising that research on classroom interaction and language difference among Spanish-speaking Mexican American students has found that their interaction strategies are often unsuccessful in mainstream, monolingual classrooms, leading to dire consequences for their academic success. In a study of mainstream and bilingual primary classrooms (McClure, 1978), bilingual Mexican American kindergartners failed to respond to teacher questions in mainstream classrooms approximately 50% of the time, whereas Anglo American kindergartners failed to respond only 15% of the time. Mexican American children were also found to volunteer to answer questions less frequently and to join in choral responses less often and less enthusiastically than the Anglo American students in mainstream classrooms. When visitors came to the mainstream classroom, Mexican American students were less apt to ask them questions than the Anglo American students. Mexican American students were also less likely to address comments to the teacher of a mainstream classroom, but more likely to ask questions than the monolingual English students. In their bilingual classrooms, however, the interaction of Mexican American students closely resembled that of their Anglo American counterparts in the mainstream classroom. For example, they volunteered answers and asked questions of visitors. This study suggests that the findings of differential treatment research, which also found less interaction by Mexican American students, were likely influenced by language difference as well as ethnicity. Language difference appears to have an effect on bilingual students' willingness to interact in mainstream classrooms.

Perhaps bilingual student willingness to interact varies because when bilingual children are given a chance to use either language, they prefer to ask questions in the language in which they are most proficient (Rodríguez-Brown & Elías-Olivares, 1983). Moreover, bilingual students are very sensitive to the language context and even in bilingual classrooms may feel inhibited to use Spanish because of subtle indications that English is preferred (Sapiens, 1982). Vásquez (1993) found that important cues are sent to students about which language is preferred in the classroom. When she tried to create a bilingual–bicultural after-school program, she found that students clearly preferred to use English over Spanish while taking part in her program. Balanced bilinguals chose English and even those students with little competency in English preferred to use the little English they had. She concluded that the children preferred to speak English because the program could not escape appearing to be a school-like environment. Because Spanish is generally less-preferred in school, the children followed that rule in the after-school program.

Successful classrooms with bilingual Mexican American students have been found to use both English and Spanish openly (Ammon, 1985). Reyes and Laliberty (1992) found fourth grade students in a mixed NS–NNS bilingual classroom more successful when the teacher provided an environment that validated the use of both English and Spanish and encouraged writing and "publication" in Spanish as well as English. Bilingual Mexican American students have been found to write more in journals in which they feel free to write in both their languages than in journals in which they are required to use English only (Reyes, 1991).

Although the language differences of Spanish-speaking Mexican American students can lead to interaction differences in the classroom, it is not only the students who interact differently. As was found in research from the differential treatment perspective, teachers interact differently with these students, too, often to the students' disadvantage. Teachers' interaction with bilingual Mexican American students may discourage them in the classroom. Laosa (1977) found that Spanish-dominant second graders make more attempts than monolingual English Anglos or English-dominant Mexican Americans to gain the teacher's attention but receive more disapprovals from the teacher and less academic information. Laosa concludes that if the trend of discouragement and decreased academic information continued for the Spanish-dominant students, it could turn into "disruptive attention-seeking or . . . apathy for academic work" (p. 62).

Indeed, there is evidence to suggest that Laosa's prediction is accurate. Three types of "maladjustments" have been found in Spanish-speaking Mexican Americans who were identified by their teachers as exhibiting frustration, anxiety, aggression, and avoidance: "underparticipation," characterized by a preference to be left alone and unnoticed; "overparticipation," an obsession with schoolwork; and "selective participation under protest," students who were disruptive and defensive. According to Trueba (1983), these manifestations of stress were the result of being Spanish-speaking and having less experience in schooling and literacy (in English or Spanish) in a monolingual, monocultural school environment where students did not know the expectations.

As I noted earlier, some teachers purposely do not call on nonnative speakers of English for fear of embarrassing them. This behavior can lead to the inappropriate assessment of bilingual students. Carrasco (1981) found "Lupita," a Spanish-dominant kindergartner born in Mexico, was not called on in either whole class or small group discussions. The teacher explained that "because of Lupita's history and home background and her lack of the skills required to participate effectively in these [class] sessions, she decided not to humiliate or embarrass Lupita in front of her peers for not being able to answer or perform adequately" (p. 169). However, the teacher did not observe many scenes witnessed by the researcher that proved Lupita to be competent enough to complete her own work and to help her friends complete their work, as well. The teacher's assumptions led her to misassess Lupita's abilities. Teachers also have been found to misassess bilingual Mexican American students when they rely on pronunciation as an indicator of reading comprehension in English (Díaz, Moll, & Mehan, 1986) and when they observe bilingual children in a single context that does not reveal their strengths in English (Carrasco, Vera, & Cazden, 1981).

Research on language difference and classroom interaction among Mexican American students adds another component to the myriad factors that influence the interaction of Mexican American students in the classroom. Student use of language in the home and teacher attitudes toward students as a result of ethnicity and interaction style are not the only factors of importance when considering Mexican Americans in the classroom. In numerous ways language differences may affect how teachers and students perceive and interact with one another. Language differences may also help explain the findings of those studying from the cultural mismatch and differential treatment perspectives, who have focused only on ethnicity.

Consideration of language difference reveals once again that the silence of Mexican American students is a common phenomenon. But this perspective augments our understanding of the silence observed. Bilingual Mexican American students may be more silent in the classroom for a number of language-related reasons: because they are accustomed to a different interactional style at home; because they feel more comfortable speaking up in their first language, but know that English is expected in the mainstream classroom; and because teachers fail to call on them because they are not considered proficient enough in English.

THE ROLE OF GENDER IN CLASSROOM INTERACTION

Yet another important source of interactional difference in the classroom is gender. In fact, in every interactional situation "doing gender is unavoidable" (West & Zimmerman, 1991, p. 24) because "gender itself is constituted through interaction" (West & Zimmerman, 1991, p. 16). The importance of gender as a sociolinguistic variable cannot be underestimated. Indeed, Swacker (1975) claims that "any sociolinguistic research which does not, at least, specifically give consideration to the sex of the informant might well be of questionable validity" (p. 82). Shuy (1969) also argues that "linguistic correlates of sex differences" (p. 2) and their causes should receive greater attention from sociolinguists.

Like the research on differences across ethnicities, studies of gender have examined differences in interaction from a cross-cultural model. As Maltz and Borker (1982) explain, "We prefer to think of the difficulties in cross-sex and cross-ethnic communication as two examples of the same larger phenomenon: cultural difference and miscommunication" (p. 196). Research in the home and classroom has looked at the differences in interactional styles of males and females, and it has also begun to examine gender-based differential treatment by teachers. But few studies have looked at the interactional influence of both ethnicity and gender as cultural factors in a single study. As two of the cultural groups in which individuals operate, however, it is necessary to consider the possibility—nay, probability—of both influencing interaction in the classroom.

The cross-cultural study of gender and language use is based on the notion that, not unlike separate cultures or subcultures, women and men develop different "languages," "codes," or "voices" through which they are socialized to interact differently (Maltz & Borker, 1982; Tannen, 1990a, b). Lakoff (1975) argues that women are socialized to be more "polite" than men through the use of tag questions, rising intonation, and lexical choices; whereas Gilligan (1982) has found that women and men speak differently about moral problems, with men referring to an ideology of "justice" and women to one of "care."

Such differences in language socialization lead to differences and sometimes difficulties in the interaction of men and women and even boys and girls. Studies have found that children begin to use language differently at a very early age. Sheldon (1990) found that among three year old friends, "conflict talk" was sex-differentiated. Boys used a more aggressive discourse style and had more direct conflict in their interactions, whereas girls attempted to lessen conflict through the use of a more collaborative discourse style.

Males and females become both increasingly different in their interaction styles and increasingly aware of these differences in each other as they grow older. In a study of children's typically male and female behaviors, Whiting and Edwards (1973) have found that children learn to differentiate between typically male or female lexical features, such as "damn" versus "my goodness" early, and by the time they are in the sixth grade they are nearly as accurate as adults in doing so (Edelsky, 1977). Moreover, 8–13-year-old black girls use directives differently than black boys to construct the social organizations typical of their same-sex groups (Goodwin, 1980). And although they use similar strategies in telling stories, they do so for different purposes, with boys using stories to continue arguments and girls using them to alter relationships within the group for the present and future (Goodwin, 1990a, b).

Boys and girls use differing conversation strategies for creating and maintaining "conversational involvement" that remain virtually unchanged as they grow older (Tannen, 1990a). Girls in second and sixth grade speak for relatively long periods of time on a few subjects, whereas boys speak on a wide range of topics, giving only a short period of time to each. In tenth grade boys talk on fewer subjects than they did in second and sixth grade, but they nevertheless develop them in less personal ways than tenth grade girls.

Studies of adult male–female interaction have found that gender-related interactional differences continue into adulthood. In same-sex conversations, middle-class Anglo American adult males and females rarely interrupt each other, but when they do, the interruptions are fairly evenly distributed between the two parties. However, in cross-sex dyads, there is significantly more interrupting, and it is almost completely initiated by men (West & Zimmerman, 1983; Zimmerman & West, 1975). From recordings of male–female interaction in the homes of three Anglo American married couples, Fishman (1983) found that women are relegated to doing the "shitwork" of interaction (p. 99). That is, they are responsible for initiating topics through the use of questions and with the use of attention-drawing phrases and topics that are either dropped or picked up, depending on the desires of the men.

The interactional differences between men and women found outside the classroom are also found in it, where these differences affect student progress and success. As Coates (1986) explains, "In the school setting, this differing understanding of when to speak, when to remain silent, how to mark speech for politeness, when it is permissible to interrupt, and so on, helps to contribute to different outcomes for girls and boys" (p. 156).

Studies from the cross-cultural perspective have identified typically female adaptations to the schooling situation. One finding—the silence of female students—is a common theme throughout the research on gender in classroom interaction. Females in British secondary schools have been found to use silence as a successful adaptation to the expectations of school, although the women were known to be talkative and even rowdy outside of school. Their silence was considered "self-imposed" (Stanley, 1986, p. 280), making the women "active participants" in the construction of their silence. The silence was found to coincide with teacher expectations for successful female students. Female British secondary students also employ strategies that are found in the "local female culture" outside the classroom to counter various "power scenarios" by the teacher (Davies, 1983). These strategies include bargaining, humor, and femininity. Young women have even seemed unwilling to participate in class (Whyte, 1984), practicing avoidance strategies such as raising a hand when the teacher calls on someone else to look as if attempting to participate (Swann, 1988).

Although studies from the cross-cultural perspective generally conclude that young women choose to be silent in the classroom, the findings of differential treatment studies suggest that women may have little choice in the matter. There is no doubt that male students receive significantly more attention from teachers than female students, whether the teachers are male or female (Eccles & Blumenfeld, 1985; Morse & Handley, 1985; Serbin, O'Leary, Kent, & Tonick, 1973). Teachers also look at the boys in their classes more often, usually because the teachers plan to call on one of them (Swann, 1988). In nine first and fifth grade classrooms, boys had the teacher's attention 39% of the time, whereas girls had it 21% of the time. The rest of the time, attention was given to both boys and girls together (Eccles & Blumenfeld, 1985). Boys have also been found to monopolize classroom resources, such as lab equipment (Whyte, 1984), and to interrupt during classroom discussion more than girls (Swann, 1988).

Whether teachers can change this phenomenon remains in question. Although one study by Whyte (1984) suggests that teachers with a desire to do so can change their predilection to call on boys and can provide more equal access to resources in the classroom, Spender (1982/1989) found they couldn't. When she and her colleagues at the secondary and college level made a conscious effort to pay as much attention to the women as to the men in their classes, they still spent only an average of 34–38% of their time talking to women. Even then, the teachers felt they had spent too much time with the women, and the men in the class complained that they weren't getting enough attention.

In nearly all of the studies of differential treatment and gender, teachers were found to give more attention to male students, leaving the females in relative silence. But most of this research has been conducted with Anglo (American or British) participants. Little is known about the gender differences in the classroom interaction of students of other ethnicities. However, it is not sufficient to study one without the other. As bell hooks (1989) notes, "sex, race and class . . . *together* determine the social construction of femaleness" (p. 23).

Although there have been no studies of ethnicity, gender, and language in a comparative study of interaction, studies that combine gender and ethnicity as possible factors affecting interaction suggest the importance of such research. Studies of linguistic differences between males and females within an ethnic group (Nichols, 1980, 1983; Shuy, 1969) rarely describe their interaction, particularly with other ethnicities or across languages for comparison. Nevertheless, these studies reveal that there are differences in interactional intention and interpretation across both ethnic and gender groups. Moreover, these differences may lead to differential treatment based on gender and ethnicity in the classroom. For example, the same statements made by a member of the opposite sex can be interpreted quite differently depending on one's ethnic heritage (Tannen, 1982). Moreover, rather than adjusting to different communicative styles with constant contact, differences can sometimes become exaggerated with repeated contact, increasing the lack of understanding. Although immigrant families may begin to lose the language of their culture by the third generation, the communicative strategies of their culture may still affect their interaction. In the classroom this phenomenon can lead to interactional differences to which teachers respond negatively.

A study of six first grade classrooms with black and white students found that "students' schooling experiences are differentiated in systematic ways by their race-gender status" (Grant, 1985, p. 72). Girls had "warmer, more positive contacts with the teachers" than boys, and whites had more positive contacts than black students, with the following order of warmth from the teacher: (a) white girls, (b) black girls, (c) white boys, (d) black boys. The actual amount of teacher attention given students follows the same rank order as relative warmth. White females were found to initiate more friendly, personal "chats" with the teacher than any other student groups, and teachers were more apt to give "special assignments" requiring responsibility and involving leaving the classroom to white girls. Males, in general, were most apt to initiate and to "challenge." The teacher gave black males the most control-directed praise and disciplined them the most (Grant, 1985).

When examining classroom interaction for gender difference, silence again becomes a prevalent finding. Studies suggest that women tend to be silent for reasons not unlike those found in the research on Mexican Americans—because of their socialization, a lack of teacher attention, and to some extent, an unwillingness to initiate. In fact, all of the research on the classroom interaction of Mexican Americans and the classroom interaction of women, no matter what the research perspective, finds silence again and again. And silence is what I found, not only in the specific example of a community college composition classroom, but also in the community in which the course was taught. What might be the cause of this silence? Is it just a conflict between the interaction styles of the home and the school? Is it only the unfair treatment of Mexican American students by their teachers? Is it language difference or gender difference? All of these explanations play a part in the silence observed as does the larger sociocultural context of silence in the classroom, which has an influence as well.

Some would suggest that the silence of Mexican American students is a response to classroom interaction that legitimizes and reconfirms the status quo in society, particularly the prominence of Anglo American culture and values. When examining why some minorities fail in school and others don't, Ogbu (1978) and Ogbu and Matute-Bianchi (1986) maintain that there is a need to consider larger sociocultural forces at work in society, especially the linkages between the school, the economy, and the beliefs of students and their parents regarding the role of school in becoming gainfully employed. They state that "caste-like minorities," that is, minority groups such as the Mexican Americans, who have been "incorporated into a society more or less involuntarily and permanently through slavery, conquest, or colonization and then relegated to menial status" (Ogbu & Matute-Bianchi, 1986, p. 90) exhibit "secondary cultural differences" that develop "after two populations have come in contact, especially in contact involving the subordination of one population by the other" (p. 97). The secondary cultural differences of caste-like minorities result from their "subordination" and "exploitation" in mainstream society. In school these differences serve to create and maintain tension between minorities and the majority group. As such, they become marked and lasting, taking on a significance of their own. In this way, secondary cultural differences become secondary cultural discontinuities that create educational difficulties for minority students. Ogbu and Matute-Bianchi state that secondary cultural differences and discontinuities are "usually more a matter of 'style' than 'content,'" and they argue that "communication style" discontinuities are the result of such secondary cultural differences (Ogbu & Matute-Bianchi, 1986, p. 97). From this perspective, the silence found among Mexican American students is indicative of secondary cultural differences resulting from their situation in society as caste-like minorities.

Erickson (1987) also posits a societal explanation for differences between successful and unsuccessful minority students. He argues that we should consider teaching and learning as political acts, where "learning what is deliberately taught can be seen as a form of political assent. Not learning can be seen as a form of political resistance" (p. 344). According to Erickson, in cases where minority students have educational success despite differences in the communication styles of the teacher and student, political assent has occurred; the students trust in the legitimacy of the institution to further their interests and needs. In cases where they are not learning, students and their parents may be consciously, but more likely unconsciously, distrustful of schools and their representatives in response to the perceived labor market or in response to problematic cross-cultural communication. Therefore the trusting relationship necessary for learning and educational success does not form.

Erickson uses resistance theory to create an explanation of minority student achievement in which "labor market inequity as perceived by members of a domestic (caste-like) minority and conflictual teacher–student interaction that derives in part from culturally differing communicative styles can both be seen as impediments to the trust that constitutes an existential foundation for school legitimacy" (1987, p. 345). Consideration of resistance and the labor market theory is particularly pertinent in the study of older students, according to Erickson, because students' distrust in the school's ability to prepare them for work increases as they come closer to the reality of the job hunt.

Unlike other perspectives on the relationship of Mexican American interaction in the classroom and school achievement, Erickson and Ogbu account for agency on the part of the student as well as the teacher. According to Giroux (1983), resistance theory "restores the critical notion of agency" to educational theory (p. 260). He argues that other theories are unable to:

> provide any major insights into how teachers, students, and other human agents come together within specific historical and social contexts in order to both make and reproduce the conditions of their existence. . . human subjects generally 'disappear' amidst a theory that leaves no room for moments of self-creation, mediation, and resistance. (p. 259)

Consideration of the effects of secondary cultural differences and labor market inequities on the interaction of Mexican American students, particularly adults, accounts for the influence of larger societal factors on day-to-day classroom behavior.

Moreover, the notion of student response to such factors in the classroom eliminates an assumption common in much of the research: that what is observed is predetermined, culturally or otherwise. The silence of Mexican American students does not occur in a vacuum. Larger societal factors and students' responses to them in the classroom also play a role.

I wrote this book to provide a rare look at the interaction of adult Mexican American students and their Anglo American instructor as they managed to teach and learn in a basic writing course. I also wrote it to develop existing notions of cultural mismatch in communication styles by considering a broader range of possible influences and motivations in student and teacher discourse, including differential treatment, gender- and language-related differences, secondary cultural differences, labor market inequities, and resistance. This study explores the varying social contexts and participant perspectives that influence communication in the classroom. It examines the interactions between Anglo American teachers and their adult Mexican American students by exploring patterns of interaction in the classroom and their variations in content and structure within and across ethnic, gender, and linguistic groups. Sources of interactional difference are found in both teacher and student characteristics and perspectives and in larger sociocultural influences, that is, political, economic, cultural, and linguistic factors.

In the next chapter I describe how I entered the community and the classroom I studied. I explain how I collected and analyzed the data at a number of levels to make sense of the silence I observed. Chapter Three presents current and historical sociocultural data about the community and the college to document the varying contexts that influence what occurs in the outreach program and to illustrate the pervasiveness of silence in the community—past and present. In Chapter Four I introduce the participants in detail, particularly their personal backgrounds, educational experiences, and personal motivations or "key themes." This information helps reveal their perspectives on the interaction in the classroom. Chapter Five describes the variations in interaction surrounding course assignments as well as how the participants understood those differences, focusing, in particular, on how silence manifested itself as a result of the course curriculum. Chapter Six describes in detail the variation in structure and content of classroom talk, including how it changed in differing contexts and how participants understood those changes. Again, patterns of silence and voice are recurring themes. In the closing chapter, I consider the findings of this study in relation to what we already know about the classroom interaction of Mexican Americans. I explore how the consideration of culture, language, gender, and the larger societal situation develops our current understanding of the classroom interaction of Mexican American students, and I suggest what these findings mean for other classrooms and communities.

2

STUDYING SILENCE IN CONTEXT

We shall be able to interpret meanings and meaning-making in a
principled manner only in the degree to which we are able to specify
the structure and coherence of the larger contexts in which specific
meanings are created and transmitted.
—Bruner, 1990, pp. 64–65

Because of the social nature of language and learning and the role
of schooling in society described in Chapter One, I designed this
study to collect and analyze data at four levels: the level of the
community, the level of the college, the level of the classroom, and
the level of the individual "focal" student. These differing levels
need to be considered in order to interpret and understand what
is observed in the classroom. Only by connecting the macro-level
sociocultural situation in which the outreach program existed to
the micro-level analysis of interaction in the classroom and the
individual participants in the study could an increased understanding of the classroom interaction of Mexican Americans be
achieved. I agree with Ogbu (1982) who writes:

> The language, cognitive, motivation, and social competencies which
> parents and other childrearing agents seek to inculcate in the
> young—depend on historical and contemporary economic, social
> and political realities of the population and not merely on the teach-
> ing competencies of its adult members. (p. 254)

In this chapter I will describe in detail how I conducted the
research project that is the basis for this book, including where it
took place, who I studied, and how I collected and analyzed the
data.

APPLETON

The site for this study was a community college outreach program in the primarily agricultural community of Appleton[1] off scenic Highway 1 in Central California. Anglo Americans and Mexican Americans alike have noted that Appleton resembles a town in México. According to a one-time Appleton resident, the central plaza of Appleton looks like a *zócalo* (town square) in México at times.

> Each Sunday, Hispanic farm workers and food-packing workers and their families gather in the plaza, as they do in parks throughout Latin America, to enjoy themselves and to socialize with friends and neighbors.

> The lonely men who've left their wives and children south of the border and come to the [Appleton] Valley to toil and earn money to feed their families sit on benches on Sundays—their day off—and chat softly in Spanish. They look enviously at the men fortunate enough to afford to have their wives and children with them, the workers whose little girls and boys are dressed in their finest outfits each Sunday when they gather in the plaza after Mass. (Quarnstrom, 1990, p. 1B)

An oral history of longtime Appleton residents describes the town during the summer season as follows.

> It seems the place is three-fourths Mexican in the summertime. On Thursday nights everybody gets dressed up and goes downtown, if not to buy anything, just to check each other out. The boys watch the girls and the girls watch the boys, families walk down Main Street together, the old men sit in the park and talk. Appleton is alive! It's a true little México. (Starkey, 1978)

Similarly, during a recent Cinco de Mayo festival one Mexican American proclaimed to a reporter, "This is México, *chiquito!*" And another declared, "This is a part of México we stole" (Trevino, 1990, p. 1).

Many Appleton residents do not consider this comparison to México complimentary, a point I will discuss in greater detail in Chapter Three. Nevertheless, it is understandable that people perceive Appleton as Mexican. For nearly a decade Hispanics, primarily Mexican Americans, have been the majority in the town. In 1980, there were already more Hispanics than Anglos in the town (49 and

---

[1] The names of people, places, and publications have been changed as necessary to protect the anonymity of the participants.

45%, respectively). And by 1990 61% of the the town's population was Hispanic, whereas 33% was Anglo, 4% Asian or Pacific Islander, and less than 1% Black (Zabin, 1991). However, this count is probably low. Local census workers state that the 1990 tally missed nearly 200 homes and all of the Federal Emergency Management Administration-sponsored trailers (byproducts of the 1989 Loma Prieta earthquake), not to mention the homeless and others who are habitually undercounted in census years. Also, because of the confusing way that questions about ethnicity and race were worded on the census, many Appleton Hispanics were reported to have identified themselves as "Other" rather than Hispanic ("Census Committee," 1990; Zabin, 1991). In 1991, the mayor of Appleton estimated the actual Hispanic population of the town at between 65 and 67% (Revised Minutes..., 1991).

Agriculture and related businesses are the primary industry in Appleton. Strawberries are the number one crop, with production yielding $58.9 million in 1990 or 40% of the strawberries produced in California. Lettuce, cut roses, and apples are the next largest money-makers (Brazil, 1990; "Santa Cruz County's logging," 1990). Broccoli, cauliflower, brussel sprouts, and artichokes also are major crops planted in the area. As a result, Appleton leads the nation in the agriculture-related business of frozen food processing, with more than 600 million pounds produced in 1989 (Brazil, 1990). Two frozen food plants in the area employ over 2,250 seasonal workers (Appleton Valley Chamber of Commerce, 1991).

UCLA sociologist David Hayes-Bautista says that the people of Appleton are "test-driving the future of California" (Brazil, 1990, p. B1). Because the demographics that existed for Hispanics in Appleton at the time of the study were similar to those projected for the year 2000 for the remainder of California and the Southwest, Appleton was a prime location for a research project in cross-cultural interaction. The results of this study provide an interesting preview of our future classrooms and communities.

Most of the people walking down Appleton's Main Street appear to be Mexican American. The men, in blue jeans, straw cowboy hats, and well-worn cowboy boots, travel alone or in pairs. The women often accompany each other and have several children walking in front, behind, and next to them. Many stores have Spanish names and signs, and much Spanish is heard on the street.[2] Across the street from JCPenney's is *Joyeria de Appleton*, a

---

[2] This description of Appleton is based on observations of the town before and after the Loma Prieta earthquake of October, 1989. Some of the buildings and businesses described no longer exist as a result of the physical and economic devastation of the earthquake.

jewelry store for the Spanish-speaking. Downtown Appleton has numerous taverns advertising *cerveza* (beer) with dusty neon signs, and *taquerias* (taco stands) abound on the main thoroughfares, where ownership changes but the menu remains constant. Three major grocery stores in town cater to the Mexican American population. These stores sell homemade tortillas, tamales, and carnitas and carry chiles, spices, produce (plantain, tomatillos, cactus), meats (brain, tongue), and drinks *(aguas frescas)* that are difficult to find in other grocery stores and supermarket chains.

Despite Appleton's many similarities to a Mexican village—the look of the plaza on a Sunday afternoon, the agricultural economy, the mere number of Mexican Americans on the street—one difference is outstanding: the Mexican Americans in Appleton hold little power in the community—political or economic. Because of their historic position in the community, a fundamental gap exists between the situation of Mexican Americans and Anglo Americans in this community, a gap that pervades virtually every aspect of public life in the town. In the next chapter, I will analyze the rift between Mexican Americans and Anglo Americans in Appleton in more detail, focusing particularly on political, economic, social, and educational points of contention and the attitudes in the community that are revealed in them.

ENGLISH 10 AT PORTOLÁ COMMUNITY COLLEGE'S APPLETON CENTER

The main campus of Portolá Community College (PCC) is 12 miles north of Appleton, high atop a hill overlooking the Pacific Ocean, in a small, wealthy, largely Anglo American, beach community called Shoreline. The only ethnic breakdown available for the main campus includes students at the Appleton Center outreach program, as well. These statistics show a total campus population for spring 1990 of 83.3% Anglo; 10.5% Hispanic; 2.9% Asian or Pacific Islander; 1.2% Black–African American; 1.2% American Indian; and 0.9% Filipino. (See Table 1 for campus-wide statistics from other semesters I was in the field there.)

The college was founded in 1959, and construction was completed in 1962. Originally designed for 2,500 students, the school has had three major expansions and now enrolls between 13,000 and 14,000 students each semester (Gallagher, 1989). It is expected that PCC will grow another 4,000 students by the year 2000 (Alvarado, 1990a). Prior to the completion of the campus buildings, PCC offered evening classes in Appleton at the local high school. But once the main campus was open, classes were no

Table 1.
Appleton Center Ethnic Breakdown*

	Enrollment by Semester (%)			
Ethnicity	Fall, 1988	Spring, 1989	Fall, 1989	Spring, 1990
Anglo	83.9	83.3	83.6	83.3
Hispanic	10.3	10.3	10.4	10.5
Asian/Pacific Islander	2.8	3.1	2.8	2.9
Black/African American	1.1	1.2	1.2	1.2
American Indian	1.0	1.1	1.1	1.2
Filipino	0.9	1.0	0.9	0.9

Note. From [Portolá] College Fact Book, 1990-1991, by R.G. Rodriguez, 1991, Portolá College, Office of Institutional Research.
*Main campus and off-campus sites combined.

longer available in Appleton on a regular basis, until the creation of the outreach center almost 30 years later.

According to the Mission Statement, the college's purpose is to "prepare students to transfer to a four-year institution, provide preparation for employment through occupational training programs, provide basic skills education, and offer opportunities for lifelong learning and continuing education" (Catalog, p. 10). PCC has an excellent transfer record, the measure of success for most community colleges. In the state of California, it is sixth out of 107 in sending students to four-year universities. The school's statistician points out that if this ranking were based on percentages rather than raw numbers, PCC would be even higher—probably third or fourth in the state in transfers (Office of Institutional Research, 1990–1991, p. 62).

PCC's excellence may be illustrated by a few recent awards. The college was selected by the American Association of Community and Junior Colleges as one of 25 sites nationally for the development of an NEH-endowed program entitled "Humanities Connection" ("Portolá picked," 1990). PCC also has a nationally recognized literary magazine that won the Community College Humanities Association "Best Community College Literary Magazine Award" in the Western division. This magazine has the unusual feature of a "writers from a second language section" ("White Pine Review," 1990).

PCC has several programs to support Mexican American students. In spring 1989, the main campus began the Puente Project, an intensive English composition, counseling, and mentoring program designed to improve the retention and transfer rates of Mexican American students. From the outset, it had impressive results, with 28 of 30 students from the first basic writing class (English 10) moving up to English 15, a course required for transfer to a four-year university. This is a considerably higher passage rate than that for Mexican Americans in mainstream composition classes (Wagner, 1989). PCC has also started a program in Appleton to encourage students to graduate from high school and attend college. In 1991 they awarded eleven middle school students $1,000 scholarships to be redeemed at PCC if the students graduate from high school. All were awarded to Mexican American students ("Proud Winners," 1991).

The English class I chose to study was offered in the Appleton Center outreach program created by PCC. The motivating force behind the creation of the Appleton Center was an anonymous donation to the college of $15,000 for the express purpose of "increasing the College's presence" in Appleton ([Portolá] College Governing Board Meeting Minutes, March 2, 1987, p. 8) through "the establishment of an Educational Outreach Center offering an array of educational offerings and support services tailored to the specific need and desires of the [Appleton] community" (Preliminary Planning Report, 1987, p. 2). The planning committee created, and the Board approved, the following goals for the center:

1. Provide initial preparation for transfer to a 4-year institution, initial preparation for employment, and opportunities for continuing study.
2. Create a learning environment attractive to students and faculty and conducive to student success.
3. Increase the number of students from the Appleton area who enroll in [Portolá] College.
4. Allow for expansion of course offerings that are now restricted by space limitations on the [Shoreline] campus. (Preliminary Report, p. 2)

To implement these goals, the school planned to: "Provide courses meeting the needs of the target population" and "employ teaching methodologies appropriate to the adult learner and responsive to cultural differences" (Preliminary Report, p. 3).

As noted in Chapter One, very few Mexican Americans attend college, and the majority of Mexican American students who do attend a post-secondary institution attend a two-year community, junior, or technical college. Therefore, my best opportunity for capturing the interaction of Mexican American adults in the

classroom was at a community college. However, because of the
dearth of Mexican Americans attending college, opportunities to
observe more than a very few Mexican Americans in any typical
community college course are limited. But this outreach program's location in a majority Hispanic community assured a large
number of Mexican American students.

The Appleton Center was located in a relatively new downtown
shopping center with access both from Main Street and a cross
street. The equivalent of several stores had been rented and set up
as three classrooms, a reception area, and an administrative office.
To reach the center from Main Street, one passed under a royal
blue awning next to JCPenney's, through a glass-roofed arcade of
stores and offices, and into an open-air courtyard with two levels of
store and office space around the perimeter. The shopping center
was owned by a member of the Mexican American community and
housed many of the Mexican American-owned businesses in town.
In addition to the Appleton Center, the mall had a deli selling lus-
cious homemade Mexican food where students and tutors spent
their breaks, and I occasionally tutored students there. Other
spaces held a beauty salon, a bookstore (with irregular hours), a
United Farm Workers office, the offices of a Mexican American community activist, a health clinic catering to the Spanish-speaking, a
tax consultant, and a considerable number of unrented spaces. The
Center classrooms and office space opened onto the courtyard
where trees and foliage were planted in cement boxes. PCC had
purchased white wrought iron tables and chairs for students to
gather around between classes and during breaks.

The reception area was run by one or two bilingual
(Spanish–English) office personnel. Just before classes on Monday
evenings, it was usually full of students, teachers, and tutors, with
as much talk in Spanish as in English. The phones were usually
ringing, teachers were using the receptionist's stapler behind the
counter, and students were borrowing the keys to the bathrooms,
which were kept on the reception counter. There was one copy
machine (usually in operation); one bookshelf, which held textbooks, college catalogs, and schedules for sale; and a table of free
literature about financial aid, academic programs, and upcoming
events. The college newspaper, the locally published bilingual
newspaper, and other free community papers were also available.
Posters advertising upcoming community or PCC events were
hung on the walls and the doors. Apparently, PCC recognized that
a significant portion of its clientele at the Appleton Center were
Spanish-speaking. One door in the reception area led to a small

office with two desks for the acting Dean and the counselor, who were at the Appleton Center only on a part time basis. This area was also used occasionally by the teachers and tutors for discussing plans for the evening classes, assessing student writing, or tutoring students individually.

The classroom in which English 10 met was also adjacent to the reception area. It was a long, narrow room with indoor–outdoor carpeting and no windows. From an imaginary line at the classroom door forward to the front of the room was the teacher's area. A large conference table and plastic chair served as her desk. In front of the desk was a wide aisle from the door separating her desk from the student desks. Behind the teacher's desk, on the front wall of the classroom, hung a chalkboard. A second chalkboard was on the left wall of the classroom. The desks were five across and nine deep. During the last semester I was there, three desks in the center of the last row were mysteriously replaced with two conference tables at which four students sat. Students sitting in the back, nine desks deep, were very far indeed from the teacher, who generally stayed out of the rows of desks unless working with students individually or returning student papers.

On Monday evenings three levels of English met simultaneously at the Appleton Center: English 5, English 10, and English 15. Three tutors were provided Monday evenings to "float" between the three English classes as needed. Classes met from 6 p.m. to 10 p.m. The four hours of class time in English 10 were generally divided in the following way: from 6:00 to 6:15 students entered the classroom, the teacher informally answered student questions and/or met with the tutors and other English teachers to plan the tutors' activities for the evening. During the beginning of the semester, attendance was taken at this time, too. From approximately 6:15 to 7:30, *English Workbook* (grammar and usage) assignments were discussed. Usually the tutors were in the classroom and, along with the teacher, they met with students individually to check students' answers to the assigned tasks and to respond to any questions they might have had about the assignment. If the tutors were not available (because they were in another English class), the time might be used to go over the assignments as a whole class. In either case, some of the more difficult workbook problems were often discussed with the whole class.

Then there was generally a short break, during which students walked down to the deli or asked the teacher questions in the classroom. When class resumed, the next hour and 15 minutes was usually spent with the teacher and the tutors giving individual help to students on drafts of their papers. If papers were just returned to students, time was spent with the teacher and the tutors talking to the students individually about comments the teacher had made on their papers, answering any questions that the students might have, and making suggestions for revision. There was occasionally a break after this portion of the class. The final third of class was usually spent in a whole class discussion or lecture about a writing assignment, an assigned reading (including the study of handouts created from the writings of previous students), or a combination of the two. During the first half of the semester, class nearly always remained in session until 9:45 p.m. During the last half, students usually were released earlier, depending on how much time tutors spent with students.

THE STUDENTS, THE TEACHER, AND THE TUTORS

During this study I worked with students from four semesters of English classes held at the Appleton Center, but especially those in two semesters of English 10 (fall 1989, and spring 1990), their teacher, and the tutors at Appleton Center. The students in these classes ranged in age from approximately 18 to 60 years. Some were just out of the local high school; others had been out of school for many years. Students came from various ethnic backgrounds, although most were either Anglo American or Mexican American. At least 55% of students in each English 10 class studied was Mexican American, and many were non-native speakers of English. Most worked at least part time, many full time, and many also took other classes and had families at home waiting for them while they attended class.

Students were in English 10 either because they had been placed in the class as a result of a holistically scored direct assessment of their writing that occurred upon enrollment in English at PCC or because they were former English 5 students who had been promoted to English 10. Students have been known to call English 10 "bonehead English," although the instructor of English 10 in Appleton insists that the community college faculty do not consider it a remedial course. I observed these students during classes, worked with them in one-to-one tutorials during class (as directed by the teacher), and chatted with them during breaks and before and after class.

Five students became focal students for this project, one from the first semester of my second year there and four from the second semester of year two. Because I did not want to impose myself on the normal functioning of the course, I did not select particular students. Rather, they selected themselves. I offered my services as a tutor outside of class (a service that was otherwise unavailable to these students in Appleton) in exchange for their being focal students in this study. In each semester four to five students responded. I chose as focal students those who met with me for the longest period of time. The focal students include two males and four females who ranged in age at the time of the study from 18 to 37 years. All were Mexican American. In this section I will briefly introduce them. You will learn much more about them in Chapter Four.

Juanita

Juanita was 22 years of age at the time of the study. She was the only focal student born in the United States. Born in Appleton, she attended the Appleton Valley schools K–12. Her first language was Spanish, and she recalls that she did not start speaking English until the third grade. Juanita taught herself to write in Spanish and was able to correct the writing of bilingual teachers at the elementary school where she worked as a migrant aide four days a week. Juanita was in her second semester at the community college the semester I began working with her. She was taking 12 units, including one called "La Mujer" about Chicana issues and one about Chicano psychology. She was attending Appleton Center with the intention to earn an AA degree and eventually transfer to the local University of California campus, where she would work toward her certificate as a bilingual teacher.

Amado

Born in Michoacán, México, 27-year-old Amado had lived in the United States for 18 years the semester he was in English 10. After attending first grade in México, Amado enrolled in the third grade in Appleton and attended Appleton Valley schools until graduating. At home and with his friends, he spoke Spanish, whereas at school and at work he spoke English. He said he was teaching himself to write in Spanish, although he didn't think he was very good yet. Amado was in his fourth year taking classes at PCC. He planned to earn his AA degree and transfer from the community college to a seminary, where he would train to become a pastor in his church. Amado volunteered as the assistant youth director of his church, worked at an industrial laundry, and took two other courses during the semester I tutored him.

Isaura

Isaura was 37 years old and married with three children at the time of the study. Born in Michoacán, México, she attended Mexican schools until the sixth grade, when her family moved to the United States. She enrolled in school in Chicago, where she graduated from the eighth grade. She had then had to quit school in order to work full time to help support her family. She recently passed the high school equivalency exam in Spanish and had been taking English classes at the Appleton Center for four semesters when I met her. She was literate in both English and Spanish. Isaura was attending classes at the Center in order to improve her English speaking abilities with the hope of getting a better job, one she assumed would require greater fluency in English. She was working as a seasonal strawberry picker at the time of the study, a job for which English was neither required nor used. English 10 was the only class she was taking the semester I worked with her.

Federico

Federico was 30 years old, recently married, and the father of a one-year-old during the semester he was in English 10. He was born in México where he attended school until he and his family moved to the United States when he was 10 years old. He was enrolled in several different school districts around the Monterey and San Francisco Bay Areas before his family settled down in Appleton, where he eventually graduated from high school. After high school Federico immediately went into the Navy, returning to Appleton again after finishing his tour of duty. He held two jobs while taking English 10: one as civil servant in the Appleton sewage treatment plant and the other as a waiter at an upscale restaurant in a tourist town 40 minutes from Appleton. His goal was to get an AA degree and transfer to a four-year college where he could work on a degree in engineering. Although a fluent Spanish speaker, he had not developed his early Spanish literacy.

Mónica

Mónica was 19 years old at the time of the study and in her second semester of classes at Portolá. She was born in Guadalajara, Jalisco, México, and came with her family to the Appleton vicinity when she was one year old. She completed all of her schooling in the Appleton Valley schools. Her first language was Spanish, and it continued to be the language of the home. She was living with her parents and five brothers and sisters while attending college. She began learning English when she entered kindergarten and did not read or write Spanish. Mónica completed beauty college during the semester in which I worked with her. She was also taking two other courses and working part time at a local drug store "for retail experience." Mónica planned to get her AA degree in business so that she would have the necessary background to open her own beauty salon.

I worked extensively with these students on their writing, tutoring them both in and out of class. I interacted with the focal students during class, as a part of tutorial–student interaction in the classroom. I also spoke with them informally before and after class and during breaks. I answered their whispered questions to me during teacher lectures and whole class discussions, and they phoned me frequently, sometimes just to set up a meeting, other times to consult about specific problems that had arisen while writing. I also met with focal students at their request outside of class to tutor them on their writing for class. The students decided where these meetings would be held. Mónica usually suggested that we meet at the public library, across from the town plaza. Sometimes the library would close before we had finished working or it was a Sunday when the library was closed all day, so we would meet at the deli in the shopping arcade near the Appleton Center. Juanita also suggested that we meet at the library, as did Amado once. Another time, a Sunday evening, Amado and I were forced to meet in one of the few public places open in Appleton, the local Dunkin' Donuts. Another time we met in the courtyard in front of the Appleton Center, where I also met with Federico. Both Amado and Mónica apologized to me for not inviting me to their homes, explaining that it was too noisy to work there or that there was a family party that day. Isaura regularly invited me to her house, where I got to know her husband and three children. I was always offered fresh fruit and homemade *agua fresca* when I went there, and I was showered with gifts of food each time I left.

All official classroom interaction between the teacher, tutors, and students was in English, but talk about what happened in class occasionally occurred in Spanish in unofficial peer interaction and in tutorials with me. I was able to follow what students were talking about in Spanish, but I did not join in the Spanish conversations. Instead, I responded in English to statements and questions that were made in Spanish. Although my relative lack of proficiency in Spanish and my Anglo American heritage could be considered a limitation by those, such as Zinn (1979), who argue that "insiders" have a greater ability to gather and interpret data in communities of color, students evidently felt comfortable speaking Spanish and codeswitching in my presence, a subtle sign of social acceptance. (See Gumperz & Hernández-Chávez, 1972/1985 and Valdés-Fallis, 1978, for further discussions of Spanish/English codeswitching.) Moreover, my ethnic difference from the focal students may actually have led them to be more forthcoming in their talk with me than had I been from a similar background. This argument is suggested by the research of Tixler y Vigil and Elsasser (1976), who found that Chicanas were at least as frank with an Anglo American interviewer as with a Chicana interviewer and sometimes more so.

The Teacher and the Tutors

The teacher for English 10 at the Appleton Center was a monolingual English, Anglo American woman who had taught 17 years at PCC. A tenured faculty member, Carol had served in a variety of administrative posts, including chair of the English department and chair of Women's Studies. She made efforts to stay abreast of current research, theory, and practice in composition by taking sabbaticals to teach in a nationally acclaimed writing program and to take graduate courses on language and literacy education. Carol was highly committed to the outreach program in Appleton and to the Mexican American students at the school. For example, she had been instrumental in instituting and maintaining in-class tutoring in the Appleton Center English classes, and she advocated making computers and computer writing courses available to students there. She was also a strong proponent of bringing the Puente Project to PCC, a program that has been on the main campus for several years now.

During the two years I was at the Appleton Center, the tutors were three men and a woman, all Anglo American, and all with extensive experience in writing and tutoring. Two were students at PCC who also tutored at the writing center on the main campus. They received their AA degrees in English during the time of the study, with one transferring to the creative writing program at the nearest campus of the University of California. A third tutor had already received his BA in creative writing from the same UC campus; the fourth was the director of the writing center at a local high school and left the Appleton Center after the first year of the study to take a position as editor of the newsletter published by the local National Writing Project affiliate. Three of the four tutors were published writers, two were journalists, and one was a poet and short story writer. Although two of the tutors had some Spanish-speaking abilities, I never heard either of them converse with students in Spanish.

TUTORING AND RESEARCHING AT THE APPLETON CENTER

My entry into Appleton Center life was made particularly easy by my prior acquaintance with the teacher of English 10, Carol. Carol and I met in a graduate course on language and literacy while she was on sabbatical and I was taking courses for my doctorate. During this time I learned of her work at the Appleton Center. Once she resumed teaching at the College, I asked for permission to observe her class at the Appleton Center. She suggested that I work as a tutor for the Center instead. I accepted her offer, and my observations began.

My primary method of data collection was participant observation. The degree of my participation and observation varied during my two years in the field. During the first year of participant observation, I worked with two others as a tutor in the Appleton Center English classes. We traveled among the three English classes as the teachers requested, doing individual or small group tutoring, depending on each teacher's plans. It was during this period that I chose a single classroom in which I could more closely observe during my second year of research at the Center.

I decided to limit the study of classroom interaction to English 10 for several reasons. First of all, English 10 was a basic writing or remedial writing course. Credit for the course was not transferable to a four-year university. As mentioned in Chapter One, basic writing courses such as this are particularly crucial points in the college careers of Mexican American students. Students' success or failure in these courses may influence not only their success in college but also their decision to stay in college at all. I believe a description of the interaction in classrooms that have such an impact on the lives of Mexican American students is of vital importance.

Second, although I would have preferred to study English 5 because students in that class were considered to have the poorest English skills, and therefore, I assumed, they were most likely to be at risk for failing or dropping out, because of a staffing

change there was considerable doubt that I would be able to conduct this project in that class. The next level of basic writing,
English 10, was taught by Carol who had first told me about the
Appleton Center and who had originally invited me to observe and
tutor in the program. In addition, she encouraged a research project in her classroom and was certain to teach the course there for
at least one more year. Therefore I selected her English 10 class as
the focus of the project.

During the first year I collected the following types of data: field
notes, photocopies of essays written by students whom I had
tutored extensively in class, teacher assignments and handouts,
course texts, and teachers' written instructions to the tutors. By far
the most extensive data collection method, narrative field notes,
were written after each four-hour meeting of the classes. Classes
met 30 times during the two semesters for a total of 116 hours of
participant observation during the first year. Observation focused
on students with whom I regularly worked, the kinds of literacy
activities and teaching in the three classes, and conversations with
the teachers, tutors, and students regarding the program. I also
wrote analytic observer comments comparing the activities in each
class and student response to them. After reviewing these reflective
notes it became clear to me that teacher and student beliefs and
concerns about the nature and purpose of schooling and literacy
education could be discerned from an analysis of their actions in
the classroom and their informal statements on the topics over
time. Moreover, some teachers and students had differing beliefs
and concerns that likely affected the conduct and effectiveness of
classroom lessons. These concerns were related to these individuals' lives outside the classroom, making apparent the importance of
personal histories and the sociocultural situation in understanding
the classroom interaction I observed.

To further investigate these issues, I focused on the English 10
classroom during my second year at the Appleton Center. I quit
working as a paid tutor, instead volunteering to be a fourth tutor
who would spend all of her time in English 10. As described earlier, the teacher in English 10 used the tutors a minimum of one
hour per class session. This schedule meant I would have many
opportunities during regular class meetings to work with students
individually as well as to observe whole class interaction. Class
meetings during the second year totaled 29, or 109 hours, of participant observation. Again, I took extensive field notes. I also collected all class assignments, all focal student papers, the teacher's
comments on the focal student papers, and the teacher's grades

for the classes. Although I spoke with the teacher frequently about the students and her teaching, recording this in the field notes, I also audiotaped discussions with the teacher after each semester of the second year for a total of five hours.

During the first semester of year two (fall 1989) my field notes focused on teacher–student, tutor–student, and student–student interaction. I also tutored focal students outside of class at their request, writing extensive field notes after each tutorial session ended. The focal student that semester was Amado. In the field notes for these meetings with him, I noted his questions about, problems with, and apparent beliefs about school, English 10, and writing. I also noted information about his personal and educational history that seemed relevant to his current concerns and beliefs. I tutored Amado outside of class four times for a total of approximately four hours. In class I tutored him frequently, working on grammar exercises, returned essays, and rough drafts. I also audiotaped some tutorial sessions with Amado, collecting about one and one half hours of tutorial tape.

During the second semester of year two (spring 1990), I increased my data collection in the classroom to include not only field notes, but also audiotapes of every class session, creating a corpus of over 55 hours of classroom interaction, including approximately 10 hours of tutor–student interaction. In addition, I taped over 20 hours of tutorials with students outside of class. Most of these sessions were with four new focal students: Mónica (11 hours), Isaura (six hours), Juanita (three hours), and Federico (two hours). As I began data analysis, I conducted follow-up interviews with available informants (teacher, tutors, Isaura, Amado, and Juanita) to gain additional information to confirm or call into question my understandings of their perspectives. All of these interviews, except those with the tutors, were audiotaped as well.

During the first year, I began collecting data on the Appleton community by reading the local paper and historical and current literature about the area, and by listening to student, teacher, and tutor comments about the town. This level of research continued into the second year, with the addition of my attendance at local community functions. During the second year I began collecting data about Portolá Community College and the Appleton Center. I met with the Director of the Office of Institutional Research at the college to obtain statistical and survey data about the students. In addition, I visited the Office of the President to research the creation of the Appleton Center.

The goal of my data analysis was a rich description of the formal English literacy learning environment of these Mexican American adults, moving from a broad view of community, school, and program to succeedingly narrow, but more detailed, pictures of these students in the classroom context, and finally as individuals with personal histories that they brought to their various understandings of the interaction in the composition classroom. The analysis reveals how classroom interaction influences and is influenced by the personal histories, classroom context, and larger social–historical factors in which students and their teachers are immersed. This analysis required multiple sources of data and multiple methods of data analysis at all levels.

The broadest level of analysis provides a general description of the social, educational, and linguistic contexts in which these Mexican American adults were learning to read and write English. This analysis was based on field notes gathered during both years of the study, secondary research into the historical and contemporary concerns of the community, and demographic information from the community college. Analysis at the level of the community began with regular reading of the local newspaper to discover current "points of contention" in the community that revealed and contributed to the ethnic strife evident in the community. These themes were readily apparent from their frequency in the papers, the number and type of letters to the editor they inspired, and the community response to them. These "points of contention," which I will discuss in detail in Chapter Three, were found in all aspects of community life: political, economic, cultural, and educational. They included a lawsuit regarding the lack of Hispanic representation on city council, a 19-month strike in the local frozen food processing plants, an uproar over the second annual Cinco de Mayo fiesta, and a lack of access to adequate education because of segregation and limited bilingual education programs.

After it became apparent that through all these issues ethnic battles of power and oppression, of silence and voice were being fought, I continued to follow these issues during my two years in the field. It was necessary to learn the status and history of these points of contention if I was to interpret successfully the perspectives of people who had been living in this community for most of their lives and for whom these ethnic battles and their histories had shaped, in part, their ways of understanding and responding to the world, including whatever transpired in the composition classroom. This level of analysis helped me to understand the varying social and educational contexts and perspectives influencing interaction in the classroom by describing the sociocultural situation in which the outreach program exists.

Analysis of statistical and survey data gathered at the level of the community college was conducted primarily by comparing differences in the student populations of the main campus to those at the Appleton Center, in terms of their ethnicity, language background, and educational goals. I researched the creation of the Appleton Center to gain an understanding of the institutional intentions with regard to the Center and to compare the institution's statement of purpose with students' expectations of the program. Both comparisons provide more information about the situation in which the program exists, in this case, at the level of the college rather than the community. The analyses reveal vast differences in the student body at the outreach program, an outreach program that is nevertheless administered by the main campus. They also reveal vast differences in the interests and concerns of the administration and the students regarding the outreach program.

The next level of analysis provided a picture of the sociolinguistic and interactional environment of the classroom, relying heavily on field notes written during the second year of the study and audiotapes of classroom discourse gathered during the second semester of year two. I completed this analysis for three different types of interaction that regularly occurred in the classroom: official whole class discussions, official one-to-one interaction with a tutor, and unofficial interaction among peers. Transcriptions were made as accurate as possible at the lexical level. See Appendix A for a list of transcription conventions used in this work.

For the analysis of whole class discussions, transcriptions of four typical whole class discussions (eight hours or approximately 316 pages of transcript) were selected to represent typical lessons from the beginning to the end of the second semester of year two. After two years of experience observing in the class, it became easy to identify a typical lesson. The topic was either students' assigned reading, workbook exercises, or composition assignments. It did not involve a guest speaker. It was not interrupted by unforeseen circumstances, such as a power outage or a sudden change in tutor scheduling. In terms of structure and content, these typical lessons began to appear quite similar over time—they had patterned opening, middle, and closing sections.

First, the whole class discussions were analyzed thematically to gain insights into the topics of concern to the teacher and the students, using the episode, a series of turns on the same theme or topic, as the unit of analysis. "Key themes," that is, recurring top-ics of importance, were found in the talk of the teacher and the students. These themes served to help elucidate how the teacher and the students understood and responded to particular interac-tive situations in the classroom. For all participants, key themes were inextricably tied to their personal histories, past educational experiences, first language, and culture as well as to the larger sociocultural milieu in which the outreach program existed.

Second, the transcripts were analyzed to discover the "partici-pant structures" or "structural arrangements of interaction" dur-ing classroom lessons (Philips, 1972/1985, p. 377). In the classroom participant structures are "ways of arranging verbal interaction with students" (Philips, 1972/1985, p. 377). The basic unit of analysis for this work was the speech event, which is any activity that is "directly governed by rules or norms for the use of speech" (Hymes, 1974, p. 52). The participant structures were analyzed quantitatively to determine differences in frequency of turns and turn types (e.g., initiation, response) for different ethnic- and gender-based groupings in the various interactional contexts of this study. Participant structures were also analyzed qualita-tively to identify and describe the types of interaction strategies used in varying contexts and to examine for the effect of language and cultural differences. Data from the detailed field notes written during this time provided yet another source of evidence for the analysis of the structure and content of classroom discourse.

The analysis of the structure and content of classroom interac-tion was not limited only to a study of talk in the classroom. Interaction surrounding course assignments—the handouts, the student essays, the teacher's feedback—was also analyzed for interaction patterns based on culture, gender, and language. Patterns and strategies in student and teacher response were dis-covered and related to their interaction in classroom discussions. Furthermore, these data were culled for information regarding focal students' personal, educational, and linguistic histories in an attempt to gain insights into the sources of individual students' beliefs and concerns and the interactional differences observed.

I designed this study to allow for a naturalistic understanding of how Mexican American adult students and their Anglo American teacher interact in the basic writing classroom. In order to allow for consideration of a broader range of influences on the negotia-tion of classroom interaction, I took particular care to gain a full understanding of both the macro-level sociocultural situation in which the outreach program existed and the micro-level analysis of interaction in the classroom. Such an approach deepens our current understanding of cultural difference and literacy education. The interaction one can observe in the classroom is but a small part of the lives of those studied. The interaction is affected by the personal experiences of those involved and the sociocultural situation in which the participants exist. Although it is difficult for anyone not a part of that environment to completely grasp it, in order to gain a fuller understanding of the causes, motivations, and meanings behind what is observed in the classroom, it is necessary to learn as much as possible from the macro- and micro-levels beyond the classroom.

3
A HISTORY OF SILENCING

Our [Mexican American] history, or that part of it within the American
community, has all too frequently been one of inability to speak up,
to speak out, or to speak at all on the issues that concern
us. Specifically, our exclusion from the institutional life of American
society and from the forums it provides has kept us from being heard,
even when our voices have been loud and our concerns compelling.
—Madrid, 1986, p. ix

In order to understand the broader factors that directly and indirectly influenced the classroom interaction, particularly the
silence of the Mexican American students, I spent two years learning as much as I could about the political, economic, cultural, educational, and linguistic situation of the Appleton community. I
delved deeply into the local history and current affairs of the town
to learn more about life in Appleton. Although it is impossible for
me to present the complete history of Appleton or to document
fully its currents situation, certain "points of contention"—or
sources of repeated conflict in the Appleton community in the past
and the present, such as political representation or linguistic
access to education—illustrate how the same problems that
plagued Appleton nearly 150 years ago still exist today.

Conflict between Anglo Americans and Mexican Americans has
been the overarching theme in Appleton community interaction
from the Mexican American War to the present. Through this conflict Anglo Americans have usurped and maintained power, both
political and economic, while simultaneously attempting to eradi-
cate the unique cultural attributes of Mexican American society,
resulting in a deepening divide between Mexican Americans and
Anglo Americans. A literal and metaphorical silencing of Mexican
Americans can be seen as the common thread running throughout

49

the otherwise disparate topics I will present. As Madrid suggests in the quotation opening this chapter, despite their attempts to be heard, Mexican Americans in Appleton were excluded from participation and power through pervasive silencing.

To address the *social* context, I begin by providing a view of typical political, economic, cultural, and ethnic issues that affected Mexican Americans in the Appleton area at time of the Mexican American War (1845–1848), and later I illustrate how these same issues are sources of conflict or "points of contention" in the community today. This information is important for understanding the classroom experiences and interaction observed. Then, I present a brief overview of the *educational* situation of Mexican Americans in California, both historically and at present, followed by a description of what is known about Mexican American education in the Appleton area in the past and where the current "points of contention" surrounding education are at present. Last, I present the current educational situation of Mexican American students at the Appleton Center through an examination of the creation and development of the Center as an outreach program of Portolá Community College.

Given the vast history of Mexican Americans in California, numerous points of contention were salient in the data; however, I will only review a sufficient number to offer a sense of the historical and current interaction between Mexican Americans and Anglo Americans in Appleton. Moreover, it is beyond the scope of this chapter to provide all of the relevant historical data for any one theme, instead I describe only exemplary interaction surrounding themes in the distant past and the present rather than attempting to provide an exhaustive summary of all available data.

SILENCING IN THE COMMUNITY

Interaction between Anglo Americans and Mexican Americans in Appleton is shaped by the past: the history of Mexican American and Anglo American interaction in California and in Appleton. The single most important factor in this past is the Mexican American War and the laws and uncodified, but no less fixed, modes of interaction that resulted from it. As soon as Mexicans were conquered militarily, relationships changed to reflect that. As McWilliams has astutely observed: "It is only within the framework of this age-old conflict [exemplified by the Mexican-American War] that it is possible to understand the pattern of Anglo-Hispano cultural relations in the Southwest today"

(McWilliams, 1948/1968, p. 98). The interaction began with conflict and division; in the case of Appleton, it continues in much the same mode today. One way in which the Anglo Americans have attempted to maintain power over the Mexican Americans has been to silence them in as many arenas of life as possible—political, economic, cultural, and ethnic.

The themes of suffrage and political representation shortly after the Mexican American War provide examples of the attempted silencing of the Mexican American political voice by the newly empowered Anglo Americans. With the conquest of the Northern Territories by the United States in 1848 came the most obvious loss of Mexican American political power vis-à-vis Anglo Americans. It is self-evident that there would be problems between Mexican Americans and Anglo Americans. Having just fought a war, each still considered the other the mortal enemy. The Treaty of Guadalupe Hidalgo, signed in 1848, promised that those Mexican citizens who chose to become citizens of the United States would have all of the rights of other United States citizens. The key section of the treaty with regard to citizenship reads:

> The Mexicans who . . . shall not preserve the character of citizens of the Mexican Republic . . . shall be incorporated into the Union of the United States and be admitted at the proper time (to be judged by the Congress of the United States) to the enjoyment of all the rights of citizens of the United States according to the principles of the constitution; and in the mean time shall be maintained and protected in the free enjoyment of their liberty and property, and secured in the free exercise of their religion without restriction. (Treaty of Guadalupe Hidalgo, as quoted in Weber, 1973, p. 164)

Though an apparently innocuous, even generous statement, it had several problems. First of all, because citizenship was not immediately granted, there was no guarantee that it would be and, according to Griswold del Castillo (1990), attempts were made to prevent it. That detail notwithstanding, the treaty reads as if those who chose to become citizens should enjoy "all of the rights of citizens of the United States," such as the right to vote, the right to representation, the right to due process under the law, and equal protection under the law. But there is much evidence that these rights were continually denied or in various ways eroded as the Anglo Americans came into greater numbers and influence in California. The end result, despite what the Treaty of Guadalupe Hidalgo promised, was that in fact most Mexican Americans could not vote, could not be on a jury, and were denied other rights guaranteed to Anglo citizens of the United States (Acuña, 1988).

As early as they could, many Anglo Americans in California attempted to disenfranchise Mexican Americans—even before they were officially citizens of the newly formed state. When the California constitutional convention convened in 1849 to outline the laws of the new state, there was a proposal that suffrage should be granted to "every white, male citizen of Mexico who shall have elected to become a citizen of the U.S." (Griswold del Castillo, 1990, p. 66). But only those Mexicans of direct descent from the Spanish explorers could meet the "white" criterion. Most Mexicans were of Indian and/or African heritage. Furthermore, in Mexico, all "civilized" men, whether they were Indian, Hispanic, Black, or a combination thereof, were granted the right to vote.

Because only six to eight of the 48 representatives to the constitutional convention were Mexican,[1] there was little done to oppose the proposal (Pitt, 1966). Although all of the Mexican delegates reportedly argued against the criterion, Griswold del Castillo (1990) states that no changes in the constitution were made as a result of their arguments; the representatives concluded that Mestizos were "not in fact American citizens" (p. 67). Heizer and Almquist (1971) concur that "Indian and African minorities were . . . barred from the right of suffrage" (p. 104). Some historians disagree on this point, however. Pitt (1966) maintains that the wording of the constitution was changed to grant suffrage to "certain Indians" (p. 45), and Weber believes the constitution was written to prevent "completely disenfranchising Indians" (Weber, 1973, p. 148). Whatever the case, the "right" of suffrage for former Mexican citizens in the United States was, from a constitutional perspective, uncertain at best.

Pitt (1966) provides a description of the types of difficulties Mexican Americans confronted in the 1853 elections in Los Angeles as a result of their ambiguous status:

> Since citizenship was a vaguely defined status, arguments arose constantly at the polling window . . . that So-and-So was born in Mexico, or was an Indian or a transient, and thus ineligible to vote. Irregularities occurred often. (Pitt, 1966, p. 132)

Spanish-speaking Mexican Americans had even more difficulties taking part in elections as the state constitution's promise to translate all laws into Spanish was never fulfilled nor was polling

---

[1]Pitt (1966) claims there were eight Hispanic representatives (p. 45). Griswold del Castillo (1990) states there were six (p. 66). McWilliams (1948/1968) argues there were seven (p. 129).

information translated (Acuña, 1988). Bilingual election materials were not required in California until 1975, and only then as a result of the Federal Voting Rights Act. In fact, until 1970 there was a provision in the California constitution making the ability to read English a prerequisite for voting.

Few data exist on suffrage in the Appleton area in the mid to late 1800s. Published polling lists from the time reveal relatively few Hispanic surnames. A list of voters from nearby Loma Linda in 1868 shows only 23 of 329 voters had Hispanic surnames. An 1871 Appleton poll list with 714 voters lists: "Californians [Mexican Americans], 58; Americans, 504; Irish, 59; English, 16; Scotch, 5; German, 16; Prussians, 10" (Lewis, 1976/1986, p. 9).

The loss of Mexican American political power in the northern portion of California, near Gold Country, was a matter of sheer numbers (Acuña, 1988). As would be expected, before the Mexican American War, Mexicans were nearly 100% of the population, but the combined effect of the war and the discovery of gold was a population explosion. The population of California more than doubled in just one year, from 115,000 in 1849 to 380,000 in 1850, and nearly all of the newcomers were Anglo American. Although the Mexican American population grew from 13,000 in 1848 to 30,000 in 1850, also as a result of the gold rush, the increase of Anglo Americans was so much greater that by 1850 Mexican Americans were already only 15% of the population. By 1870, they were just 4% (Weber, 1973). With the Mexican American loss of majority in the state came the loss of support for the interests of the Mexican American population.

Although Mexican Americans tried to remain involved in governing California, they were quickly and effectively eliminated from positions of power, or "silenced" politically. By 1851 there were no more Mexican Americans in the state senate. By the 1860s there were only a few Mexican Americans in the state assembly, and by 1880 there were no people with Spanish surnames in elected positions anywhere in California (Acuña, 1988). As mentioned earlier, in 1849, when there had been 30,000 Mexican Americans and a total population of 115,000, only six to eight delegates of 48 to the constitutional convention were of Mexican descent. Although Mexican Americans were one fifth of the population, they were only given one sixth to one eighth of the delegates to the convention.

Anglo Americans have also attempted to silence Mexican Americans economically by unilaterally divesting them of property and other sources of capital. With much land to settle and defend in what is now the Western United States, both the

Spanish and Mexican governments made "land grants" to individuals who had in one way or another served them (often through the armed services) faithfully. In California, these various grants became the many *ranchos* of Alta California. Like all property, these grants were guaranteed by the Treaty of Guadalupe Hidalgo to new Americans who were formerly citizens of Mexico. However, this aspect of the treaty, like that pertaining to citizenship, was effectively rendered null and void—in this case, by additional legislation.

In establishing the Land Act of 1851, the U.S. government unilaterally decided that legal claim to every existing land grant had to be proved or it would be reverted to public property or turned over to the challenger, if there was one. Eight hundred and thirteen cases were decided in California, each taking an average of 17 years to settle (Weber, 1973). This legislation proved to be an expensive proposition for all land grant holders as they had to retain lawyers, which tied up capital in the form of land and cattle (Acuña, 1988). Many grant holders in Northern California were driven off their land by squatters or bankruptcy while their cases were pending. Given the primarily agrarian economy of Northern California, the loss of land as a result of these suits effectively eliminated the economic "voice" of Mexican Americans while simultaneously adding to Anglo American economic power.

Just such a battle over land titles clouds the history of the area of Northern California which is currently known as Appleton. The real name of the town (Appleton is a pseudonym) was derived from the surname of an Anglo American who obtained rights—under questionable pretenses—to the rancho where Appleton was established (Lewis, 1980). According to one source, the Anglo American "established an 'adverse claim' to part of the Rancho" (Koch, 1973, p. 163), a method commonly used to acquire land under the Land Act of 1851 from the well-established Mexican Americans (Pitt, 1966). Although the claim was eventually cleared, proving that indeed it was legally granted to Sebastian Rodríguez (Koch, 1973), by then the town had been renamed Appleton and the Mexican American grantee had died (Lewis, 1980). The name of the central street in town was changed from "Pájaro" to "Main Street" (Koch, 1973, p. 163), and other street names were changed to honor important Anglo American townspeople (Lewis, 1976/1986). This economic "silencing" of Mexican Americans through the confiscation of property and other basic economic rights was common in the wake of the U.S. conquest of the Northern territories of Mexico in 1848.

I chose "Appleton" as the fictitious name for this town to reflect the Anglo American nature of the town's real name. Because most cities in the area are named for Spanish saints, Native American tribes, or land grant holders, the decision to change the village name in 1868 from the Spanish name it had been given by Portolá's party in 1769, to Appleton, is not only symbolic of the attitude toward Mexican American culture at the time, but it is also symbolic of anti-Mexican American attitudes in the town at the time of this study. The manner in which the land for the town was acquired and the manner in which the town was renamed both reflect attempts by the Anglo Americans to symbolically silence Mexican American influence in the community.

Laws were passed early in California's statehood designed specifically to silence traditional Mexican American cultural practices in California, revealing a general disrespect for all things Mexican American. Various aspects of the Mexican American fiesta were targets of these laws. The first such law prohibited "'bull, bear, cock, or prize fights, horse races, circus, theater, or any place of barbarous or noisy amusement on the Sabbath'" (quoted in Pitt, 1966, p. 197). But Sunday was the traditional day for Mexican American families and friends to gather at their ranchos for festivities, including animal contests and horse racing—with huge bets on the side—and plenty of music, dancing, and imbibing. This "Sabbath law" was intended to interfere with these traditional activities (Acuña, 1988; Pitt, 1966). Furthermore, a "gambling control act" was passed prohibiting betting, an important part of these contests. The ultimate effect of the "Sabbath law" was evident in 1858 with the last recorded occurrence of horse racing and bull-fighting among Mexican Americans in Los Angeles (Pitt, 1966).

A temperance law was enacted at the same time as the Sabbath law that "the Spanish-speaking properly regarded as a direct slap at their customary celebration of holidays" (Pitt, 1966, p. 198). Weddings could last for as many as five days in the Mexican American community, and balls, including such famous dances as the fandango, were a frequent and cherished part of life. The temperance law and a $10 tax on all fandangos imposed by the Los Angeles Common Council discouraged such traditional celebrations (Pitt, 1966). Apparently, no such action was taken against equally cherished Anglo American traditions. Legislation against Mexican American cultural activities provided a further source of silencing from the Anglo Americans in power.

Even after the official end of the Mexican American War in 1848, hostilities against Mexican Americans continued. Histories of

Mexican Americans in California and the Southwest document not only the anti-Mexican American sentiment that has historically existed in the region, but also the resulting violence (Acuña, 1988; McWilliams, 1948/1968; Pitt, 1966). Anecdotal records of life in the Appleton area[2] in the past reveal similar patterns of ethnically motivated acts of violence. In his recollections of the area from 1855 to 1880, Mylar (1929/1970) describes numerous hangings, false arrests, and incidents of harassment against Mexicans in the area. Dunn (1989) describes in detail a number of lynchings of Mexicans that occurred in the last half of the 19th century amidst Santa Cruz County's "often racist white population" (p. 14), lynchings that the local papers supported.

There is little doubt that many more of these lynchings occurred than were recorded in the local history books. Lydon (1980) in his introduction to Rowland's history of Santa Cruz notes that like most local historians, Rowland "excluded the story of the poor relations that existed between Yankee pioneers and Spanish-speaking residents of the County. The racism and animosity that accompanied the ethnic diversity of Santa Cruz were unpleasant facts not to be mentioned" (p. xiv). Lydon continues his critique noting that Rowland reports a 1877 double lynching "in his facts-only style (failing to note that both men were Spanish-speaking) and closes the paragraph as if in a hurry to be done with the unfortunate event. That Santa Cruz mob action was a signal event in the history of Mexican-Yankee relations, however, as it marked the end of 25 years of mob violence against the Spanish-speaking in California" (pp. xi–xv). The term "Judge Lynch" was used frequently in newspaper accounts, suggesting that it was an accepted form of justice to Anglo Americans (Dunn, 1989, p. 13; Mylar, 1929/1970, p. 47). The *Daily Alta California*, a San Francisco-based paper of the time, indicated how commonplace such "justice" was by writing, "'It was almost a by-word in our midst, that none but Mexicans could be convicted of a capital offense'" (quoted in Pitt, 1966, p. 70).

Although the specifics may vary slightly, points of contention exist today in Appleton over many of the same issues that created conflict and effectively silenced the Mexican American population in the past: political, economic, cultural, and ethnic. Mexican Americans continue to battle for political representation, economic justice, the right to celebrate their cultural heritage, and ethnic tolerance.

---

[2] These accounts are from the three counties that intersect near Appleton: Santa Cruz, Monterey, and San Benito. These three counties were all one county of Monterey until 1874 (Fink, 1982).

Nearly 150 years later, voting and the right to representation continue to be points of contention in Appleton. In 1985, after numerous attempts to get a Mexican American on the city council with an at-large system of city council and mayoral elections, the Mexican American Legal Defense and Education Fund (MALDEF) supported a suit by three unsuccessful Mexican American city council candidates against the city of Appleton. They argued that the at-large system violated the voting rights of Mexican Americans in the community, where from 1971 to 1985 eight Hispanic candidates ran for city council, and none was elected.

The suit was heard for the first time in federal district court in 1987. At the time of the trial, no Hispanic had ever been elected in Appleton under the at-large system. Nevertheless, the district court found that the at-large system was not discriminatory. MALDEF appealed the judgment, and the district court decision was eventually overturned. The appeals court found discrimination and mandated the immediate implementation of a district election system that would provide for Mexican American representation on the city council. But the Appleton City Council appealed the decision to the U.S. Supreme Court. As a result, protests broke out in Appleton. A candlelight vigil was held outside a City Council meeting, while Mexican Americans, visibly upset by this decision, filled the meeting hall (Koss, 1989). Petitions of complaint about the city's action were submitted to the council, but to no avail. In the end, the Supreme Court chose not to hear the voting rights case, letting the appeals court decision stand.

The appeals court found voting in Appleton to be "racially polarized" based on tests of "the cohesiveness of the minority group," the "power of the white bloc voting to defeat the minority candidate," and the "actual results of minority-preferred candidates" (*Gomez, et al. v. [Appleton]*, 1988, pp. 5380–5381). In other words, the plaintiffs proved that the Mexican American voters in Appleton tended to vote as a group for specific candidates. These candidates were repeatedly defeated by candidates preferred by Anglo American voters. Low voter turnout was a major issue in the court decision. Although the City maintained that low voter turnout by Mexican Americans showed a lack of cohesiveness, the appeals court found that "low voter registrations and turnout . . . may be traceable in part to historical discrimination . . . Because they were denied access to the political processes through years of discrimination, the Mexican-Americans do not now register and vote in overwhelming numbers" (*Gomez, et al. v. [Appleton]*, 1988, p. 5383).

Despite much excitement over the victory in court, the first district elections in the city yielded only one Hispanic city council member, although three Hispanics ran. One unsuccessful Mexican American candidate, reflecting on her loss, referred to the history of Mexican American voter discrimination, saying, "'We're dealing with hundreds of years of people getting nothing out of the process'" (Johnson, 1988b, p. 10). Another said the new election system "'hasn't changed a damn thing. . . . I haven't seen progress in Hispanic affairs'" (Brazil, 1990, p. B-1). Although winning the law suit appeared to be progress for the Mexican American community, years of silencing at the polls had resulted in continuing low voter turnout, yet another form of political silence. Only after direct confrontation with the Anglo American-elected, Anglo American-run government that supposedly represented the interests of the majority Mexican Americans population in Appleton was justice finally served. It is no wonder with this kind of representation that "political despair and cynicism run so deep" among the Mexican Americans in Appleton (Johnson, 1988c, p. 12).

Adding to the sense of despair in the Mexican American community is their inability to influence their own economic situation today. Although their lands (if they own any) are not stolen, as in the past, their livelihoods, nevertheless, have been repeatedly threatened. In September 1985, 1,700 frozen food workers, mostly Mexican American women, went on strike at the two major plants in Appleton because the companies were planning to lower wages 30%, eliminate seniority, and reduce vacation time. Whereas the women had been making as much as $7.06 an hour at one of the plants, they were now expected to work for as little as $4.25 (Silver, 1989).

The *huelguistas* (strikers) stayed out on strike for 19 months and two days. Strike benefits were minimal, forcing some parents to take their children out of school and put them to work to help support the family. Other families were evicted from their homes. As many as 2,000 workers and supporters took part in protest marches. Even Jesse Jackson and César Chávez came to Appleton to show their solidarity with the strikers. Pickets regularly ended in arrests. Police brutality was common (Silver, 1989).

Over the course of the 19 months, one of the companies settled with its workers and the other company went bankrupt. The major creditor of the latter offered to settle with the workers—for $5.25 an hour and no medical benefits. The women, many of them the sole breadwinners, could not support their families on so little. Although the union recommended that they accept the package, the strikers refused, going out on a wildcat strike. With no strike benefits at all, the workers were forced to settle within three weeks. They won their medical benefits, but wages remained at $5.25.

The strike's effect on the town was devastating. One townsperson noted during the strike,"This community is shredded, just torn apart by this strike" (Silver, 1989). A local historian concluded, "The strike was a painful, deeply divisive crucible which forever changed [Appleton]" (Lydon, 1989). Of course, the most devastating effect was felt by the predominantly Mexican American workers in the plants. Despite their attempts to speak up for their economic rights, they were ultimately silenced, after 19 months of struggle.

Attempts to celebrate Mexican American culture in the community are subjected to attempts to silence today, as they were over a century again. A recent cultural event in the town, the second annual Cinco de Mayo fiesta, provides an example of how the town implicitly and explicitly discourages Mexican American culture. That it was only the second officially recognized Cinco de Mayo festival should provide some indication of how well-received the event had been in the past. This particular year (1990), the fiesta received the support of the Chamber of Commerce who felt it would be an excellent way to promote downtown business in the wake of the Loma Prieta earthquake of October, 1989.

"Fiesta Appleton" received a good deal of advance publicity. The "Official Program" for the two-day celebration was a color insert in the local newspaper (published three days before the fiesta) with 16 pages of ads, feature articles, and the schedule of entertainment for the weekend. Also, advertisements with pictures of Mexican American community leaders and their families ran in the local newspaper, the free newspapers published in the area, and the bilingual paper in Appleton. The editor of the local newspaper even encouraged people to attend, using his column on the opinion page to do so

To everybody:

The Fiesta [Appleton] is being held downtown from 10 AM to 7 PM today and tomorrow, with parades Sunday at 9:30 AM and 1 PM. It promises to be a big community event and you'll regret it if you miss it. ("To everybody," 1990, p. 12)

The plan was to cordon off Main Street, making the downtown area a pedestrian mall. Bandstands would be erected at opposite ends of the designated area. Food stands, an antique and "low-rider" car show, mariachis, ballets folkloricos, a famous Motown singer, local high school rappers, and carnival rides would provide plenty of entertainment for the estimated 25,000 who would attend.

But some members of the Anglo American community began to undermine this special event, employing a variety of tactics to do so. In the days preceding the event, the two Mexican American members of the Chamber of Commerce who cochaired the event received "grumblings and crank calls." According to one of the cochairs, the complaints were "racist comments" about closing off downtown for "those Mexicans." The cochair said that he hoped that the fiesta would provide needed "healing" of ethnic relations in the community (Heckman, 1990, p. 1).

After the fiesta, it was disclosed that an attempt to thwart the event occurred just eight days prior to Cinco de Mayo. Although the planning committee had received unanimous approval for the event from the city council months in advance, at the last minute the assistant city manager and the police chief asked the city attorney for a ruling regarding the legality of cordoning off down-town streets and charging admission. The city attorney informed the fiesta planning committee that it could not charge admission, although the committee had already advanced thousands of dol-lars for performers and security. The Mexican American cochairs questioned the city attorney until he admitted that "charging an admission would *not* violate any city ordinances or state laws [emphasis added]" and the fiesta went ahead as planned (Alvarado, 1990b, p. 1). The fiesta received positive front-page coverage on May 5th and 6th, and 22,000 attended the two-day event.

But after the fiesta numerous letters to the editor complained that the event had not been free. Businesses in the cordoned-off area banded together to write a letter of complaint to the city coun-cil citing lost business, fire hazards, and complaining customers as a result of the fiesta. The following year (1991), the Chamber of Commerce refused to sponsor the event. A much smaller festival was held for a few hours one afternoon in a public park. The only mention of Cinco de Mayo in the newspaper that year was a letter from the editor that could be interpreted as apologetic, stating[3]

> Cinco de Mayo, we feel certain, will get even bigger with the passage of time, as Anglos get into the spirit of the holiday and Latinos emerge as the largest group in California's diverse population. ("Cinco de Mayo," 1991, p. 24)

---

[3] The paper did cover a local elementary school celebration as well in 1991.

Through direct legal and indirect social pressure, attempts to silence Mexican American cultural displays still occur in Appleton today.

The current milieu in Appleton continues to be charged with ethnic tension and prejudice. Although rarely physically violent, the open hostility between Anglo Americans and Mexican Americans certainly scars just as deeply. This hostility does not even need to be sparked by a particular event. The following exchange in the local newspaper's letters to the editor occurred without apparent provocation. It was initiated by an Anglo American.

> I recently stood at the corner of East Lake Avenue and Main Street and heard a rooster crow. Is this what you want? . . . A mercado [open market] is planned for downtown Appleton. Is this Appleton for the '90s? Sounds more like Mexico than the United States. (Whittle, 1990, p. 24)

Seven days later the following response appeared:

> Mr. Whittle, your hate for Mexican people showed with every word you wrote. I am very proud of my heritage and my people, and I will never go and let a hypocrite like you go unanswered. If you don't like [Appleton] the way it is, go back [to] wherever you came from and don't let the door slam in your rear. (Cervantes, 1991, p. 24)

Nor is the open hostility between Anglo Americans and Mexican Americans limited to newsprint. The following exchanges were found one day written on the bathroom wall at the public library (in just one stall!)

1. —TODOS MEXICANOS VA A MEXICO! [ALL MEXICANS GO TO MEXICO!]
   —Get your head out of the sand. We're the majority.
      You move.
2. —Why do Mexicans always write on the walls?
   —It isn't just Mexicans, is it?

(Field notes, March 3, 1990)

Like other ethnic hostilities of the past and present, these exchanges were obviously initiated by Anglo Americans, without any apparent provocation.

Prejudice can also be found in face-to-face interactions in Appleton today, although it is somewhat more subtle. The following incident occurred at the public library while I awaited a focal student:

A Mexican American woman in her mid-40s wanted to borrow a high school equivalency exam preparation manual from the public library. The Anglo American librarian in her late 30s, refused to loan her the book unless the woman left a deposit. The librarian attempted to explain.

Librarian:	I guess I can be honest with you about what happens to these books.
Mexican American Patron:	People take them out and never bring them back?
Librarian:	No, these people [Mexican Americans] are just not accustomed to being library users. They just throw them in the back seat of the car. They get torn. (The librarian takes the piece of notepaper on which the patron has written the title of the book she wants.) For one thing, you've misspelled the title.

The open hostility between Mexican Americans and Anglo Americans that currently exists in Appleton is but the culmination of a long history of physical and emotional violence suffered by Mexican Americans in California. Politically, economically, and culturally, Anglo Americans have attempted to silence the Mexican American population, past and present. The next section of this chapter discusses how education has also played a role, historically and at present, in attempting to silence the Mexican American population in California.

SILENCING IN THE SCHOOLS

In order to understand the current educational situation in which the Appleton Center is immersed and the experiences shared by students who have been educated in Appleton area schools, it is necessary to consider from a historical perspective how this situation evolved. In this section I provide a diachronic analysis of Mexican American education in California, focusing particularly on those issues that have caused conflict and division between Anglo American and Mexican American communities in the past and that continue to be "points of contention" today. Then I present the data that exist regarding the history of education specifically in the Appleton area apropos to these issues. Finally, I use this historical perspective as a backdrop for a description of the current educational situation in the Appleton schools. Both the current and historical themes are pertinent to an understanding of the creation and evolution of the Appleton Center presented in the last section of this chapter.

The major recurrent topics of controversy and concern in the history of Mexican American education in California are fundamentally issues of access—access to an education equal to that provided Anglo American students through integrated schools and through the appropriate language of instruction. Although desegregation and bilingual education, the educational bywords for these issues, are usually considered topics of the late 20th century, the problems they respond to—segregation and English-only schools—have been in existence since the United States annexed the Northern Territories of Mexico. It is difficult to separate these two concerns when examining the history of Mexican American education as language of instruction was once used as a basis for segregation and the paradoxical mandates to desegregate and provide bilingual education inextricably bind them today. In an attempt to understand their silencing effects, however, this section has been organized into the themes of linguistic exclusion and segregation.

Most progress in the educational situation of Mexican Americans has not been the result of altruistic behavior on the part of Anglo Americans in power nor has it occurred when Mexican Americans have decried the existing situation; rather legislation and court orders have always been necessary. Madrid (1986) states it well:

> Nowhere have we [Mexican Americans] felt the burden of institutional oppression nor the weight of responsibility more heavily than in education. This supposedly enlightened institution is seemingly also one of the most retrogressive. The educational system continues to blame the victim for its own failures, rather than to adapt its methods and policies to the differing population and changing circumstances with which it is constantly confronted. (p. ix)

The history of Mexican American education in California reveals how silencing once occurred and continues to occur through a lack of access to education resulting from linguistic exclusion and segregation. Although much of what we know of this history focuses on the K–12 years, it is nevertheless relevant for understanding the educational situation of Mexican Americans at all levels in California. The problems found at these levels continue into the colleges and universities around the state. This history also provides important background information for understanding the educational experiences of the Mexican American students at the Appleton Center, because so many of them were educated exclusively in California schools.

Mexican American Education in California

With the Treaty of Guadalupe Hidalgo and the end of the Mexican American War in 1848, the English-only common school of the United States came to Spanish-speaking California. In 1849, the state constitution mandated public schooling for "at least three months a year" (Hendrick, 1977, p. 7). By 1855, all public schools in California were forbidden to teach in Spanish by the state Bureau of Public Instruction (Pitt, 1966). Because the English-only policy of 1855 effectively denied Spanish-speaking students access to a public education, statistics from the early years of statehood suggest that few Mexican American students attended public schools (Hendrick, 1977). The first graduating class from a public high school in Los Angeles in 1872 had six students, none of whom were of Spanish or Mexican descent, although half the population of the town at the time was Mexican American (Romo, 1983). The failure of Hispanic surnames to appear on documents, the lack of numbers to account for their presence in schools, the failure to mention Hispanic students in the public school records of this time, all suggest that they were not in attendance.

It is a mistake to conclude that Mexican Americans did not attend school because they did not want to or did not value it. Repeated efforts by Mexican Americans during the 1850s to have public schools taught bilingually were thwarted by the increasingly powerful Anglo Americans in the communities. In Southern California during the 1850s, a small public school that was taught in Spanish was taken over by Anglo Americans and taught in English only. And three applications for bilingual public schools in the Los Angeles area were turned down (Meier & Stewart, 1991). Where Mexican American children did attend public schools, Anglo American parents complained that they interfered with the progress of the Anglo American students and caused problems for the teachers (Pitt, 1966).

Because Spanish-speaking students were effectively denied access to public education, Mexican Americans who could afford to, the old elite of California, turned to private and parochial institutions teaching in Spanish. In 1848, 18% of the schools in the state were Catholic, and they were largely responsible for serving the students of Spanish–Mexican background (Keller & Van Hooft, 1982). The Southern California Catholic school system began as a response to the "cultural purism" of Anglo American schools, that is, their refusal to teach in Spanish or to study the Hispanic culture (Pitt, 1966, p. 228). According to Francisco Hernández, Professor of Chicano Studies at the University of California, Berkeley, "Mexican schools" were established between 1848 and 1900, not only to help maintain cultural and linguistic traditions, but also as a response to the ill-treatment of Mexican American children in the newly formed public schools. If Mexican Americans were not refused admittance to public schools outright, according to Hernández, they were ill-treated once in attendance (personal communication, February 7, 1990).

In the 1860s and 1870s, Mexican Americans ran several bilingual–bicultural schools in the Los Angeles area (Weinberg, 1977). Most of these "escuelitas" were in Southern California (Los Angeles and Santa Barbara), where the Mexican American population was relatively large. Camarillo (1979) notes that in Santa Barbara, Mexican American families who could afford to sent their sons to the mission school and their daughters to a private Catholic school in town. According to Pitt (1966), "Spanish Americans of all degrees of religious commitment sought better schooling than was then available—schooling in both Spanish and English, instead of merely one or the other. Bilingual education of any sort was the common goal of all Spanish-American spokesmen" (p. 225). Those in favor of bilingual education for Spanish-speaking students had to contend with "strong Yankee opposition," however (Pitt, 1966, p. 226).

In more recent years, bilingual education has remained an important goal for Mexican Americans, and opposition to it has remained just as strong. From the late 1960s to the present, the emphasis of much litigation and protest has been on creating appropriate bilingual and bicultural contexts for the education of Mexican American students. In the late 1960s, Mexican American groups began calling for bilingual and bicultural education, primarily the Association of Mexican American Educators formed in 1965 and the Mexican American Legal Defense Education Fund (MALDEF), established in 1968 (Camarillo, 1984). In 1966 the first bilingual education programs in the state of California were established (Keller & Van Hooft, 1982). One year later, Title I of the Elementary and Secondary Education Act (ESEA) provided funding for the educationally "disadvantaged" and was eventually interpreted so that it could fund ESL and transitional bilingual education programs in California. In 1968 Title VII of the ESEA, the Bilingual Education Act, took over funding for bilingual education in California.

In 1974 all schools with 20 or more non-English proficient students were required to have a transitional bilingual education program. This was the same year that the *Lau v. Nichols* case determined that any child with limited proficiency in English who did not receive proper "remedies" was denied his or her educational rights (Keller & Van Hooft, 1982). Although Chinese students were the plaintiffs in the Lau case, it was thought that Spanish-speaking Mexican Americans would also gain considerably as a result of the decision (Meier & Stewart, 1991). By 1976, however, the San Francisco Unified School District still had not responded to the decision and the U.S. District Court was forced to order compliance, insisting that the district implement an acceptable Master Plan for bilingual–bicultural education (Keller & Van Hooft, 1982).

After this landmark decision, legislation supporting bilingual education seemed to increase. Federal guidelines for the enforcement of the Lau decision were completed in 1975. The "Task Force Findings Specifying Remedies Available for Eliminating Past Educational Practices Ruled Unlawful Under *Lau v. Nichols*" or "Lau Remedies" required identifying and assessing students with a mother tongue other than English and then providing transitional bilingual education. This was quite different than the ESL programs that had been previously recommended (Hakuta, 1986). And the Chacon-Moscone Bilingual-Bicultural Education Act was passed in California in 1976 also in response to *Lau v. Nichols*. The act required the availability of a bilingual education program for every Limited English Proficient and Non-English Proficient (LEP/NEP) student in the state (Keller & Van Hooft, 1982). Despite all of the gains of the 1970s and 1980s, the Bilingual Education Program and four other educational programs were "sunsetted" in California in 1987, leaving funding for bilingual education in the state in jeopardy. As long as certain federal mandates remained in place, the bilingual programs in California could continue to function. But if that safety net were lifted, the state was no longer in a position to fund such programs. Without bilingual education programs, LEP students would have to be mainstreamed immediately, leading to a series of obvious educational difficulties for both the students and their teachers.

In higher education in California, language also serves to restrict educational opportunities. The way this works is related to the three-tiered public college system. For admission to either of the first two tiers—the University of California (UC) or the California State University (Cal State) systems—all citizens and resident aliens are required to take a college entrance exam, usually the SAT. This exam is given in English only and, in addition to math, measures verbal skills. The need to score well on the verbal portion of this exam prevents most Mexican American LEP students from gaining admission to one of the top two tiers in California. International students may be admitted, however, on the basis of their Test of English as a Foreign Language (TOEFL) scores.

Whether citizen, immigrant, or foreigner, all students admitted to the universities must take a writing placement exam. On the basis of this exam students are placed into ESL, basic/remedial, or regular freshman composition courses. Because the SAT prevents most LEP citizens from being admitted to the UC or Cal State systems, the majority of students in ESL courses at UC and Cal State institutions are international students. A rare citizen who managed to be admitted on the basis of the SAT but tested poorly on the placement exam may also be in an ESL class, but most who exhibit some non-native features in their writing will be placed in a basic or remedial writing class. Unfortunately, the basic writing classes are usually taught by graduate students or lecturers completely unfamiliar with and untrained in teaching writing to LEP students. ESL courses do not count toward graduation at these institutions and have reduced or no credits attached to them. Therefore, although students do the work as if they were regular classes, they are essentially losing ground in their coursework toward a degree. Moreover, in the UC system, if students are in a degree program that requires knowledge of a second language, bilingual (Spanish–English) students may not use their mother tongue as one of their languages. They must master a third language.

At the community colleges, the third tier in California higher education, all students are admitted whether or not they have a high school diploma, and no college entrance exam is required. However, as in the first two tiers, all students must take a writing placement exam. Students will be placed in ESL classes, basic writing courses, or regular freshman composition classes. LEP students (citizen, immigrant, or otherwise) will generally be placed into ESL classes, but students who have only a few non-native characteristics in their writing will probably be put into a basic writing class. These students are usually not recent immigrants. Therefore, many Mexican Americans, like the students in this study, who still have some influences in their writing from their mother tongue, will be placed into such basic writing classes. Because of budget constraints, community colleges offer few, if any, support services for their LEP students. In addition, ESL classes generally do not count toward the AA or AS degree or for transfer credit.

At the college level, LEP Mexican American students may be excluded on the basis of language through a series of language examinations or at least segregated into the lowest tier of the college system: community colleges. If admitted into college, they will be placed into a program that may teach them English, but will fail to provide them with adequate support for their other classes and will put them behind in their course work and in credits toward graduation.

In addition to the historical exclusion of Mexican Americans as a result of language policy, there appears to have been exclusion from an equal education as a result of ethnicity, as well. Hendrick (1977) notes that "No political party or citizen group in California during the 1850s was prepared to consider admitting non-whites into public schools on equal terms with whites ... and no public money was appropriated for the education of non-whites as they were not included in the school census" (p. 7). The first state superintendent of schools blamed Mexican American parents for their children's lack of attendance; he said these parents were "unconvinced of the necessities of education" (Hendrick, 1977, p. 12).

Hendrick (1977) describes the period from 1880 to 1920 as one of "quiet, almost imperceptible" educational segregation (p. 71). According to Hendrick, "it was likely that most Mexican children were not attending [public] school at all during this period" (p. 81). Those who did attend school "were more likely to receive schooling that was not only segregated, but inferior in all other respects as well" (p. 82). Although the segregation of Mexican Americans in California schools was not a legislative mandate as it was for Chinese and Native American students, there is nevertheless evidence that it occurred on an ever-increasing scale throughout the 20th Century.

Nonlegislated segregation in schools occurred primarily through two methods: (a) the assignment of students to schools or classes on the basis of race or ethnicity, that is, the creation of "Mexican schools;" and (b) the placement of schools in such a way as to capitalize on residential segregation in urban areas, or the creation of "neighborhood schools" (Hendrick, 1977; Wollenberg, 1976). According to Meier and Stewart (1991), "Mexican Schools" were established as soon as a location had enough Mexican American students to hold separate classes. Wollenberg (1976) quotes an educator of the time who wrote, "One of the first demands made from an [Anglo American] community in which there is a large Mexican population [was] for a separate school" (p. 111). In 1928, Weinberg (1977) found that 64 schools in 8 counties across California had enrollments of 90 and 100% Mexican Americans.

In 1916, citizens began to publicly demand the segregation of Mexican American students (where they were not already) because of "unsanitary conditions" (Hendrick, 1977, p. 81). Later, segregation was enforced for "educational" reasons, in addition to "health" concerns. One such educational reason was the perceived need to acculturate or "Americanize" (Meier & Stewart, 1991). Another was to respond to "special needs," as determined by the results of standardized achievement and intelligence testing, which was becoming popular at the time (Romo, 1983; Wollenberg, 1976). Migrant classes were also used as a way to effectively segregate Mexican American children (Wollenberg, 1976). By the end of the 1920s, Mexican Americans constituted 10% of the state's public school population, yet they were the most segregated group in California (Wollenberg, 1976).

Examples of the extent and severity of segregation in California during the early 1930s abound (Reynolds, 1933; Weinberg, 1977). In Orange County, there were 15 all-Mexican American schools. A comparison of the facilities at these schools with those at the "white schools" revealed vast differences. On the standard scale of 1,000 (used for such comparisons), the average score for the Mexican American schools was 593, whereas the average for Anglo American schools was 714 (Weinberg, 1977). In the Imperial Valley, one 95%-Mexican school was so overcrowded that even on double shifts, classrooms had as many as 86 students per teacher (Weinberg, 1977).

It was not until the 1930s that collective action by Mexican American parents resulted in successful lawsuits and led to the creation of legislation designed to enforce desegregation. In 1931, the first recorded court action against the segregation of Mexican American students in California occurred in Lemon Grove, near San Diego. The parents of 75 Mexican American children, with legal assistance from the Mexican consul, sued the school district for attempting to segregate by building a new "Mexican" school. The parents won the case, and the children were allowed to attend school with the Anglo American population (Acuña, 1988). Although Acuña (1988) states that this case "served as precedent for school desegregation cases that followed" (p. 236)—and it undoubtedly did—the case had little immediate impact on statewide segregation (Wollenberg, 1976).

In 1946, another landmark desegregation case, *Mendez v. Westminister*, was decided in California. With plaintiffs from five school districts in Southern California, this case led to the end of California's *de jure* segregation policies, including "Mexican schools," "neighborhood schools," and the use of attendance zones to segregate (Wollenberg, 1976, p. 112). Although this decision led to the repeal of all remaining laws allowing for educational segregation based on race or ethnicity, like previous lawsuits, it had little impact on de facto segregation in the state (Meier & Stewart, 1991).

In 1955, the National Association for the Advancement of Colored People and Alianza Hispano-Americana, a Mexican American organization founded in 1894 to "maintain political representation as well as continue the contribution of Mexican-Americans" (Acuña, 1988, p. 96), sued the El Centro, California school district for segregation practices against both students and faculty. Only after an appeal to the circuit court was a decision rendered in favor of the Mexican American students and their teachers.

Parson's 1965 study of *ethnic cleavage* in Guadalupe, a small agricultural village much like Appleton, provides an excellent window on how segregation and other discriminatory practices continued to be implemented in California. For the most part, segregation in Guadalupe's only school was achieved through an elaborate tracking system. A committee placed students in either high or low ability classes, with a clear majority of Anglo American students in the high classes and Mexican Americans in the lower classes. Placement was based on teachers' general impressions of students, their background, and to some extent, their standardized test scores (p. 271). Within these high- and low-level general classes, high and low reading and math groups were formed, with Anglo Americans predominating the high groups and Mexican American students predominating the low groups.

In Guadalupe, special classes were held for bilingual Mexican American students because they were believed to have "language difficulties"(p. 306), but this was not an enlightened bilingual program. Students were required to speak in English only, and if they disobeyed, they received a paddling. After one to two years in this special course, students were placed into a regular first grade (already one to two years behind their Anglo American peers). Many Mexican American students were held back under the guise of "need[ing] more time to learn the [English] language" (p. 262). In these ways, students were punished for having a different mother tongue and once behind in school, found it impossible to catch up. As a result dropout was a common phenomenon.

In 1966, a California State Department of Education survey found that 57% of Spanish-surnamed students in California still attended minority schools, that is, segregated schools with at least 15% more minority students than the district average (Wollenberg, 1976). However, little was done to change this situation in many of the districts across the state, including the largest. In 1970, the Los Angeles Unified School District was found guilty of segregation. Two thirds of the Mexican and Mexican American students attended predominantly Mexican schools (Wollenberg, 1976). In 1971, *Serrano v. Priest* ruled that students who attended school in East Los Angeles received an unequal education because it was solely supported by local tax dollars, which were uncommonly low because of the poor neighborhoods (Acuña, 1988). As recently as the 1980s, the school buildings with predominantly Mexican American students in the Los Angeles area "were older [than the ones attended by Anglo Americans]; . . . [and] had more students per square foot and smaller recreation areas" (Acuña, 1988, p. 390).

At the college level, segregation and exclusion were also the norm. According to Weinberg (1977), "the collegiate history of Mexican-Americans had barely begun by World War I" (p. 340). Most Mexican Americans who did attend college in those years were actually of a higher economic class than their Anglo American counterparts. After World War II, the GI Bill allowed a few more Mexican American males to attend college. As more Mexican American students enrolled in college, however, "the gap between freshman entry and graduation widened" (Weinberg, 1977, p. 341).

Manuel (1965) discusses a study of freshman enrollments at 50 California colleges in 1958. Figures from the 50 studied schools show that 5.2% of freshman were "White with Spanish-surname" at a time when 9.1% of the state population was Mexican American. The study does not, however, include college completion statistics, which can be quite another story, as noted in Chapter One.

In the late 1960s, California still had only token Mexican American enrollments in four year colleges and universities. In the heavily Hispanic Los Angeles basin, San Fernando Valley State College had only seven Mexican American students enrolled in 1967, and at the University of California, Los Angeles, Mexican Americans made up 2.3% of the undergraduates in 1968 (Weinberg, 1977). In 1970, Mexican Americans made up 6.2% of all undergraduate enrollment in California at public and private, two- and four-year institutions, but 15.9% of the population in California (Casso, 1975). Figures repeatedly show the underrepresentation of Mexican Americans on California college campuses.

Open enrollment at community colleges has allowed more Mexican Americans to attend college than ever before. Yet, in the heavily tracked, three-tiered public higher education system in California, few Mexican Americans are able to attend the best institutions and fewer receive four-year degrees. The four-year public universities in the state remain highly selective in their admissions. For example, the University of California system admits the top 10% of the state's high school graduates and the California State University system admits the top third of high school graduates. Because of the poor academic preparation of Mexican American students resulting from the segregation and lack of linguistic access described earlier in this chapter, only 4.9% of Mexican American high school graduates in 1983 were eligible for admission to the UC system and only 15.3% were eligible for the Cal State system (Cepeda, 1986). In the same year, 78% of Mexican American students that were enrolled in California institutions of higher education were enrolled at the community college level. Few of these students ever transfer to four-year institutions. Of the 5,000 transfers from the community colleges to the UC system in 1983, only 400 were Hispanic (Cepeda, 1986). Leakage from the academic pipeline continues for Hispanics in California's public universities. At the University of California, Berkeley in 1982, the five-year graduation–retention rate was only 46% for Chicanos as opposed to 72% of white students (Thompson, 1987). In other words, less than half the Mexican Americans who attend a UC system school stay on to earn a four-year degree. In the Cal State system, Whites complete their degrees at twice the rate of Chicanos—15% of Chicanos complete them and 34% of Whites do (Office of Student Research, 1983).

California's treatment of Mexican American students reveals a history of unequal education as a result of segregation and lack of linguistic access. This history has led to low achievement and high dropout rates for Mexican American students throughout the state. Students in Appleton have also had these educational experiences, and as a result they suffer from the same consequences.

Mexican American Education in Appleton

In Appleton, acts of covert, if not overt, discrimination have occurred as a result of de facto segregation in the area school districts and through a failure to provide linguistic access to education. A knowledge of this history helped me to better understand the educational context of the Appleton Center, the educational system where most of the Appleton Center students were, and the educational histories of the Appleton Center students.

Few formal records of the early years in Appleton schools remain. Fires and the constant reorganization of school districts have helped create this dearth of information. Nevertheless, there are occasional lists of pupils, captions to old class photographs, and, of course, faded memories of long-time residents. In all such data, there are no Hispanic surnames among the students listed in the Appleton area until well into the 1920s (Lewis, 1976/1986, 1980). One Anglo American growing up in a nearby community remembered attending school with every nationality "except Japanese and Chinese" (Mylar, 1929/1970, p. 30), but there is no record of such a multiethnic environment in the Appleton schools. Another neighboring community had one Hispanic surname on its class roster of 45 pupils in 1866 (Malmin, 1982), although the census of 1850 showed Spanish-speaking people to be the majority in the area (Lydon, 1985).

From 1910 to 1940 there were no Mexican American high school graduates at Appleton High, although nearly 50 Asian American students graduated. It was not until the 1940s that the first Mexican Americans graduated. In 1940, three of the 295 students who graduated from Appleton High were Mexican American. By 1960, 16 of 316 or 5% of the graduates were Mexican American. At this same time, 26% of the junior high school graduates were Mexican American (see Table 2).

Table 2.
Graduation Rates Appleton High School by Year and Ethnicity

Year	Total Graduates (Raw)	Mexican American Graduates (Raw)	Mexican American Graduates (Percent)
1940	295	3	1
1945	150	3	2
1950	309	4	1
1960	316	16	5

Note. From *In Struggle: Mexican Americans in the [Appleton] Valley Schools, 1900–1979,* by Ruben Donato (1987). Unpublished Doctoral Dissertation. Palo Alto, CA, Stanford University, pp. 85–89.

In 1945, the Appleton area had as many as 24 small school districts. Through a series of unifications and consolidations, they were reduced to five, the two largest being the Shoreline and Appleton districts (Donato, 1987).[4] Unifying districts was a nationwide educational trend after World War II, and the State of California pressured large districts such as Appleton and Shoreline to consolidate. However, Shoreline communities had been resistant to unification with Appleton as early as 1946. They were "disturbed about mixing their children with others of different socioeconomic backgrounds," those from "the indigent areas across the [Appleton] River" where the Mexican American laborers lived (Donato, 1987, pp. 66, 69). By 1960, Shoreline had twice refused to take part in the unification study required of all California districts. They wanted to remain "'economically . . . socially . . . culturally and [ethnically] different from [Appleton] schools'" (quoted in Donato, 1987, p. 77). In an effort to avoid unification with Appleton, Shoreline schools went so far as to attempt consolidation with a smaller, more Anglo American district to the north, even though that district was in poor financial condition. Finally, after considerable pressure from the state, Shoreline and Appleton consolidated in 1964 to form the Appleton Valley Unified School District (AVUSD).

During the late 1960s, increased immigration and permanent settlement of Mexican Americans in the Appleton area and the accompanying *white flight* of Anglo American residents from central Appleton led to downtown Appleton schools becoming mostly Mexican American. By 1967, Mexican American students comprised 27.5% of the district's enrollment, and most of them attended the Appleton area schools. To make ethnic division in the district even greater, in the late 1960s, a new high school was built to ease overcrowding at Appleton High School. Placed squarely in the middle of the Shoreline community, attendance was drawn from the Anglo American neighborhoods surrounding it. This de facto segregation occurred despite a 1966 notice from the California State Department of Education that declared the district "racially isolated," with 7 schools in the district officially segregated (15% above or below the total district percentage of minority students) (Donato, 1987, p. 241). By 1971, 11 schools were racially isolated.

According to Donato, "integrating Anglo students from the North with Mexican American students in Appleton was unacceptable to school authorities and to Anglo residents of [Shoreline]" (Donato, 1987, p. 207). Therefore, the district's 1971 state mandated desegregation plan took full advantage of the 12 miles between

---

[4] Unless otherwise noted, the information in this section is from R. Donato's 1987 doctoral dissertation, *In Struggle: Mexican Americans in the [Appleton] Valley Schools, 1900-1979.*

Shoreline and Appleton by dividing the district into north and south zones. All attempts at desegregation were carried out within zones only, not across zones. Essentially, two minidistricts were created with no cross busing. Statistics for desegregation were also determined from the school populations within the zones, not the district as a whole. Within the zones, few schools appeared racially imbalanced, but in the district as a whole, schools were grossly out of line with federal mandates. In effect, the district had created an Anglo American zone and a Mexican American zone. It is no surprise, then, that in 1979 the district was 81st on a list of 100 of the most segregated districts in the nation, according to the Department of Health, Education and Welfare and the Office of Civil Rights (Donato, 1987, p. 237).[5] One disgruntled member of the Community Desegregation Advisory Committee commented:

> Those who wanted to prove *de jure* (intentional) segregation would only have to point to [Shoreline] High School and [Shoreline] Junior High Schools. They were built where only white people live. If someone took it to court and said these schools were built here recently so that the people in this area wouldn't have to mix with Mexicans, it would be hard to prove that that wasn't the reason the schools were built where they [are] located. (Donato, 1987, p. 235)

In 1989, a bilingual task force recommended a review of the district's 1980 desegregation plan after finding that segregation of the district was worse in 1989 than it had been in 1980. In 1980, six schools had at least 75% ethnic minority enrollment. In 1989, there were six schools in the district with more than 80% minority enrollment and two more were at 79% ("Last Desegregation," 1990). The 1980 plan included the use of magnet schools (all but one were placed in the Shoreline area, so only Appleton area Mexican Americans were bused, not Shoreline Anglos), re-drawing attendance lines, and refusing transfers of Anglo American students out of Appleton area schools (Johnson, 1989b). In the fall of 1988, the district began to implement a four year plan to move more than 500 students from the downtown Appleton attendance areas to the suburban Shoreline high school in an attempt to deal with the segregation. The projected minority enrollment at the two institutions after the completion of the moves was 70% minority at the downtown high school and 5% minority at the suburban high school (Trevino, 1988a). The adjustment was going to be smoothed out in the following way: "School staff will

---

[5] This list was based on a survey of 6,069 school districts nationwide.

not attempt to treat them [Mexican American transfers from Appleton High School] different from their Anglo counterparts. . . . 'We want to be careful not to consider them anything else than members of the freshman class' a school ESL instructor said" (Trevino, 1988a, p. 13). At the time of this study, the district had yet to require any busing of Anglo American students from Shoreline into the Appleton area.

A Mexican American member of the 1989 review committee called the desegregation plan of 1980 a "hodge podge," a plan in "disarray" that was "unproductive and harmful" (Alvarado, 1990c, p. 9). According to Alvarado, one committee member said "district officials in the past have essentially ignored some of the schools in Appleton that come close to or surpass the 80 percent mark [for racially isolated schools]. . . . The district implemented desegregation policies . . . had little or no effect on these schools. Since there isn't much response from the Hispanic community, the district thought it could do whatever it wanted. . . . 'That's no way to run a business and that's no way to run a district'" (1990c, p. 9).

At the desegregation review hearings, parents complained of unfair allocations of desegregation funds. They claimed the monies were siphoned to magnet schools with rather low minority enrollments in the wealthy Shoreline part of the district rather than being used in the Appleton schools with high minority percentages (Ball, 1989). The review committee found, indeed, that none of the racially impacted schools in Appleton had received any of the district's $1.1 million desegregation budget (Johnson, 1990). Furthermore, the district had failed to apply for racially isolated minority funds available from the state for six to eight eligible schools; those schools were not receiving any desegregation money at the time either (Alvarado, 1990c).

Like the history of segregation in the district, the story of bilingual education in the AVUSD is also full of evidence that the resources necessary to provide an adequate education for the Mexican American children it served were never allocated. Although Mexican American community members spoke out in protest against the district's approach to educating NEP and LEP students, their concerns were largely ignored. Bilingual services were provided to students in the district only under the threat of state and federal reprisals.

In the late 1960s, instruction in the Appleton Valley schools was English only and as the district director of instruction admitted, the "curriculum was not only 'oriented to middle class values of the community' but it also excluded the whole essence of the

Mexican American student" (quoted in Donato, 1987, p. 102). At the same time, an Anglo American researcher studying the high dropout rate in the Appleton High School cited social rejection by the school as the major cause of dropouts. A grassroots organization, Comunidad Organizada Para Educación (COPE), and previously unorganized parents became active, attending school board meetings and asking questions of administrators. The parents were concerned primarily with teachers' attitudes toward Mexican American students. One parent at a local school board meeting summed up the parents' feelings.

> Teachers fail to regard Mexican Americans as first class citizens . . . they take the attitude that Mexican American students are wasting their time in the classroom and should go out [and work] in the berry fields. (quoted in Donato, 1987, p. 101)

In 1969, COPE discovered that none of the Title I monies designated for disadvantaged students in the district were being used to educate Mexican American children (unless they were in special education classes), although such a use of Title I funds was generally accepted elsewhere. In the AVUSD these monies were being misused for such purposes as the purchase of audiovisual equipment for mainstream classes. COPE demanded that the district use Title I money to provide bilingual aides in the classroom, free lunches for children from low income families, training programs for teachers of nonmainstream students, and a more multicultural curriculum. The school board denied every request the organization made. The flat denial of the school board led to a walkout by Mexican American students at Appleton High School; these students demanded that COPE's requests be met by the school board. The school board finally granted one request: a community advocate who would work as a liaison between community groups, parents, and the school board.

With the help of the community advocate, COPE developed a proposal based on Title I funding for a K–3 bilingual–bicultural program at an elementary school with a high Mexican American enrollment. The school board again refused the group. COPE resorted to petition drives and attending board meetings en masse, but the school board continued to balk, citing a lack of funding and a lack of evidence that bilingual programs enhance students' educational experience. Convinced that the community advocate was inciting COPE, the school board fired her and eliminated the position. With the help of sympathetic educators at the local University of California campus, COPE was able to gain federal and state grant money for the proposed bilingual–bicultural program and the district was obliged to provide it. As a result, a pilot bilingual–bicultural classroom was established in the district in 1972 .

The bilingual–bicultural school issue led to a great deal of tension in the community. Anglo American residents verbally attacked COPE and the entire Mexican American community. Letters to the editor of the local paper were full of racist statements. One resident called the issue a "'racial battle'" (Donato, 1987, p. 120). Many thought the event "scarred the community . . . believing the [Appleton Valley]'s ethnic relations would never improve" (Donato, 1987, p. 124).

After the creation of the bilingual–bicultural school, little happened to provide special instruction for Limited English Proficient students. In 1975, only 11.7% of the Limited and Non-English Speaking (LES, NES) students in the district received any type of bilingual instruction. In 1976, six ESL programs were added at other elementary schools, but even with the new programs, the percentage of LES and NES students served in the district increased only slightly to 12.5%.

Bilingual education became an issue in the community again after the *Lau v. Nichols* decision in 1974 and the passage of the Chacon-Moscone bill in California. Unpleasant memories of the conflict surrounding the bilingual–bicultural school slowed any enthusiasm the district might have had in creating the bilingual Master Plan mandated by the state. A bilingual advisory committee was created that ultimately recommended a combined approach to transitional bilingual education: Spanish first, then English and Spanish used interchangeably. It was recommended that seven schools in the district be made "fully bilingual" (Donato, 1987, p. 182). Twenty percent of the district teachers volunteered to study Spanish and earn bilingual teaching certificates.

However, there was opposition to increased bilingual education in the district. An Anglo American parent–teacher group opposed development of the Master Plan because they "wanted to stop the expansion of bilingual education in the [Appleton] schools" (Donato, 1987, p. 187). According to the organization, bilingual education "was a costly, time-consuming program that was alienating parents, frightening students, and confusing teachers" (Donato, 1987, p. 188). Many teachers were afraid they would lose their jobs because they did not speak Spanish. The group had a petition drive, gathering 1,200 signatures against the plan and promising they could muster 5,000 more.

Although they had procrastinated for years, the district was granted a two-year grace period in 1977 to comply with state mandated bilingual education requirements, pushing the date ahead to 1979. Ultimately, the board passed a Master Plan, but so late that they had to rush to pilot it midyear so they could correct any problems before the Fall, 1979 deadline. The school board passed the plan, largely because it was mandated by the state, and it was not welcomed by many in the district. This period was so unhappy that one school board trustee noted that the desegregation plan (the board's next task) was difficult to face because the school board and the community "had not recovered from the Bilingual Education Master Plan" (Donato, 1987, p. 216).

After the creation of the Master Plan in 1979, no progress in the area of bilingual education occurred until another state action (or inaction) provided the necessary impetus. The *sunsetting* of the Bilingual Educational Program Act in June, 1987, led to the creation of a Bilingual Task Force in the district in order to evaluate the existing bilingual education Master Plan and to recommend changes. From the creation of the Task Force to school board approval of the recommended changes, 19 months passed (Johnson, 1989a). Once the recommendations were submitted to the school board, study session meetings became "public forums for complaints about the current system—slowing down the process of review" (Trevino, 1988c, p. 11). Board attitudes about bilingual education became apparent, as one member "wanted assurances that Hispanics are not given preferential treatment over other students" and another suggested that the bilingual program be called "English-language enrichment program" rather than "language enrichment program," revealing his prejudices against the Spanish language component of the program (Trevino, 1988b, p. 11).

The debate over bilingual education continued in the letters to the editor. The following letters are typical of those that filled the editorial pages of the local newspaper on a regular basis. One Anglo American mother complained that her daughter could not get into an English-only classroom. She concluded:

> It is no wonder why all the private schools in the [Appleton] Valley are doing so well. The [AVUSD] is turning into a private institution, English-only no need to apply. (Yetter, 1988, p. 24)

An advocate for bilingual education once wrote wearily that she had had "14 years of battling the same uninformed opinions and illogical reasoning surrounding bilingual education" and hoped that people would not "demoralize and destroy the successful bilingual programs we have" (Moran, 1990, p. 13).

In an unusual move, the bilingual task force found that 4,000 LEP students in the district "would remain educationally handicapped as long as their schools and classrooms are segregated" (Johnson, 1989b, p.1B); they recommended that the school board immediately set up an integration task force (Johnson, 1988a, p. 1B).

At the time of the study, the Appleton Valley School District had the third highest concentration of LEP students in the state of California (Johnson, 1988a). One third of the students at Appleton High School were classified LEP (Wagner, 1989). At the same time, Mexican American enrollment decreased with each successive high school grade level in the school district. In the ninth grade, 77% of the class was Hispanic, by the twelfth grade only 66% was Hispanic (Chamber of Commerce Grant Proposal). The graduating class at Appleton High School was less than half the size of the ninth grade class four years before (Johnson, 1988a). In 1989, the downtown Appleton area schools exceeded 80% of minority students, whereas Anglo Americans comprised more than 80% of the students in the outlying suburban area schools (Johnson, 1989b).

The same issues of access to education and the language of instruction that have plagued the schools in Appleton in the past continue today. Although the Mexican American community has spoken out repeatedly, the school board has refused to listen. Educational practices that have contributed to the silencing of Mexican Americans for generations in California continue in Appleton: a lack of access to an equal education as a result of segregation and language of instruction. The next section reveals how similar issues are apparent in the education offered to Mexican American students at the Appleton Center.

Mexican American Education at the Appleton Center

Students at the Appleton Center did not necessarily receive an education that met their needs, a stated objective of the outreach program. In this section, I present information that reveals how the primarily Mexican American student body at the Appleton Center, like Mexican Americans at other educational levels in Appleton, were segregated in unequal facilities that provided inadequate programs for bilingual students and failed to meet other specific educational needs. By comparing the goals and intentions of the students in Appleton with the goals of the school administration, it became apparent that the special needs of the Appleton clientele were not addressed, and by comparing student services of the PCC main campus with those at the Appleton Center, I learned that Appleton students did not receive the same educational benefits as those students on the main campus.

Surveys of student ethnic backgrounds reveal a striking difference between the student body of the main campus of PCC and that of the Appleton Center.[6] To illustrate this point, I will discuss figures from the two semesters I worked with focal students: Fall, 1989 and Spring, 1990. As Table 3 shows, at the Appleton Center in Fall, 1989, Hispanic enrollment was 48.9%, whereas Hispanic enrollment for the entire college was 10.4%.[7] Anglo enrollment at the Appleton Center was 43.3%, whereas on the main campus Anglo enrollment was 83.6%. In Spring, 1990, 43.7% of the students at Appleton Center were of Hispanic descent, while the figures for the entire college showed only 10.5% Hispanic enrollment. During the Spring of 1990, a full 48% of the students attending the Center had a first language other than English. Most of these students spoke Spanish, although there were some Tagalog and Portuguese speakers at the school.

Table 3.
Appleton Center Ethnic Breakdown

	Enrollment by Semester (%)			
Ethnicity	Fall, 1988	Spring, 1989	Fall, 1989	Spring, 1990
Anglo	54.0	49.6	43.3	50.6
Hispanic	38.3	44.6	48.9	43.7
Asian/Pacific Islander	3.0	3.0	2.8	2.8
Black/African American	1.4	1.5	0.9	0.3
American Indian	1.4	1.3	0.9	1.0
Filipino	2.1	2.2	3.2	1.6

Note. From [Appleton] Center Final Report, Portolá College, 1989, p. 6 and [Appleton] Center Annual Report to the Governing Board, Portolá College, 1990, p. 8.

A classroom survey conducted in Fall, 1989, revealed more than ethnic and linguistic differences between Appleton Center students

---

[6] All surveys were designed and conducted by the administration of Portolá Community College. Some were created by the acting Dean of the Appleton Center, whereas others were created by the Office of Institutional Research. The ethnic terms used here, as elsewhere, are those of the statistical survey.

[7] Unfortunately, the only ethnic breakdown for the main campus includes off-campus sites, as well. Therefore, the PCC figures include the students of Appleton Center.

and those on the main campus. Questions about educational goals, desire to attend the PCC main campus, and full-time/part time status revealed additional differences that were not well-considered by those planning for the Appleton Center. Many Appleton Center students were not familiar with the main campus of PCC or with the geographic area in which it exists, about 12 miles north of Appleton. To some students, Shoreline was considered literally "over the hill" from Appleton, because one must drive out of the Appleton Valley to reach the northern beach communities, including Shoreline, the site of PCC's main campus. As one counselor who worked part time in Appleton put it, "Portolá College [main campus] . . . still seems over the horizon to some Appleton students. Some folks do not know where Portolá is" (Hudson, 1988, p. 4). When students were asked if they would take classes at PCC if they were not offered in Appleton, 26% answered that they would not. Fifty percent of the students taking classes in Appleton that semester were not taking any courses on the main campus. In answer to a question about why they were attending classes in Appleton, 72% answered that they did so because it was close to home; another 31% answered that they did so because it was close to work; but 12% also stated that they chose the Appleton Center because it was easier to find their classes there than on the main campus. One of the focal students in this study, Amado, described how new Appleton students feel on the main campus: "Hey, the guy is new in, in college, and it's hard enough being in that, showing up to that class, that classroom, much less telling him where to find something up in the I-O-whatever building, OK?" Students attended the Appleton Center because of the proximity to home and work and because of the small size of the campus. At least one fourth of the students said they would never take classes on the main campus in Shoreline.

Another difference between Appleton students and those students on the main campus was the extent to which the student body was part-time. Nearly all of the students at the Appleton Center were attending classes on a part-time basis. In the Spring of 1990, 91.7% of students taking class there were part-time; only 8.3% were taking classes on a full-time basis. However, at the main campus, during that semester, as many as 25% percent of the students were attending on a full-time basis. For Appleton students, this meant that the best class time was evening, after work. Forty-six percent of students attending the Appleton Center stated that weekday evenings were the most convenient time for taking classes, but on the main campus *prime-time* was weekday mornings.

Student bodies at the two locations also varied in terms of their goals. A comparison of responses to a follow-up survey of students from PCC[8] and a survey of students at the Appleton Center reveals that although the top three reasons for attending classes at the institution were the same, namely transferring to a four-year institution, receiving an AA degree, and changing careers, the order of importance to each group was *completely reversed*. Although 31% of students at the Appleton Center were attending classes with the intention of receiving an AA degree, only 5% of those attending PCC had this as a goal. Although another 31% of students in Appleton were taking classes as part of a career change, only 15% of PCC students had that as their goal. Finally, although 25% of students at the Center planned to transfer to a four-year university, 35% of those students polled from PCC had this as their goal.

A comparison of student goals and objectives with those of the program reveal that the program was not designed to meet the specific educational needs and desires of Appleton Center students. As stated in Chapter 2, the goals for the Center created by the planning committee and approved by the Board were to:

1. Provide initial preparation for transfer to a four-year institution, initial preparation for employment, and opportunities for continuing study.
2. Create a learning environment attractive to students and faculty and conducive to student success.
3. Increase the number of students from the [Appleton] area who enroll in Portolá College.
4. Allow for expansion of course offerings that are now restricted by space limitations on the [Shoreline] campus. (Preliminary Report, p. 2)

Two of the four goals developed for the Center, however, refer specifically to the College's needs, not students' needs: (1) "Increase the number of students from the Appleton area who enroll in Portolá College;" and (2) "Allow for expansion of course offering that are now restricted by space limitations." Both the acting dean of the Center and the teacher of English 10 interpreted the first of these goals as a desire to have students transfer from the Appleton Center to the main campus. In other words, the Center was to function as a recruitment program of sorts for the main campus. The

---

[8] Again, the only survey data for the main campus include figures from the Appleton Center, as well.

student survey information previously reviewed, however, suggests that this was an unrealistic goal for 26% of the students taking classes who simply would not—or could not, as was most often the case—take any class offered at the main campus. Tactics used to encourage more Appleton students to use the main campus (such as limited course offerings) did not favor students who were not able to leave Appleton to take classes on the main campus.

Additional proof that the administration had no plans to provide a full range of educational opportunities to students is found in yet another goal in the planning report: "Provide *initial preparation* for transfer to a four-year institution, *initial preparation* for employment and opportunities for continuing study [emphasis added]." Thus, it is apparent that there was never an intention that degrees or certificates could be earned at the Center. The types of classes planned for the Center also reveals this. They were selected to meet "three educational needs—learning skills, general education, and *introductory courses* in degree programs [emphasis added]" (Board minutes, May 4, 1987, p. 62). This focus on introductory and initial preparation runs counter to the primary goal of students attending the Center: receipt of an AA degree. As the English 10 teacher explained in an interview, the acting Dean never intended to offer complete degree programs.

> He never wanted to provide a full range of courses so that people could just go to [the] Appleton [Center], perhaps for their whole two years, or however many years it took them to get out of there. He never saw that as the function.

Considering the fact that 31% of the students attending the Center planned to receive an AA Degree and 26% of the students indicated that they could not take classes at the main campus, it appears that some students who wanted to complete an AA Degree but could not go to the main campus to do so, would not be served. Several students I worked with over the course of my two years in Appleton expressed the desire to be able to take all of the courses they needed to complete a degree at the Center. In fact, one focal student, Isaura, expressed the belief that all of the courses necessary for an AA Degree *could* be taken at the Center.

The second Appleton Center goal that speaks to PCC's needs rather than those of the students', "allow for the expansion of course offerings," reveals planning based on the needs and patterns of the main campus, not the Appleton Center. "The availability of a facility during the day would permit us to offer a wider variety of courses and to offer courses during the prime time between eight o'clock and 1 pm [sic]." This quote from the May 4, 1987, Board of Trustee meetings' minutes illustrates a fundamental lack of understanding the needs of the students that the Center was to serve. A "prime-time" of 8 a.m. to 1 p.m. was fine by main campus standards, where the majority of full-time and only some part-time students attend classes. Yet, survey information, previously reviewed shows that 46% of the students at the Appleton Center considered weekday evenings as "prime-time" for classes at the Center, not mornings.[9] Furthermore, PCC did not meet the needs of the community in terms of the number of course offerings; there were not enough sections of English courses to meet the demands of the community. The teacher in English 10 reported that she had cut off her waiting list at 12 students one semester.

The Board of Trustees also showed a lack of commitment, or at least an ambivalence, toward maintaining a lasting presence in Appleton. The Planning Committee proposed two options for the creation and development of the Center. The first, Option I, was presented as a completely developed plan attached to the Planning Committee Report. Clearly, this was the Committee's recommended approach to setting up the Center. Option II offered to: "reduce the scope of the project planned . . . to bring total project costs within a predetermined revenue and expenditure level " (*Preliminary planning report* . . ., 1987, p.6). The Board chose Option II, the less expensive and less educationally complete of the two plans.[10]

Another indication of the Board's lack of commitment is evident in their decisions regarding a school plant. From the outset of the program, the Board of Trustees chose to lease space for the Center at a shopping mall on a short-term basis, at ever-increasing rates, rather than make plans to buy or build its own facility designed specifically for teaching and learning. This fact was not lost on the Appleton community, which was brought into the development planning process in the second year of the Center's existence. The Appleton Center Advisory Committee unanimously passed a recommendation that "the college begin a process for the establishment of

---

[9] This notion of "prime-time" has not changed in scheduling classes at the Center. When computer classes were finally introduced at the Center the semester after I left, classes were scheduled for mornings, much to the English 10 teacher's dismay; she knew many students would be unable to attend.

[10] Two other options, "abandon the project" and "provide other direction" were also given to the Board at this time.

a more permanent center for the college in Appleton" (Annual Report [Appleton] Center, 1990–1991). With this recommendation, the advisory committee made evident its concern that the college could leave the town with little notice.

In addition to failing to provide access to degree programs at the Center, a lack of course offerings at convenient times for Appleton students, and an apparent lack of commitment to maintaining the Center on a long-term basis, support services were severely limited for students attending the Appleton Center compared to those available on the main campus. During my two years there, an advisor was available to Appleton students only one and one half days a week, and only during hours when most students worked: Monday 9–5 and Tuesday 9–2:30. Here, again, the Center failed to consider the needs of part-time students.

Although there is little doubt that the Appleton Center planning committee knew they would have many bilingual and LEP students if PCC held classes in Appleton, no specific mention of meeting the language needs of students was made in the committee report. Although ESL courses were offered at the Center, they required that students attend two ESL classes each semester (one in writing, the other reading and discussion) for a minimum of eight to twelve hours a week. Two to four of these hours (the discussion class) met only during the workday in Appleton. Although such concentrated practice would certainly benefit students, the realities of students' lives in Appleton prevented many from taking advantage of the program. Moreover, no special support services were provided for LEP students at the Center—for example, there was no bilingual tutoring or translating.

The main campus had a fully staffed writing center available where students could receive individual tutoring on their writing either on a walk-in or appointment basis. The Appleton Center, however, had no such facility, and there was no tutoring beyond that available during classes on Monday evenings. Furthermore, none of the English instructors held office hours at Appleton; yet, the English 10 teacher in this study held a minimum of five office hours a week on the main campus. There was also access to computers on the main campus, but none was available to Appleton students. There was no access to library facilities in Appleton, although an unsuccessful attempt to establish a relationship with the public library had been made. The lack of library facilities was a particular hardship for English 15 students because they were required to complete a major library research paper unit as a part of the course. During the two years I was in Appleton, this part of the course was never taught.

Students in Appleton paid for health services, like all PCC students, but there was no clinic or health care professional available to students in Appleton, itself. Registration materials were purportedly available at the Appleton Center, but there had been at least one complaint made to the Board of Trustees that the Center had not received the schedule in time for students to mail in preregistration materials by the deadline (Kitts, 1990). As previously mentioned, PCC was committed to having the Puente Program at the college. However, this intensive English composition course, designed to improve the transfer rate of Chicano students from two-year to four-year institutions, was not housed in Appleton, where the majority of the Mexican American students attended, but on the main campus, further limiting the opportunities of the Appleton Mexican American population.

In interviews, the teacher of English 10 voiced similar concerns about the Center. She recognized that the main campus did not provide the support that it might.

> I feel like the Center is such a second class citizen. It is. I think the students are treated pretty shabbily all in all. And yet the school makes great hay, public relations hay out of having that outreach, applying for Title III [funds]. . . . I know it costs money [to have the Center], but I can't believe that there aren't sources to find that money. If you really apply to the state. You've got this group of, this potential population that everyone is talking about needs to be educated—there's money out there.

According to the teacher, the acting Dean of the Center at this time was more interested in developing community contacts than in providing for the educational needs of the students. The teacher explained:

> We [teachers] were in a position of constantly proving to him that these were at-risk students who needed a lot of individual help if they were to stay in school. I mean that's the . . . educational part that he didn't get. His bag was going out into the community. He's a real PR kind of person.

The Center was providing a second-rate educational experience for Appleton's largely Mexican American enrollment. Moreover, PCC lacked any intent of providing a more complete or permanent educational program for Appleton students, although the students and the community expressed the need for such changes. In fact, the differences between the main campus in Shoreline and the Center campus in Appleton were remarkably similar to the differences between the Shoreline and Appleton K–12 schools in the Appleton Valley Unified School District. In both cases, Mexican American students have been denied access to an educational experience equal to that of Anglo American students.

The sociocultural and educational situation in Appleton is reflective of a century and a half of Anglo Americans' attempts to silence the Mexican American population in the state despite, as Madrid mentions in the opening of this chapter, attempts to be heard. Little changed during those years. In the 1850s, points of contention between the Anglo American and Mexican American communities existed around issues of political representation, economic justice, cultural expression, and ethnic intolerance. These points of contention continue to exist today. Students in the Appleton area, like most of those in the study, have spent nearly all of their lives in this environment, an environment that attempts to silence the Mexican American voice at every turn. The schools in California and Appleton have attempted to do the same with Mexican American students. Through linguistic exclusion and segregation, Mexican American students have received an inferior education and learned that, according to the schools, they are not worthy to receive an education equal to their Anglo American counterparts. Students at the Appleton Center also suffer from an unequal education in comparison to the largely Anglo American population enrolled at the PCC main campus. They, too, suffer from exclusion from certain programs and a lack of linguistic access. The information gathered from carefully examining the social and educational context of the Appleton Center helps explain the interaction in an Appleton Center classroom, particularly the silence. In the next chapter, I reveal more about the students, their teacher, and how their personal histories also influenced classroom interaction.

4
STUDENT AND TEACHER VOICES

> Silencing permeates classroom life so primitively as to render irrelevant
> the lived experiences, passions, concerns, communities and
> biographies of low-income, minority students.
> –Fine, 1989, p. 155

Individuals' unique experiences affect their perspectives on interaction and their responses to it. Often, as Fine suggests in the preceding quotation, these experiences are never acknowledged in the classroom. In order to interpret the classroom interaction I observed from the perspective of the participants, I needed to understand more than just the social, linguistic, and educational contexts described in the previous chapter. I also needed to explore the "passions, concerns . . .and biographies" that inform interaction in the classroom. The salient themes in the talk of the teacher and the focal students helped elucidate their interaction in the classroom. These key themes appeared as naturally recurring topics in the talk of the individuals involved: teacher and students.

Because interviews were informal without protocols, participants raised topics and returned to them at will. Therefore, key themes such as "education of the Spanish-speaking" were discerned with relative ease and assurance. Informal interviews have their shortcomings, however, in a certain unevenness in the data collected. Information on particular topics, including educational experiences, personal background, and student goals, may have more or less detail, depending on a participant's interest in that topic. Viewed as a whole, however, the information about the focal students reveals several unique responses to a single unifying circumstance: being Mexican American students in English 10 at the Appleton Center.

All of the focal students had at least one key theme recurring in their talk, as unique as each one of them. Although the themes

89

were different, their source and the way that they were enacted was uncannily similar: These themes were the students' responses to their past experiences with the Anglo American society, in either a political, economic, educational, or other manifestation. It was through the filter of these past experiences that they interpreted and responded to what happened in the English 10 classroom, both socially and academically. The key themes discussed in this chapter provide an important link between the social, educational, and linguistic contexts of the outreach program discussed in Chapter Three and the interaction of the students and the teacher that are analyzed in Chapters Five and Six.

Furthermore, without prompting, all students volunteered information about the ways that the education system was either failing generally or had failed them specifically. Some considered this failure to be related to issues of ethnicity and language use—that is, some seemed to think it was only failing Mexican American or Spanish-speaking students—whereas, others found it failed everyone, regardless of ethnicity or language background. They all revealed feelings of inadequacy regarding their English writing skills (a common feeling among bilinguals, in general), but often accompanied statements of these feelings with complaints of inadequate composition instruction in their schools.

The first section of this chapter presents each of the five focal students who were briefly introduced in Chapter Two, providing descriptions of their past educational experiences and discussing the various key themes that inform an understanding of their perspectives on the classroom interaction that will be described in Chapters Five and Six. Then, I present background information about the teacher of English 10, Carol, providing a description of her experiences as a teacher and administrator at the community college and an analysis of the themes that recurred in her many talks with me, themes that are important in understanding *her* perspective on the interaction in the classroom.

THE STUDENTS

Juanita

Twenty-two years old at the time of the study, Juanita was born into a family of migrant workers in California. She explained in a tutorial that she "travelled from place to place because when the winter came there was no work here in Appleton." When she was growing up, her family also spent at least one month every winter in Mexico visiting family.

Juanita had all of her schooling in the United States, but because she frequently missed school, she was labeled a migrant student and received special tutoring. Her experiences as a migrant student in largely Anglo American schools and her experiences learning English in English-only classrooms have influenced not only her current attitudes toward education, particularly English classes, but also the direction of her career, and, as will be discussed later in this section, her key theme. She was a migrant aide at a local elementary school, with a career goal of becoming a bilingual elementary school teacher. In a conference with her teacher toward the end of the semester, she said that she hoped to transfer from the community college to the nearest campus of the University of California for her bilingual teaching certificate. She planned to get her teaching credential by the time she was 30.

Juanita's first language was Spanish. Because she attended predominantly Anglo American Shoreline area schools in the Appleton Valley School District, she learned English in English-only classrooms. She explained:

> Nothing was bilingual . . . it was kind of hard, you know, for me when I was growing up because, you know, I had to learn everything, you know, catch up fast, you know, because I didn't know any . . . English . . . until I was like probably in the third grade. . . . Well, I was always, I remember being in the lowest group of flash cards and reading and stuff.

As a migrant student, Juanita met regularly with a migrant aide. Because she was pulled from her class to meet with the aide, she felt stigmatized.

> Because we used to get pulled out of class, you know . . . they [her classmates] used to tell, well, "She's kind of stupid," because I had to go to the . . . [migrant aide], and "She's stupid because that's why she has to go." I knew exactly how, you know, how I felt.

Juanita's description of her life in high school was not unlike the bleak picture she paints of her elementary years. Juanita spoke somewhat cryptically about her high school years, only saying that because she was in a school with relatively few Mexican American students, she felt isolated. Virtually her only friend in high school was her older sister. She commented to me that some of her teachers were "prejudiced" in high school, but did not go into any specifics. Instead, she just shrugged her shoulders and asked rhetorically, "But what could you do?" It was painful for her to remember those times. Juanita did mention that she had been enrolled in Basic English as a ninth grader at Shoreline High School, adding that after that she was allowed to take electives like the short story and American literature. She did not remember much about the courses though.

After her unhappy years in high school, attempting college was traumatic for Juanita. She expressed a great deal of anxiety about returning to school in general and about writing in particular. The title of her first essay for English 10 was "Coming Back to School." In it she vividly described her feelings as she first registered at the Appleton Center.

> I was very scared and my hands were sweating and I was trembel-ing [sic]. I didn't know if I could go through this. I felt like walking out of the office and forgetting about the whole thing. . . . I was scared for a long time, because I knew that I was never smart in high school and that it would be harder now that I was enrolled at Portolá. I was also very frightened, because I had lack of confidence [sic] in myself. I thought I would never make it, and I had a very low self-esteem. . . . Another reason was because I had not gone to school for four years now.

Juanita received much support from home, however, in her quest to return to school. In fact, her husband, a construction worker, encouraged her to return to school and willingly shared in the household duties so that she could keep up with her school work. She explained:

> Another reason that I decided to come back was because my hus-band encouraged me to think about presuing [sic] higher education. He told me that I should think about my future ten years from now, that time flyes [sic] by fast and before I know it, I will accomplish my goal. He also told me he would help me in any way he could and not to worry about having dinner ready or doing a lot of house work around the house but to concentrate on school, which is more important.

Juanita's mother also encouraged her educational pursuit. In Juanita's second essay, she wrote about her mother, whose formal education ended in the second grade, concluding: "She [Juanita's mother] wanted her children to have an education, because of the fact that she was denied one."

Juanita's experience with her first English class at the Appleton Center, the semester before she was in English 10, had not been a happy one for her. In our first tutorial, she described how her experience in English 5 had made her feel worse about her writing than she had before she returned to school. She complained that the teacher was not interested in helping her with her writing, the school had wrongly assessed her ability, and the tutor she worked with in English 5 classes made her feel terrible about her writing. She described those feelings to me with a great deal of hurt and anger in her voice.

> Steve [the tutor] made me feel like, really like a nobody, you know, like I really don't know how to do, you know, anything, like my writing was just terrible, you know. And here I was I already thought that, and he made me believe it more (laughs), you know. It's like, 'Hey why did you do this?' you know, and I really felt bad.

These feelings about her writing had not faded by the time she reached English 10, nor did they dissipate during the course. At various times during the semester, she commented on her feelings about writing with statements such as, "I think that my writing is really terrible," and "Writing, I think it's the hardest thing. . . . I don't even know if I'm going to pass this class, this is how bad I feel about writing."

Although Juanita was discouraged by her experience in English 5, she was nevertheless certain that her English skills were considerably better than those of her classmates in English 5, many of whom were just out of ESL classes. After all, she reasoned, she had done all of her schooling in English and in the United States. She was also convinced that she had not learned anything in English 5 and that going through it again would not help improve her writing. Therefore, when she was recommended by her English 5 teacher to repeat the course, she unofficially challenged the recommendation; she signed up for English 10 anyway. Juanita passed the in-class assessment and was allowed to stay in English 10.

Although Juanita felt great trepidation about writing in English, she was not as fearful of writing in Spanish. Juanita had taught herself to write in Spanish. Although she modestly insisted that her writing was poor because she had learned "*sin acentos*," many of the bilingual teachers that she was an aide for relied on her expertise in Spanish writing. As she said, "My writing is even better than their [the teachers'] writing, and they went to school to learn that writing. And even on like some words, they even ask me, and I even know them. And they've gone to school for I don't know how long."

A commitment to the education of Spanish-speaking students was the basis of Juanita's current and future career choices. It was a concern she spent a lot of time pondering, and this key theme ran throughout her tutorials and her talk in class. During an in-class tutorial, Juanita explained why she would be a good bilingual teacher in the future by linking it to her own past experiences.

> I think that I know exactly how they feel because migrant students, everything is more difficult for them, because these migrant students have to move from place to place and financially, there's a lot of problems in their homes because of that. And I think that they need more attention, you know, from their teachers, and I kind of remember feeling the same way, too. I remember I had a migrant aide, also. . . . And I remember that I felt good going to her. . . . because she was like the only person I could tell my problems, because I thought that she would understand me better. . . .[I want to be a bilingual elementary teacher for migrant students] because I want to help . . . because I understand how . . . I know their background, I know their culture.

Juanita was particularly concerned about the lack of discipline that she saw in classes where she was an aide and about a lack of fluency in Spanish among the teaching staff, a factor that she believed contributed to the breakdown in discipline. In our tutorial, she elaborated on how "knowing their [the students'] culture," would make her a better teacher. She explained that because she was Hispanic, she would command more *respeto* (respect) and her fluency in the local variety of Spanish would enable her to understand everything the students said. She added:

> Being an Hispanic teacher would probably make them, you know, I think that they would like kind of like respect me more. . . .*Y, y también* [And, and also] just because, also because they know that I know good enough Spanish and they'll understand because *muchos maestros no saben mucho bien en español* [many teachers do not know Spanish very well], you know, *tienen los cosas que están diciendo, como* [they have things that are said, how], how do you say, um, *como se* [how do you], when you use, um, other langu-well other words that you use in Spanish that . . . because teachers only understand what's from the book, *y yo entiendo todo* [and I understand everything] . . . I understand *todo que están diciendo y muchos maestros no saben lo*

que están diciendo, y si están diciendo cosas, [I understand everything they are saying and many teachers do not know what they are saying, and if they are saying things], you know.[1]

She said that children were not learning in either language in the classes she observed and that parents were frantic, because they needed someone in the family to learn English to transact the family business. Parents did not have time to learn English because they were busy working to support the family.

In addition to her work as a migrant aide, Juanita was taking classes such as Chicano Psychology and La Mujer that would prepare her to work with migrant students.

Mónica

Mónica was born in Guadalajara, Mexico. Nineteen years old at the time of the study, she was the eldest daughter in the family, with one older brother, two younger brothers, and two younger sisters. When she was one year old, her family moved to the United States from Mexico because her father, who had been working for several years in the United States, had bought a house in the countryside near Appleton. Her parents farmed the land they owned until it became too much work for the two of them. Then, they moved into the town of Appleton to work in a local food processing plant. As a child, Mónica traveled to Mexico occasionally to visit her grandmother. She had not been there recently, however, because most of her family had moved to the United States and therefore, her grandmother came to the United States to visit instead. Mónica's first language was Spanish, and she continued to use Spanish with her parents, her grandmother, and with many of her friends.

Mónica had attended downtown Appleton schools and graduated from Appleton High School. In tutorials, she frequently mentioned how little writing was taught throughout her schooling in the Appleton Valley Unified School District, a frequent refrain of other students, as well. These discussions also revealed the anxiety she experienced as a result of school writing tasks and little confidence in her own abilities as a writer.

In high school, she took a college preparatory English class, but felt it was "too hard," so the following year, she took an intermediate level class. In her junior year, she took American Literature and "Sports English." She was not required to take any English

---

[1] As discussed in Chapter Two, students occasionally code switched during our tutorial sessions and during unofficial peer interaction. Code switching is a normal linguistic occurrence in bilingual communities.

classes in her senior year, so she didn't; no one advised her otherwise. She commented to me that she was "so dumb in English" because she took only electives "like home ec" in her senior year and had forgotten "everything about English."

Sports English, according to Mónica, "was, like, watch movies and read a magazine and, like, maybe, talk about one athlete, write about that athlete. . . . They [the teachers] had a little paper thing: date, time, hour, period and then write on those three lines. It's like everyday we did that." Evidently, the only writing required for that class amounted to filling out this reading log daily. Her American Literature class did not provide many more writing opportunities than her Sports English class: "Just like, um, reports like for a book, read the book, but then other than that, just talk in class." She remembered that there was not much writing assigned in her junior high school English classes either, although she had always wanted to have more writing assigned. She told me:

> I used to like for them to give me a hard report so I could try to figure it out myself, but they never did. And so that's why I never learned to like express myself or anything. That's the way I feel. . . .
> I still like that [a challenging assignment], but I just don't know the way to start it, you know, 'cause I never learned to.

Despite her fears about writing for school, Mónica enjoyed writing for herself. She had kept a thirteen page journal of the days following the Loma Prieta earthquake in the Appleton area; she said she wrote it "just for herself," and she brought it to one of our meetings to show me. She also told me that she wrote fairly regularly about other topics, such as her boyfriend. She said that when she "gets going," she usually writes "a lot," but, she warned me, there were "no commas" in it. To my knowledge, Mónica did not read or write in Spanish, as she never mentioned it to me.

Mónica started attending PCC immediately after high school graduation, attending a local beauty college simultaneously. Planning to get an AA Degree in Business Administration in preparation for opening her own beauty salon, she took three business classes during her first semester. She enrolled in English 10 during her second semester at PCC. According to Mónica, she had been too busy with beauty school and college to keep a job. During her semester in English 10, she graduated from beauty college and immediately found a position as a cashier at the local pharmacy in order to gain experience handling cash and working cash registers.

Although she told her manager that she could only work limited hours because of school, she was frequently called in to work at the last minute, sometimes even when she was supposed to be in class. On those occasions, she would have to leave class early or arrive late. In high school, Mónica had worked as a receptionist in a beauty salon and as a volunteer in the local hospital.

Mónica was formally assessed into English 10 by the campus-wide assessment procedure. Her counselor (a Latino male), however, advised her to start in a lower level of English—English 5. According to Mónica, he told her it was "better to start at the bottom." During the first evening of class in English 5, she was again assessed and again told she should be in English 10. She was then moved into Carol's English 10 class.

As the semester wore on, Mónica increasingly confided in me about tensions in her relationships with friends and family. Mónica's response to, or perhaps refuge from, the conflicting pressures of her parents and friends was to remain devoted to her family and others who needed her and to place school well above socializing on her list of priorities. This desire to maintain traditional values of the Mexican American home was a key theme in Mónica's talk and writing. She told me, "Most of my friends, thirteen of [us] are really close, all of them have kids, except me and Marisa. Most of them are not married." This situation caused her a good deal of distress because her parents were afraid that she would follow her friends' example and, as a result, they set many limits on Mónica's social life. She explained her parents' position, "They think I'm going to get a bad influence from them [her friends]."

At the same time, Mónica experienced pressure from her girlfriends to act more like them. When Mónica was younger, she would sneak out of the house, but as she grew older she came to understand her parents' concerns and to respect their authority while she was still living in their house. Nevertheless, she was still called on occasionally to lie for a girlfriend by telling the girlfriend's parents that their daughter was spending the night at Mónica's house when, in fact, the friend was out with a boyfriend.

Mónica had decided not to spend too much time with her own boyfriend, against the advice of her friends and sisters. Although she had been seeing the same young man for four years, a star soccer player at the high school, she said they had only had a few "real" dates (that is, going out alone), most of the time they just hung out at each others' houses with their families. She says, "He respects me. He doesn't tell me what to do, *I* tell *him*."

During the semester Mónica was in English 10, her mother had two major operations (the sixth and seventh operations Mónica remembered her mother having). As eldest daughter, Mónica was responsible for taking her mother to the doctor, picking her up from the hospital, talking with the doctor about her mother's prognosis, taking care of her bedridden mother when she returned home, helping to make meals, and babysitting her youngest brother, Miguel, who was seven years old. In her first paper, she wrote that since the Loma Prieta earthquake, she had been afraid of another quake that would hurt or kill her or a family member. She even considered dropping out of school. She wrote: "I just thought that since time was limited, why continue school? I would just spend my time with my family." Mónica also took care of an elderly neighbor. Although the woman was bitter and treated Mónica poorly, Mónica visited her regularly, washed and set her hair for free in her home, and fed the woman's cat when the woman did not feel up to it.

Mónica insisted that school was more important to her than her relationship with her boyfriend. She had made it clear to him that school came before he did on her list of priorities. Her brothers were also supportive of her schooling, and her father told her it was "OK" for her to go to school, adding that he only wished that he "had had the opportunity to go to college." During one tutorial, while informally discussing another student who had failed to show up to a tutorial session, I concluded that the student "must have been busy." Mónica corrected me rather brusquely stating,"You have to make time for English; I do. I only visited my mom [in the hospital] for one hour today. It was a decision, a choice." Another clue about her dedication to her education and about the support she received from those around her to pursue it, was a trinket on her key ring: a picture of Mónica in her high school graduation gown. Her boyfriend had given her the key ring with the picture already in place. Mónica referred to herself as a "nerd." She was seen regularly at the public library doing her homework.

Isaura

Isaura was a 37-year-old woman who came to the United States from Mexico when she was 13. She grew up and attended elementary school through the sixth grade in the tiny village of San Antonio Ocampo in Michoacán. She moved with her family from Mexico to Chicago, where part of her mother's family already resided. She attended seventh and eighth grade in Chicago, but after the eighth grade, she had to quit school to help support the family; she was one of 13 children. She went to work in a dingy, "depressing," box factory until her family decided to move to California to work in the fields.

At 20, she married and began working with her husband in the strawberry fields of Central California, where she has continued to work for the last 17 years, every April to November, six days a week, nine hours a day. She had three children, aged 16 years, 10 years, and five weeks when the semester began. Isaura and her husband have done well enough financially to build a house in Mexico and to put a down payment on a home in Appleton. Her goal for the course was to improve her English-speaking skills in order to get a better job. As I will discuss in more detail later, this goal became part of her key theme throughout the semester.

Isaura used Spanish both at home with her husband and children and at work in the fields. The children usually spoke to each other in Spanish (except for when they fought, according to their mother, then they used English). English language newspapers, magazines, and television were omnipresent in her home, however.

In her first essay for English 10, Isaura described her educational experiences in Mexico and the United States. She explained why she only went through the sixth grade in Mexico.

> I went to school until grade six. It was the highest grade that was available in the village. In order to continue studying, we needed to go to the nearest city that was half of an hour away from the village and we needed to take the bus very early in the morning. I wanted to continue studying but my parents didn't let me go. They put the excuse that it was too risky for a girl to be waiting for the bus at dawn.

Once the family moved to Chicago, however, she was able to attend junior high school. She said she was happy to be able to continue her education, but she explained:

> The first year I went to school was very difficult because I didn't understand the teachers, and I had no friends. I was beginning to learn English when my parents took me out of school because I had to work. I felt very disappointed because I couldn't go to school anymore.

She was proud of having graduated from the eighth grade, nevertheless. She wryly commented to me that at the time, she "didn't know it was nothing."

Isaura returned to adult school just a few years ago and earned her high school equivalency in Spanish. The semester we worked together was her fourth semester at the Appleton Center. In the first semester, she took an advanced ESL class, then two semesters of English 5, and finally English 10. She had taken a course in Early Childhood Education at the Center, as well. A highly motivated student, Isaura reported frequently staying up until two o'clock in the morning to read or write for English 10, often after working all day in the field. Her husband took care of the baby while she attended class and when she met with me for tutoring. According to Isaura, he encouraged her to continue with her schooling. He often asked me how she was doing.

Isaura's experience in English 10 was a phenomenal success, according to Carol. She earned an A– from the notoriously hard grader. However, when I talked with Isaura after she completed the course and received her recommendation to English 15, she said, "In case I go to school next year, I think I have to enroll in the same 10 or 5, no?" In other words, Isaura felt that she should take the same level English class, which she had just passed with an A-, over again, or go to an even lower level of English, a class she had already taken twice. When I asked Isaura why she felt that way, considering her A– in English 10, she said, "I think she [Carol] gave me an A because I do the homework two or three times." Despite her good grades in the class, Isaura's opinion of herself and her English remained negative. Isaura did not credit herself with having made progress in her English, despite her teacher's judgment to the contrary. At various times in the course, she indicated her belief that her English skills were "the lowest of everybody" in the class. When asked how she could reach such a conclusion, she said, "I think I have low self-esteem."

Her feelings of inadequacy in English notwithstanding, Isaura reported reading frequently in both English and Spanish, depending on if the reading was interesting, not what language it was in. Although she had early training in Spanish composition, Isaura preferred to write in English now, insisting, "I don't remember anything about grammar from Mexico. . . . I have forgotten everything."

Like many Mexican Americans in Appleton, Isaura had directly experienced economic and, closely related to this, educational oppression. She tied her current educational goals to economic issues, as well, and this became her key theme throughout tutorials. She frequently spoke of how the English language might help Mexican Americans get more desirable jobs. Isaura wished to stop working in the fields. Her goal in English 10 was to learn to speak English more fluently in order to get a job that did not require manual labor. She talked about the relationship between English and work in a tutorial session with me, saying, "In the place that I work I don't need the English. I know it is necessary that I know it, but ah, I know that I have to look for another job. . . . I think my English is very limited." Isaura felt that she needed to learn to speak English better in order to get a better job. Because of her goal, she questioned the value of courses and activities that did not seem as if they would help her reach this goal.

In our first tutorial outside of class, Isaura asked me to explain the different types of English classes at the community college. It was during this conversation that she first openly questioned how learning academic discourse would help her reach her goals:

> Kay: They teach other 15 level courses, 15b, 15c, so there is more English that you can take, and they are more difficult in things like, one of them will focus on, um, writing a research paper, so it's really very academically oriented . . .
> Isaura: But do you think that's important for people who want just to work in, ah, let's say a store or school or something?
> Kay: Uh uh [no].
> Isaura: Do you think you need that?
> Kay: Uh uh [no].
> Isaura: That's what I think too.

These same types of questions came up in other tutorials later in the semester. For example, when the class was comparing and contrasting the educational experiences of Maya Angelou and Frederick Douglass, she asked if I thought she would need this "stuff" in order to work where they spoke English. Again, I had to admit that I didn't think so.

Although Isaura had doubts about the practicality of English 10 for her needs, she had little difficulty completing the assigned tasks successfully. However, she did not believe she was any closer to her educational or economic goals at the end of the semester.

Amado

Amado was a 27-year-old native of Michoacán, Mexico, who had lived in the United States since the third grade. He was one of eight children and still lived at home. At home and with his friends, Amado spoke Spanish; at school and at work, he spoke English. He planned to transfer from the community college to a seminary, where he would train to become a pastor in his church. Amado was taking two other courses at the college, working 21 hours a week in an industrial laundry, and volunteering as the assistant youth director for his church during the semester I worked with him. He had been a gang member during his high school years and for four years thereafter.

When he was one year old, Amado moved to Tijuana where he lived until he was eight, attending the first grade there. He began his U. S. schooling in the Appleton Valley School District shortly thereafter. He vividly remembered attending first grade in Mexico, stating, "I learned a lot when I was there. They grade you by from 1 to 10. . . . I was getting all 10s." He compared his schooling in Mexico with his elementary school experience in the United States in the following way: "Here [in the United States] they didn't teach me nothin.'"

His description of elementary school in the United States could also be said to characterize his high school experience. He described his education at Appleton High School as generally poor. He related the story of one bilingual math class in which the teacher joked all the time and cancelled class on Fridays to teach disco lessons. Amado flunked the class. He explained to me, "If he [the teacher] didn't care, we didn't care. . . . Nobody respected him. . . . I never did learn anything in that class."

The two English classes he remembered from high school were "Sports English," which he said he flunked, and a ninth grade grammar class, in which he received a D. Amado admitted that he did not apply himself much in these classes, explaining, "I was kind of weaker to the, the outside environment, OK, not the intellectual environment, or thing, you know. And I was always going out with my friends and partying. And doing this and that, you know. . . . I was into gangs, you know." He said he managed to avoid both reading and writing in high school by either "copying off of somebody" or going "to the end of the book [to] find out what it's about."

Amado claimed that he "never did read nothing" in high school and he "never did do any essays" there either. He said, "I kind of did enough just to pass by, you know. At the high school, if you're always there, you know, they'll just kind of give you a grade, or something, pass grade." If a teacher did ask him to write, he completed it as quickly as possible, using the following method: "Just deliver it on the same day you're gonna hand it in. Just write a page on it, you know. Not even time to think about it, you know. Just hand it in." Amado's high school teachers did not seem to discourage this approach to writing, since he said, "They accept it, fine, you know. You get a passing grade."

Amado said he was the only one of his friends from his junior high class to actually graduate from Appleton High in his year. He connected this to the fact that they all had "Spanish names," like his. Amado almost didn't graduate himself. Everyone assumed he would drop out like his friends, and he was behind 20 credits just one semester before graduation. However, Amado's mother "kept pushing" and "pushing" him because "she wanted her kids to get educations." She convinced Amado to enroll in adult school during the spring of his senior year, and in two months, he had made up the credits. As a result, Amado was the first person in his family to go through graduation ceremonies at the high school; none of his three older brothers and sisters had made it that far (neither had two after him).

Amado went to work right out of high school, cutting celery in the fields for a large unionized grower. Here, he not only made money, but also a reputation for himself as "tough" in his gang. With his money from cutting celery, he did what everyone in the gang admired: He got a car and spent the rest on drugs. Thanks to his mother, however, he experienced a religious conversion that indirectly led him back to school.

When Amado decided to return to school four years after high school graduation, he found that his old ways of approaching school did not suffice. He was placed in English 5, which he failed twice before being promoted to English 10. He explained his difficulties to me.

> I couldn't pick up the idea of how to begin writing, you know. . . . I had to still clear up, you know, get used to the habit of studying, you know, because from four years being out of high school and forgetting the habit of studying, which I never did have.

Although finally promoted from English 5 to English 10, Amado dropped out during his first semester in the course because his father who "drinks a lot" was "messing up." He took English 10 a second time, but he only received a "C," which prevented him from moving to English 15. He took a third English 10, in which he says he did "excellent," so he was promoted to English 15. However, on the first night of English 15, as a result of the in-class writing assessment, he was asked to once again move to the 10 level, Carol's class.

In Carol's class, Amado felt he made real progress for the first time. He commented, "I worked really hard. That was my first semester I really worked really hard. And I found through, through that semester I found a lot of things, a lot of new things, and a lot of errors I had made before." But Carol felt that Amado had made no progress at all, commenting to me that he "stood perfectly still" in his writing ability. She said, "I feel his weakness, as a student and as a writer, is that he doesn't work hard enough. . . . He just, he didn't go back to learn from his mistakes."

After completing his fourth semester of English 10 and his *seventh* semester of English at the community college, Amado still felt his position as a student was somewhat tenuous.

> What I'm trying to do still is trying to get on the steady line. . . . Well, I'm kind of, like, trying you know. I'm on it, trying to stay on it, you know. But before I was trying to get on it, you know. Now, now, now, that I'm on it, I have to kind of watch out and stay on it, see.

Despite Amado's many unsuccessful experiences with English classes in school, he did a considerable amount of reading and writing outside of school, much of it connected to church activities. A devotional book led Amado back to school and provided inspiration when things did not go well there. As assistant youth director at his church, he helped direct "Bible Bowl" contests between churches. To prepare youth for tests on various books of the Bible, Amado developed an elaborate system for creating practice questions and answers from the Bible. He also wrote a weekly sermon to deliver to the youth. He was learning to write in Spanish in his spare time, and he wrote letters in Spanish to a girlfriend in the San Joaquin Valley.

Prior to his enrollment in PCC, Amado experienced a religious conversion that made him realize that the church was a gang member's only hope of a future. He explained how he reached this conclusion.

> What really, really helped, made me feel secure in church, you know, is that I had, I was better off, you know, I had a future. Because out there, I didn't have a future because all of my friends were in jail, or they were dead, or they were married, having a lousy marriage. And

I really thought about that, you know. What is it that I'm gonna do, you know? Where is it that I'm gonna end up? There's only three ways for me to go, you know. Once you're out on the street, that's where you're gonna end up.

Throughout the semester, the key theme in Amado's talk and writing was how religion could save Mexican American youth. He planned to become a minister to the Spanish-speaking community of Appleton because, he explained:

If the Lord did that for me, you know, to just clear my mind, well, if He did that for me, I want to do something for Him, you know. Not because I owe Him, no. Because I feel that if he did something good for me, I can do something good for somebody, you know.

He decided he would attend a seminary in Northern California rather than one in Mexico because "If I want to live here, I should graduate here. Problems are different here than in Mexico."

As assistant youth director at his church, he was already encouraging teenage gang members to stay in school and go to college.

If someone doesn't know really what they want to be, that's no reason to stop from going to college, you know. . . . They should just keep on going. On the way, while they're studying, while they're in college, something will turn up, you know. They'll grow up, they'll know more about life, they'll know more, they'll have more knowledge, and they'll have more, ah, options to choose. I can go on and on, harangue on that subject.

Amado was proud of the fact that several youth from his church had taken his advice and were currently enrolled in adult education classes to prepare for the high school equivalency examination.

Federico

Federico was a 30-year-old male enrolled in English 10 for the first time. He moved with his parents from Mexico to the United States when he was ten and one half years old. The family of ten initially stayed with friends in a nearby town, but the Federal Housing Authority moved the family to a labor camp on the outskirts of Appleton, which he described as a "cluster of huts." He said their place was "adequate" because it had cooking facilities and heating, unlike much migrant housing.

After two months in the labor camp, the Housing Authority found the family an apartment and both of Federico's parents found work. When his father got a job at the Ford plant in the next county, the family moved again. In just a few years, the Ford plant closed, and Federico's family moved back to Appleton. It was not until well after Federico graduated from high school that his parents were able to make a down payment on a house.

Federico entered the Navy after finishing high school. After completing his tour of duty, he returned to Appleton to marry and start a family. He had a one-and-a-half-year-old son at the time of the study. At the end of the semester, he and his wife were in the process of making a bid on a house in the upscale Shoreline area. Spanish was Federico's first language and the language he still used at home. Work, however, was strictly English only.

Federico held two jobs while he was taking English 10. One was a civil servant in the Appleton sewage treatment plant, the other was a waiter on weekends in a coastal resort town. During the last month of class, he quit his job as a waiter so he could give more attention to his school work. His goal was to get an AA Degree and transfer to a four-year college so that he could work on a degree in engineering.

Federico did not talk much about his educational experiences, perhaps because it had been over ten years since high school, or perhaps, because he was so consumed with talking about the social and political situation in Appleton—his key theme. In commenting on all of the moving around his family did in his youth, from Mexico to Salinas, to Appleton, to Santa Clara and back again to Appleton, he made the comment, "I still suffer the effects of all the hopping about." He lamented the fact that he didn't have a stronger background in English, explaining, "I de-emphasized English too much. I put it aside, but it's hurting me now. Math, you know, ask me anything."

Federico was nearly sent from English 10 to English 5 as a result of his in-class assessment. The teacher had described it as "sketchy" and suggested to him that he move down. Federico made a successful argument to stay in the class, and the teacher came to consider him "the best writer in the class," after the first paper was revised.

Federico wrote outside of class for a variety of reasons. He kept a journal of incidents at work that he felt were unjust or irregular in some way. He wrote letters to the editor of the local newspaper and had them published (I will discuss one of these in the next section). Federico's one-and-a-half-year-old son already played on the computer keyboard while *Papi* wrote and had (unfortunately) learned how to turn the computer on and off. Federico never mentioned if he could read or write in Spanish.

Federico had experienced prejudice and discrimination first hand in Appleton and observed it elsewhere in the town. The key theme in his talk and his writing was the wrongs that had been done against Mexican Americans in the Appleton area, the causes of those wrongs, and how they might be righted. Although Federico claimed that his days of speaking out against injustice were over now that he had a family to consider, these topics continued to concern him deeply.

Shortly before he was enrolled in English 10, Federico had observed a series of incidents at work in the city's water and sewage department that he summarized as "incompetence at all levels," including the misuse of power, drinking on the job, and, in his case, unfair labor practices. At work, he felt "humiliated every day" because people who had less seniority than he were getting paid more. He asked for a raise, but was told he was not qualified, even though he had more experience on the job than others. So he took the state exam and received the necessary certificate, but management said his qualifications were "marginal" even with his Navy experience and the certificate. They finally agreed to interview him for what Federico described as the position he was already filling. This was the last straw.

Because most of the supervisors and those who were getting paid more than Federico with less knowledge and experience were Anglo American, Federico suspected discrimination. He made formal allegations of all of the wrongdoings he had observed, only to be thanked by his supervisors for alerting them so they could begin a coverup of the wrongdoings. This experience was completely disillusioning for Federico. He considered himself an American, part of a country that proclaimed equality for all, yet he felt discriminated against. He explained:

> I still remember . . . the day when my chest kind of swelled up and my, I got all pumped up about the National Anthem playing in the background, and I'm graduating and, you know, boot camp, and God, you know, I'm here I got my clean uniform, and, um, it was the closest I could get to the first ranks and, um, I remember that and compare it to what I was going through [at work].

He said he felt he had to speak up for himself and for others who had been and would be wronged: "My motivation stems from some deep-seated belief of America. . . . Where else can I go where it's going to get better? It's not. I can't go anywhere else. . . . This is my community," he insisted.

In Chapter Three, I described the battle between the Appleton City Council and the local Mexican American population over representation and voting rights. Federico was so incensed by the entire affair that when the Supreme Court refused to hear the city council's appeal, he wrote a letter to the editor of the local paper. He said, "One night I just sat down and [thought] 'Gosh, when are these things going to change?'" The letter began by pointing out that finally, justice had been served in the case. It continued by indicting the local Anglo American community for a number of injustices against Mexican Americans that continued to exist in the town:

> Mayor Betty Murphy's insistence on continuing belligerence is but one more brick on [sic] the wall that her kind has built for so long. A barrier that's responsible for the lot of this community's woes. We do not have to rely so heavily on agricultural product processing for our livelihoods, our kids should not have to be deemed lesser peasants by their Anglo counterparts (a cause for not a few academic failures). In short, our community would be better served by individuals interested in issues other than land development, ones able to to transcend the travesty of land devaluation due to new neighbors of Mexican descent. . . .
>
> We shall overcome.
>   Federico L. L.
>   Appleton

Federico had gone to city council meetings "a couple of times." He explained, "This is back when I was, like, God, seeking a forum where I could lay out the facts and uh, gosh, you know, I'm kind of disgusted now. It's not just local, it goes deeper than that." He was reluctant to divide positions on the issues strictly along ethnic lines; Federico always added a disclaimer to his statements about Anglo Americans. For example, in one of his papers he wrote,"I can find several examples in my own life where the compassion and understanding of key people of Anglo Saxon ethnicity helped me become what I am today." In a tutorial, he elaborated:

> I still have the notion within me that I can do anything I want and change anything that I want to change, that I would like, in my life and that, that just doesn't come from within, you have to, I have

acquired it from others. And, you know, I'm not rac-, I'm the last person that you would deem a racist, but I, I have had the necessity to acquire it from mostly the Anglo culture, and so it's, um, my anger is not racial, it's more, um, this is America, dammit, how can this be happening, you know. This stuff's not supposed to happen here, it's supposed to happen in South America or Mexico . . . what about us?

When asked if he was currently involved in any of the attempts to get Mexican Americans elected to city council seats, Federico responded:

I prefer not to get involved in what went on anymore because it does me no good. I just get frustrated and I think too much and I'd just rather do what's best for myself and my family now for several reasons. One, I feel better and two, I'm not risking. If I become involved in a lawsuit. . . .

These concerns did not keep Federico from talking or writing about the issues.

The past educational experiences and key themes of the five focal students in this study provide valuable insights into the varying social, educational, and linguistic perspectives that students brought to their educational experiences and to their interaction in English 10. All of the focal students may be considered Mexican American based on the definition I gave in Chapter One, however, there were differences among these focal students that are worth considering. Differences in nativity, in number of years in the United States, in use of Spanish and English (and literacy in each), in educational backgrounds (including how long they were educated in Mexico or the United States), and, of course, experiences in Anglo American society, all served to influence how each Mexican American student interacted in English 10.

Although one purpose for presenting these focal student voices was to illustrate the variation among the students, another purpose was to reveal their similarities as a result of living in the Appleton area for years and having been subject to similar experiences as Mexican Americans there. Recognizing the similarities in student experiences that result from the local history and current situation described in Chapter Three is important for understanding how the group as a whole may interpret classroom interaction and how classroom interaction might be designed to take these similarities into account.

Although the students had differing educational experiences (Amado and Mónica probably had the most similar experiences as they attended many of the same schools, albeit eight years apart), their experiences, in various ways, provided specific examples of past and present attempts to silence Mexican Americans educationally (as described in Chapter Three). The five students experienced a lack of educational attainment and a lack of access to an equal education. Students who attended Appleton High experienced segregation both within the district (Appleton vs. Shoreline) and within the school (Sports English rather than college prep English). Both Juanita and Isaura were hampered in their educational pursuits by their lack of bilingual instruction. Most of the focal students felt they had experienced, to one degree or another, an inadequate and unequal education, particularly with reference to English and writing instruction. Although they recognized the shortcomings of their schooling, this did not prevent them from feeling that they were in some way responsible for the inadequacies of their education. Both Juanita and Isaura mentioned that they had "low self-esteem." This statement might have been made by all the focal students, especially the women. None felt good about himself or herself as a student, especially as a student of English composition. Accompanying this low self-esteem was a fear of school writing tasks that interfered with their attempts to improve their writing. Despite these feelings about school-based literacy, all focal students engaged in a variety of literacy practices outside of school, a number of them doing so in two languages.

All of these students had highly developed abilities in their first language. However, this fact was lost on their teachers throughout K–12 and even at PCC. Formal and informal assessment procedures at the college did not evaluate languages other than English, even for students placed in ESL classes. There is no evidence to suggest that these teachers would have known how to use their students' language and literacy skills in L1 as a resource for developing the students' L2, if they had acknowledged the existence of such skills. Throughout their academic careers, these students were seen as having limited abilities and limited potential because their L1 abilities were not made worthy of consideration. These factors contributed to students being placed in low level English classes and repeatedly taking the same basic writing courses, left on their own to make connections between their two languages.

These frustrating experiences and a lack of understanding and recognition of their abilities led, in part, to the lack of self-esteem many of these students felt. The students came to see themselves as their teachers did—inadequate. The low expectations of teachers and administrators are evident in classes that were "dumbed down" such as Sports English, in classes cancelled for disco lessons, and in counselors at the high school who do not recommend a college prep curriculum for these students (e.g., four years of English) or in counselors at the community college who suggest that students take the most basic English class, even if they place out of it. If highly motivated students, such as those in this study, were feeling pressure from the educational system, how must average students respond? Many of the case study students received much support and positive feedback for their educational efforts from home, mitigating the negative messages received from the schools and dispelling the myth that Mexican Americans do not value education.

Finally, the tenacity of these students in the face of the most disheartening of educational experiences provides yet another point of comparison. For many, the reason for persevering was related to their key themes: getting a better job, becoming a pastor, earning a teaching credential. Juanita explained it to me like this, when I asked how she kept going after the negative experiences she had described:

> Because I know that I need this English class for what I want to do. And I know that I need to improve, and I know that I have to, you know, keep going and not give up because then that will be the end of it. . . if I think that way. I think that you have to think positive, not negative, and if there's someone that wants to put me down, well fine, that person has a problem.

The key themes of the focal students have a commonality in that all are responses to the situation Mexican Americans faced in Appleton; they vary according to how the situation has particularly affected (usually negatively) each personally. Most were concerned not only with their own situation, although that surely provided the initial impetus for the focus on their particular key theme, but also with helping other Mexican Americans who had been similarly affected. These key themes played an important role in the classroom interaction described in Chapters Five and Six.

THE TEACHER

Like the focal students, the teacher's perspective was revealed through key themes as well. Carol's past experiences, personal and professional, also influenced her understanding of and response to interaction in the classroom. Carol had her 25th anniversary as a teacher of college-level English during this study. Seventeen of those years she spent at PCC. Her BA was in English with an education minor from a private Catholic institution in the East. She described her undergraduate training as "classic, liberal arts—in the old style," including the canon of English literature with philosophy and theology, as well. Her first college teaching experience was as a TA while getting her MA Degree and working toward a PhD in English. She described her MA program as "The old MA, where you had to know everything from Beowulf to Hemingway;" her dissertation topic was Jacobean Tragedy. During these years, she taught one year at the high school level in Philadelphia city schools and worked with youngsters in a Montessori program, as well.

Carol claimed that she was never formally trained in writing pedagogy and for this reason, she spent at least two sabbatical leaves working to improve her knowledge in this area. One year, she took courses in composition research, theory, and pedagogy at UC Berkeley, whereas another year, she learned "by osmosis," as she put it, while a visiting lecturer in the UCLA Writing Program. These experiences served to reinforce her belief that "literature is the best training that you can get to teach comp[osition]" because both require text analysis. She also believed, however, that teachers of writing needed some composition theory, and even more important, they needed practical advice for applying that theory to the classroom. She explained, "It's one thing to say writing should be taught as a process, but what does that mean when you're actually in the classroom?" She was fully aware that the way writing is taught in school is "sometimes turned to ends that have more to do with the school running smoothly" than with the writing process. These perspectives on the teaching of writing are important for understanding Carol's interactional decisions surrounding composition instruction that will be analyzed in Chapter Five.

In a typical semester, Carol taught four courses with approximately 30 students each. All of these, except the class I studied, were conducted on the main campus of the community college in Shoreline. She usually taught two composition courses and two literature courses, but no composition course below the basic writing course English 10. She admitted to me, "I don't go below 10 because I don't feel very good with very basic writers." This feeling was not uncommon among the English teachers at the Appleton Center; at least one teacher requested that he not be reassigned to English 5 in Appleton because he felt he "needed some questions answered about teaching basic writing," especially to non-native speakers of English.

The key themes that recurred in Carol's talk were naturally centered on teaching, her life's work. They focused on her goals for

English 10 students and how she determined "where students were" in terms of those goals. Both of these key themes help to elucidate her interpretations of student interaction in the classroom, as well as her own choices related to this interaction. Carol's first key theme was her goal for all her English 10 classes, whether they were taught in Appleton or Shoreline: to prepare students for English 15 and any future academic writing they would face. Carol considered her basic writing course an integral part of the sequence needed for the AA Degree at the community college and for eventual transfer to a four-year college or university. She remained absolutely consistent in this goal throughout the two years of the study, and it provided the primary motivation for most of her interaction in the classroom or related to it. Nearly every time we talked, she mentioned this goal in one way or another.

Because both English 10 and its counterpart at the same level, English 11, could serve as the last English class required of a terminal AA Degree student at the college and as a prerequisite for English 15, transfer level English, there was a history of controversy surrounding the teaching of these two courses. Carol's role in that history sheds light on her belief that English 10 should cater to students who planned to take English 15 for transfer to a four-year university.

According to Carol, there was "terrible acrimony" in the department over a course called English 10/15 in the early 1980s. As the name suggests, the course was a heterogeneous mix of students that were considered to be at two different levels of ability, English 10 and English 15. Carol, who was department chair at the time, favored dividing the course into two separate courses, but many of the faculty opposed the idea. Eventually, the stalemate was decided by the University of California, Berkeley, which threatened to eliminate transfer credit for the course if it was not divided. Although the course was indeed split, it was not because the department had reached any consensus on how such courses would or should be taught.

By the time the course was officially divided, Carol was no longer department chair. The new chair wanted to create an English 10 level course that would address the needs of terminal AA Degree students and other students who did not have a degree goal at all, but were taking the class to improve job skills or simply for enrichment. After all, he reasoned, the majority of the students in English 10 level classes fit one of these two descriptions. Carol said the new department chair wanted "really good classes at the 10 level because this may be the last exposure to lit[erature] they [the students] have or to writing or to using writing as a way of expressing themselves." He wanted classes "where you wrote about a film and you wrote about sports and you wrote about yourself and you wrote journals, you wrote about fine art, anything that would be really interesting to these folks." This class was to be the only type of its kind offered at the English 10 level, however, and Carol felt that the needs of the prospective transfer students would be ignored in such classes. Carol explained, "There needed to be a generic class for those who wanted to take, who had to take 10 level, but then were going on to 15. . . . You had to look out for the transfer student in the works."

Carol insisted that a course be created for these prospective transfer students, and it was named English 10. The course designed for the other students became known as English 11. Still, the controversy over English 10 and English 11 had not ended at PCC. Because there was no formal method for directing students into one course or the other, both English 10 and English 11 classes had students with a variety of educational goals. Many in English 10 were terminal AAs or enrichment students and many in English 11 were university-bound. So, the curriculum for these courses continued to be an issue. Some of the English faculty questioned whether English 10 should be taught as preparation for 15 and transfer since a good number of students in every section were not transfer-bound. Carol was concerned that English 11 would not provide adequate preparation for English 15. She said: "I worry about these 11s because I'm afraid they're having a good time writing . . . not getting enough, um, practice in the kinds of writing that will help [them] get through 15." Carol's position on the controversy has remained unchanged over the years:

> If you think of that class [English 10] as a terminal class, which is the way some people think about it, people are going to take it to get their AA or their AS Degree, it's the last comp[osition] course they're going to take, if I thought of 10 in those terms, I'd run my class completely differently, you know, you'd want 'em, they'd write journals and poems and stories and have a wonderful time, enjoy writing. . . .

> [But] I don't want them to get scared when they hear "I want you to compare this to this," or "I want you to write an argument about," or "I want you to write a persuasive essay about" or "I want a propositional paper on" I mean I don't want them, even from the 10 level on, ever to be scared when they hear "I want you to analyze, I want you to summarize," 'cause teachers, their teachers in the future, . . . they're going to just say that.

In this quotation, Carol reveals how the constraints of the English sequence affected her decisions about course content and methodology. If the course were truly the last English course the students would ever take, then she could let them enjoy themselves, but because this class was also a prerequisite, she felt compelled to prepare them. The notion that one cannot have fun in a course designed to teach academic writing speaks to her definition and understanding of writing and helps explain why she approached English 10 as she did.

In addition to the constraints of the English department course sequence, Carol's method of teaching English 10 was also influenced by the perceived expectations of her colleagues. She felt that in order to maintain respect in the department, her English 10 students must do well in her colleagues' English 15 courses, and she held her colleagues to the same standard of review:

> I realize . . . that the techniques I use in comp[osition] are really different from what I use when I don't think "This student is going on to somebody else's class." That's when I feel the pressure. . . . And I mean I've made the mistake too. People have told me, "Hey, I have your student such-and-such, and she's not making it. How did she ever get out of your class?" It's not like I'm perfect here. That's the first thing I ask when someone's having trouble, "OK, so tell me who'd you take?"

Because Carol's goal was to prepare students for English 15, she tried to gauge where students were in relation to this goal from the first evening of class. When she spoke of students' progress in English 10 and their prognosis for success in English 15, she regularly referred to the "type" of student an individual was and how that explained the student's probable success or failure. These types were distinguished from one another by age, proficiency in English, and gender. She spoke of four types, with the majority of students in English 10 classes falling into the first three groups. In her words they were called: a) "re-entry women," b) "re-entry men," c) "babies," and d) those "who've come to the States late in life."

Carol quickly and easily categorized students into one of these groups based upon her observations of students' interaction in the classroom—their actions and their talk. There were only a few times when she adjusted her initial categorization, based on such things as the first essay turned in or other information that became available during a semester. Once, Carol explained how this "typing" happens:

I mean I know it's awful to type students in that way, but um I mean at the same time you're looking at students as individuals, um, from past experience you, you I don't know quite how to put this, you assign them a, um, it's like a risk factor (   ), or prediction, you're guessing how they're going to do in the class. I'm already doing that now, it's completely unconscious, you know, you're saying to yourself, "Who's going to make it through this class? Which one of these (   ), is going to make it all the way to 15 by next semester?" You know, you're constantly making that kind of under-the-surface assessment.

Although Carol was aware of the pitfalls of categorizing students, she was also honest enough to admit that teachers (indeed, all humans) rely on past experience to interpret the present. She said that it was the diversity of the classroom that forced her to "click" into different modes of interpreting and assessing students in the classroom. She was not cognizant enough of her different types to know she had four, and she did not talk about them (except when asked to), unless referring to a specific person. These types do reveal, however, the importance past experience plays in understandings and interpretations of the present and their intricate connection to Carol's goals for the class. The following descriptions of each type, based upon interviews with Carol, also reveal how she characterized the focal students described earlier in this chapter.

According to Carol, re-entry women were the majority of her students, not just in Appleton, but in her classes on the main campus, as well. She placed the focal student Isaura in this category (with some difficulty, as will be discussed later in the chapter). Carol described re-entry women as follows:

They [re-entry women] come in, ah, sometimes they bring their children. They're going through sometimes painful separations or divorces. They're trying to get their feet on the ground and get off welfare . . . or ah recovering from drug addiction and alcohol abuse. And boy do they struggle, they work so hard, like Isaura. Isaura's a perfect example, only more so, because she's doing that backbreaking physical work.

Carol recognized too that these women were of various ethnicities and language backgrounds, noting that there were those re-entry women "who are fluent in English, even those who speak with accents, but they're confident in their ability to communicate, are very outspoken. I think the re-entry women are probably the most vocal of the groups."

Carol also spoke frequently of the re-entry men in her classes, especially in Appleton. They were significantly different from the re-entry women, according to Carol.

> This is the way most re-entry men are different than re-entry women, re-entry women are known as workhorses. I mean they just kill themselves. I teach re-entry women here [in Shoreline] and in the classes in Appleton which are made up of a lot of returning women. In general they [the re-entry women] work themselves to the bone, I mean they do more than enough. Re-entry men often, um, I think, don't have the time to, or I don't know, maybe their time is dished out, divided up in different kinds of ways.

Although the re-entry men did not appear to work as hard as the women on their writing, Carol found that, like the re-entry women, they came from a variety of backgrounds and had a great deal of confidence. She noted:

> There are different kinds of re-entry men, there are Anglo re-entry men and there are Hispanic re-entry men, and then there are Hispanic men who come from Mexico or Central America or something and then there are ones who were born here or came here at an early age, so I'd guess you'd have to subcategorize re-entry men.

She considered both Federico and Amado typical re-entry men. Commenting on Federico, she said:

> [He's] a typical re-entry man in his confidence. There's, there's a confidence about him. Again, as a thinker and as just a human being. He's not, he doesn't seem cowed, or, um, afraid of the experience of returning to school. He's not um, you know, he's mastered a lot of things in his life, he's gone through the military, who knows what he saw, he's married, he's had to go out into the work world, and he's someone who knows if he applies himself he can make it. . . . Um, um, Amado was like that. You know, Amado is the same kind of re-entry guy.

Finally, although the re-entry men may miss class or come late, she assumed it was because of work or other important obligations that men had. In the following, she spoke of Federico not living up to his potential. You'll recall she also made similar statements about Amado not working hard enough:

> I think I expected a lot of him [Federico]. I expected a great deal of him. And probably because of the circumstances of his life, he wasn't able to give it.

The third type of student Carol described were the babies. These were recent high school graduates who, according to Carol, would "monkey around" a lot. She found them unmotivated and immature compared to the re-entry men and women. She elaborated:

I think of them as babies and . . . they don't belong in school right now, they need to be doing something besides school. They treat a college classroom like a high school classroom. And it is the one kind of student that I can't deal with. . . . I just want to give them a quarter and tell them to call their mother and go home.

I mean they come in late, yeah, oh yeah, they're not even doing their work, I mean real irr-, complete lack of responsibility, complete lack of, um, I mean they're not there for any reason, it doesn't even make sense and the trouble is that they drag down the class with them, I feel like, and they get to me and it affects my morale, and I really mind that, so. . . .

I just have no patience anymore for that kind of, I don't know, I see it, I guess, as laziness. And when you have students, when 90% of the students are working mothers, like in re-entry classes, they, these young kids whose parents are sending them to school and they don't do the work, I can't even, I can't even deal with it.

You see that back corner, it's always in the back. . . . It doesn't matter, you know, Anglo or Chicano, you sit in the back of the room and don't do anything, it just pisses me off. . . . Mónica and Juanita almost fell into that category. I felt like. They were just a step, they were just a step away . . . . They did that kind of stuff, they walked out early or they didn't come to class, remember they would go—, see they did their work, they always did their work and I knew they were working with you.

The last type of student Carol regularly referred to were those who came to the States late in life. These students generally had heavy accents in English because they had been in the United States relatively few years and had had little exposure to English while here (although their proficiency could be quite good). These students were very motivated to learn English and had usually been through all of the ESL courses available to them and had taken English 5 at least once. They were able to write lengthy essays, but their limited English vocabulary and grammar prevented them from successfully competing for grades in Carol's class. As soon as Carol identified these students based on their oral skills and their age, and confirmed it with their writing, she

began to grade them with CRs (meaning "credit") rather than letter grades, because they would undoubtedly fail by Carol's standard. Carol would talk these students into taking the course
Pass/Not Pass so they could take it for a letter grade in the future.
Carol had assumed that Isaura was in this group early in the
semester, based on her classroom talk and her in-class writing,
but she revised this categorization of Isaura after she received
writing that Isaura had had time to work on at home. No special
provisions were made to help students in this category improve
their English language skills.

Knowledge of the personal and educational backgrounds of the
primary participants in this study—the focal students and the
teacher—helped me to gain insights into their perspectives on the
negotiation of classroom interaction in English 10. The key themes
of all the participants are particularly valuable in understanding
their differing perspectives. Although individuals had key themes
unique unto themselves, the themes of the focal students are similar in that they were all responses to the situation of Mexican
Americans in Appleton.

The teacher's key themes were quite different from her students'
in a large part because of her differing past experiences and her
purposes for being in the classroom. As an ABD English literature
student and highly experienced educator, her goals for this course
were to help the students develop the academic discourse that she
believed would ensure their success in future English classes. Her
notions of appropriate goals and curriculum came from her past
experiences as a student and a teacher in English departments
and from teaching students on the main campus at Shoreline for
19 years. Her goal for the class was "school for school's sake." The
purpose and motivation that was offered to students for completing the assignments was that it would help them in school. The
students' goals, however, were oriented toward when they completed school.

The focal students enrolled in this class in order to further their
goals as related to their own key themes, for example, getting a better job, becoming a minister, earning a bilingual teaching credential. This course was instrumental to reaching these goals, part of
a history of previous courses and future courses in a long process.
The students were in this class because it would help them reach
their individual goals, not because it would help them in the next
level of English. These highly motivated students received little support for their personal goals in the classroom. Instead, as Fine suggests in the quotation opening this chapter, they received repeated

messages throughout their academic careers that they were inadequate students and their goals were unworthy.

This chapter also uncovered differences in how Carol judged students' progress in the course and how students judged themselves. Carol used categories based on her initial classroom interaction with students in order to explain their successes and failures in her course. These categories helped her understand and predict "how far" students had to go before they would be ready to move on to English 15, her goal for them. Carol was well aware that she had students with limited proficiency in English in her classes. In fact, this knowledge was an important part of her categorization of students. Beyond her prediction of student success (or more accurately, prediction of their lack of success), Carol did nothing special to help these students improve as speakers and writers of English. They received no special tutoring or attention, were never assessed in their first languages, were never taught as if they had different language abilities than their monolingual English peers in the class. Moreover, she made the common error of equating ability in English with academic potential or intelligence.

The focal students, on the other hand, judged their progress in the course based on their own goals. Isaura was disappointed in her work, although she received an A-, because she believed she had not made progress toward her personal goal: learning to speak better English in order to get a job. And although Carol felt that Amado "stood completely still" in relation to her goal of moving him toward English 15, he felt that he had made progress toward his goal, compared to his previous experiences with English classes at PCC. These differences between the teachers' and students' goals made a crucial difference in how the students and teacher interacted in the classroom, as the next two chapters will show.

5

THE SOCIAL CONSTRUCTION OF SILENCE: COURSE ASSIGNMENTS

The curriculum of directed instruction, as it is experienced in real life as a learning environment, is always a matter of the content of social relations and the content of subject matter being engaged together in successive moments of real time.
—Erickson, 1982, p. 182

As Erickson notes, to understand the real life of a classroom it is necessary to consider both the subject matter and how the teacher and students interact during the teaching of that subject matter. This interaction can be both oral and written, so I examined each separately. When the teacher and the students described in Chapter Four came together in the classroom, their interaction was characterized by various types of silence. These silences occurred in a variety of forms for differing groups, depending, in part, on whether the interaction was written or oral. In this chapter, I describe the interactional variations between the Mexican American and Anglo American students and their Anglo American teacher surrounding written course assignments. In examining the written interaction in the classroom, I analyzed teacher assignments, student written work, teacher evaluations of student work, and student responses to teacher evaluation. This approach reveals how the varying perspectives and characteristics of the participants influenced the interaction observed.

COMPOSITION ASSIGNMENTS: TEACHING THE FORMS OF ACADEMIC DISCOURSE

Chapter Four revealed that one of Carol's key themes was the need to prepare English 10 students for English 15 by teaching them to read and write academic discourse. One way that Carol prepared students for English 15 was to teach English 10 as much as she taught her English 15 classes. She often made the point: "I'm running this class like a 15 class. I'm doing a lot of the same kinds of assignments, usually more difficult than the generic 10s." Carol also insisted that she taught the English 10 class in Appleton just like she taught her English 10 classes on the main campus in Shoreline. Once, when she was asked to submit an article about her class in Appleton for a special journal issue focusing on writing in the community, she commented to me that her teaching in Appleton was not an appropriate topic for this special issue because she did not consider the community to be a factor in her class. She taught the class the same way no matter where it was located.

Carol's course description for English 10 was published in the English Department Handbook, a guide designed to help students when selecting classes. Although this handbook was supposed to be available to all students, it could only be obtained at the English Department office on the main campus. It was unlikely that any students in Carol's class ever had access to it. Carol's course description suggests how she planned to prepare students for English 15.

> This section of English 10 at the Appleton Center emphasizes two principles of good writing: careful perception and clear, forceful communication. Class discussions stress the most important elements of the essay, including focus, unity, organization, paragraph coherence, transition, and effective sentences. Many class periods will be given over to one-to-one editorial sessions where close, individual attention will be given to the student's work in progress. Readings drawn from the text, *Fields of Writing*, are used to acquaint students with the various kinds of essays we'll be writing. . . . (*English Department Handbook*, 1991, p. 7)

Nearly the same paragraph was on her course syllabus that was handed out the first night of class each semester, with an additional descriptive sentence: "The chief activities of the course are writing, editing, and revising, as well as reading and discussing good models for academic writing."

Carol always provided students with a detailed assignment sheet every time an essay assignment was introduced. These handouts appeared much like business memoranda with each one following the same format, including reading assignments, writing assignments, *English Workbook* (grammar and usage) lessons, and due dates. Although Carol did not call them such, the assignments on each handout appeared to constitute distinct units, with readings and *English Workbook* assignments carefully selected to accompany the writing assignments.

All of the composition units employed the same basic assignment pattern and time frame: readings related (in content or form) to the writing assignments, *English Workbook* assignments to be done each week, one or two drafts (one per week) of the essay (to be responded to by a tutor or the teacher during class time), and a final draft that, after being graded by the teacher, could be revised and re-submitted within two weeks for a new grade. This assignment pattern was Carol's way of reconciling her belief that writing was a process with her need to evaluate students' written products.

The only writing assignments that did not allow for two to three weeks of drafting and revising were in-class writings: the writing assessment and a practice essay exam. As I have already mentioned, the writing assessment was given the first night of class as a safeguard against misplacing students. It allowed students forty-five minutes to write about a turning point in their lives. The other in-class writing, the practice essay exam, gave students an opportunity to use the essay exam structure provided in the *English Workbook* lessons. The practice essay exam asked students to describe how the attitude of the author changed in the essay, "What did you do in the War, Grandma?" by Hardy, an essay included in the course text.

English Workbook assignments remained absolutely constant throughout the two years I observed Carol's class. The text was a spiral-bound workbook of lessons and exercises in grammar and usage created by the Portolá English Department specifically for English 10. It contained lessons on sentence ending punctuation, sentence combining, commas, and other forms of punctuation. Exercises on subject–verb agreement were followed by lessons on style and usage.

The progression of assignments in Carol's class, as well as the manner in which these assignments were evaluated, illustrated the commonly held belief that written academic discourse is learned by practicing a series of composition modes distinguished by their unique organizational requirements, or forms (such as narrative and expository), in a specific order ranging from what is considered to be the less difficult personal writing, to more difficult analytical writing (Bartholomae & Petrosky, 1986; Miller, 1982; Shaughnessy, 1977). The form was the important part of the composition lesson for Carol, content was less important; once the form was mastered, anything could be substituted in for content.

During the four semesters I observed Carol's English 10 class, composition assignments only changed slightly, an assignment or two here and there each semester. In the first semester, the major assignments were as follows: (a) a "chronological description" of a day in a well-known place, (b) a "description" of behavior of an animal or human, (c) a "process–analysis" or how-to, (d) a "compare–contrast" of essays by Frederick Douglass and Maya Angelou, (e) a "problem–solution," and (f) a "final essay," a compare–contrast of three descriptions of the bombings of Nagasaki and Hiroshima. All the changes that Carol made in her assignments over the course of the study only served to hone the course into one that was better able to provide practice in academic discourse. Carol's description of her decisions regarding assignments confirmed this point:

> There are certain assignments I like to do just because they fit the goals I have for the class. I mean that's usually how I decide. It's always really carefully thought out. . . . I guess I'm trying to gauge the assignments, use them in such a way that they are developing the skills I think they need when they get to 15. And . . . that's the . . . reason for . . . a lot of those choices.

Although the names of the assignments changed, the forms they required did not. For instance, between the first two semesters, she abandoned her chronological order essay and descriptive assignments. The turning point essay that replaced the chronological assignment required students to lead up to a significant moment in their lives, describe the moment, and then tell how they changed after it—an assignment that still required a chronological organization to be successful. Similarly, the descriptive essay became the interview assignment, for which students were to write up an interview with an older relative or acquaintance, including a description of the person and of the place where the interview occurred. In other words, this new assignment was still a descriptive one. The two changes in Carol's assignments reveal the importance of these traditional forms of writing in Carol's conception of what students need in order to acquire academic discourse.

For Carol, an important part of helping students acquire the discourse of the academy was to teach them how to write about the text. To give students that experience, students had to "pull them [the texts] apart" or analyze them. The process–analysis (how-to) assignment was replaced with what came to be known as the "animals" essay, in which students summarized three short essays describing the deaths of animals and provided a summary of an experience that they had had with the death of an animal. Carol explained that although she had used the process–analysis assignment as a little bridge between personal writing and analytical writing, by changing the assignment to the animals essay, students were "getting to the text really soon." She continued:

> I like them working with that [the text], you know, as you can see from Douglass and Angelou and the Japanese one, too. 'Cause I think that these [English] 10 students are going to go to [English] 15, a lot of them, you know that's my, that's what I've got as my [goal], so I feel like they need that kind of experience.

Carol found that the most difficult essay form for students to master was the analytical essay about texts—the compare–contrast. After she had "disastrous" results on the compare–contrast of Douglass and Angelou followed by a compare–contrast final essay on which students "did the worst of everything" they had written, Carol changed the order of essay assignments. She put the problem–solution essay before both of the text analysis essays. Because the problem–solution essay used the students' own topics rather than teacher-selected texts, the change allowed students to practice the more analytical form of the problem–solution essay without the added complexity of text analysis, which was required by the other two assignments.

During the last two semesters, there were no changes in the order or content of the writing assignments. They were: turning point, interview, animals, problem–solution, compare–contrast of Douglass and Angelou, and the final essay, a compare–contrast of three essays about the bombing of Japan. In both the essay assignments and the *English Workbook* assignments, there was a distinct focus on form as opposed to content. Even though students were told what content to use, assignments were selected and arranged on the basis of the forms they required students to master.

Because the focus of Carol's assignments was primarily on form, the focus of her response and evaluation of student work was also on form. All of her responses seemed geared toward providing advice and correction in order to help students better approximate Carol's vision of the type of writing necessary in English 15 and for students' academic futures. Carol provided several different types of feedback when evaluating student essays: (a) a letter grade, (b) a lengthy end comment, including suggestions for revision, (c) brief marks on the text of student essays indicating problems with spelling, punctuation, grammar, and usage; and

(d) a quantitative analysis of the relative strengths and weaknesses of the paper, using a form she devised several years prior and has used ever since (see Appendix B).

Carol's form (clearly based on the Diederich Scale) had three categories for analysis and grading: Rhetoric, Language, and Editing. Each of these areas had two to three subheadings, with numbers for ranking the essay from 0 (unacceptable) to 5 (excellent). Each of the three areas then had a multiplier factor (e.g., the total of the subareas in Rhetoric were multiplied by five; for Language, by three; for Editing, by two). At the end of this form, she also provided a lengthy comment discussing how the essay might be revised. Letter grades were assigned to the essay on the basis of the numerical total on this form. Student grades for the course were largely determined by their letter grades on the written assignments. One semester, she provided the following chart for students on the board:

65 D	76 C+	86 B+
70 C–	80 B	90 A–
73 C	83 B	93 A

Carol reviewed the form with the entire class the first time a paper was returned for a letter grade. She explained her use of the form to her students by saying, "Students, especially in English, have told me that sometimes teachers just pull grades out of the air. . . . Sure, the grade is subjective," she admitted, "but at least I'm trying to tell you something quantitatively." She suggested that students use the quantitative analysis to help them decide where to focus their attention during revision. Each time essays were returned, Carol set aside class time for students to read over her comments, attempt to correct small problems on the page, think of how larger ones might be dealt with in a revision, and have a tutor (or Carol, who took part in all tutoring activities) attempt to clarify the comments, interpret the handwriting, and discuss revision strategies.

Each of the three major areas on the grading handout—rhetoric, language, and editing—revealed her focus on form over content in the evaluation of essays. Rhetoric, on her form, referred to the organization or form of the overall essay. The language section provided for the evaluation of good form, that is, style and word choice of essays. Finally, the editing section provided a rubric for grading form at the micro-level: grammar, usage, and spelling.

In an interview, Carol stated that although essays such as these took her an average of 27 minutes to grade, she thought it was important to return student papers as soon as possible, especially in Appleton, because the class met only once a week. She usually returned papers within a week or two of being turned in, always before the next major essay was due.

With as many as 38 students in her classes and up to four classes a semester, the "paper load" for Carol was tremendous. She admitted that sometimes she had to cut corners on her responses as a result. Although she always started out giving positive feedback, especially on the first essay, with so many papers to grade, she was not always able to give all of the positive feedback she would have liked to. In an interview, she explained:

> So you know, the kind of mistakes you can make, and the kinds of, um, I don't know, short cuts you take. I, lots of times I know when I'm correcting a paper or commenting on it that, um, what this student needs is X, and what it might mean is, um, oh let's say, oh, a lot of encouragement, talk about all the great things in the paper. But I know that if a student's going to revise the paper, that that's not what's going to help. So if I have a choice between doing the encouragement or doing, I don't know, something else that might be very beneficial, I often don't do it [the encouragement] just for lack of time. . . . And I think I do that just to make it, um, to give everyone an equal amount of time and to have it be the same kind of time, I guess, in some way. So I'm really conscious of the fact that it isn't always the most beneficial kind of correction that they can get.

The final comment was always given with the assumption that students would revise the essay for a higher grade, often with such opening lines as, "Even though you earned a good grade for this essay, I hope you'll consider revising it."

Teacher assignments and responses to student writing do not occur in a vacuum. In the following sections, I present student written response to and interaction with the course assignments and teacher evaluations, particularly how their focus on form affected student interaction.

STUDENT RESPONSE TO ASSIGNMENT STRUCTURE

The most obvious way that students responded to the composition assignments was, of course, by turning in essays—or not turning them in—as the case may be. In order to give a general sense of how students responded to Carol's plans to have them engage in writing as a process while mastering the forms of academic writing, I first describe the number of formal revisions students turned in, based on ethnicity and gender. After presenting an overall picture of the class response, I proceed to describe how focal students responded qualitatively to various assignments.

Students in Carol's class had the opportunity to revise four essays during the semester, although Carol only expected three revisions to be completed. (Students were advised against revising the fourth essay because working on it would interfere with working on the final exam essay, a take-home.) The average student in Carol's English 10 turned in 1.2 of the possible 4.0 revisions.[1] Mexican American students turned in, on the average, more revisions than Anglo American students at 1.6 revisions whereas, Anglo American students turned in only 0.9 revisions.

Within ethnic groups, there were gender differences. Mexican American women turned in 1.7 revisions whereas, Mexican American men turned in 1.0. Anglo American women, on the other hand, completed only 0.6 revisions whereas, the Anglo American men averaged 2.0. The grade book contained one possible explanation for several Anglo American women choosing not to revise: The first grade on their essays was usually so high that revision for a better grade seemed unnecessary. The reason the Mexican American men, who also turned in relatively few assignments compared to the rest of the class, chose not to revise was not as apparent. Other factors, which will be explored throughout this chapter, seem to have influenced the focal males' decisions not to revise.

Among the focal students, the differences between the male and female Mexican Americans in the number of essay revisions reflected the numbers found in the class at large. The men, Federico and Amado, each turned in only one revision during the semester whereas, Isaura turned in three revisions, and Juanita and Mónica turned in two revisions each. Moreover, the men rarely brought rough drafts of essays to class when required, but Isaura and Mónica brought a draft every time one was required (five times over the course of the semester) and Juanita brought drafts three times.

Silence in Assignment Interaction: Mexican American Focal Men

The interaction of the focal students surrounding the writing assignments revealed that the men turned in considerably less

---

[1] The quantitative data reported in this chapter is based on statistics from the Spring, 1990 semester. Most of the focal students were enrolled during that semester.

writing for credit than the women. In comparison to the women, they were silenced by the structure of the interaction surrounding essay assignments; that is, the sequence and timing of assignments prevented the men from being heard relative to the women. They did not receive the same credit from the teacher because rough drafts and revisions were not turned in when they were due. The remainder of this section will illustrate how the due dates for rough drafts, final drafts, and revisions created artificial time constraints that interfered with the processes of real writers and failed to account for the limitations on their time. Moreover, the content of essay assignments and teacher suggestions appeared to have influenced decisions to revise, as well. Finally, the men did not engage in the same sorts of social support for revision that the women did.

Once the semester was under way, Carol's essay units required a written draft in one stage of completion or another (rough, final, or revised) every week. The Mexican American male focal students were concerned with completing their assignments and revisions in a timely fashion, but for Amado and Federico, writing and revising did not follow the neat timetable required for success in the course.

In Chapter Four, Carol stated that Amado "didn't go back to learn from his mistakes." This statement was a direct reference to his failure to revise. Carol believed that Amado rarely revised because he did not have drafts in class and he only completed one revision. Yet, Amado *did* write drafts, only he did so much closer to the due date for a paper than required by the teacher for credit. By his choice, our tutorials regularly occurred just a day or two before the final draft of an essay was due. During those tutorials, I observed Amado making more than one significant change on his drafts of essays. In fact, on the evening before the final essay was due, Amado arrived to his tutorial not only with a nine-page handwritten draft, but also with two introductions that he proceeded to craft, through the classic revision strategies of cut and paste, into a single unified introduction. Although Amado was generating rough drafts and revising them, Carol never knew about them or gave him credit for them because the drafts were not prepared for class according to her schedule. Amado, who had not been asked to write or revise in high school, was learning to revise, but he had not yet learned to meet the demands of revision for school writing tasks, such as meeting due dates; as a result, his progress went unnoticed by the teacher.

Amado considered his difficulty with completing drafts and revisions one of "procrastination," which he worked to solve in a fashion that kept with his key theme: "I decided to pray for it, until it [his problem with procrastination] goes away," he told me the evening before the final essay exam was due. Then he elaborated.

> I just seem to postpone things, you know, for a little while, meanwhile, I'll do something else, or you know? And it just gets to me, catches up to me. . . . When I get home, I start thinking of the time (snaps fingers), of pressure. Work is hard under pressure. Working under the gun is hard. Thoughts just don't flow.

According to Amado, he put off his homework until it was so late that he would become too anxious to write well.

Federico, too, had difficulty with the timing and sequence of the assignments in the course. He expressed concern with finding the time to devote to writing. To of the five classes during which students were to review rough drafts with tutors, Federico brought rough drafts only twice. Although he completed all of his essay assignments, he only did one revision for a higher grade. One paper (the problem–solution essay) was so short that he did not receive a letter grade for it. Instead, the teacher gave him a CR (credit only), a mark Carol usually reserved for students she thought had second language difficulties.

Federico told me he wanted to do more revisions for letter grades and often promised me he would. He also complained that two weeks was not enough time, particularly when another essay was assigned at the same time. Once, upon receiving a graded essay ready for revision, he lamented, "I'm going to do this next one, but she gives me only so many days to do it."

The one revision he completed, on the animals essay, was due during the problem–solution unit. Although he received an A- on the revision (from a B-), the problem–solution paper was the one that was so short, he only received a CR. He simply ran out of time to write the second paper. It was handwritten in one sitting. Federico had explained to me earlier in the semester that he always writes at least two drafts of an essay on his computer before turning it in. Knowing that the essay would not please Carol, Federico confided in me as he turned it in, "I hope she doesn't bomb me, but that's OK. It's just a stopgap." The following week in a tutorial he explained what he meant by "stopgap:"

> Federico: Did you get the meaning from me? Stopgap?
>   Kay: Oh yeah. Yeah.
> Federico: I just wanted to be there.
>   Kay: Turn something in.

Federico: To let, let her know that I was still around, and I was still interested.

When he got that paper back, he told a fellow student:

She, um, didn't even give me a letter grade on it. She just wrote "credit" on it, for, you know, turning it in, because I didn't do too well on it. I, you know, wrote it in about, oh, I just, I had to be here and I hadn't had time, so I just winged it, you know, what I mean, for whatever it was worth.

After receiving the CR, Federico decided to quit one of his two jobs. He explained this to me at the beginning of a tutorial session:

I quit the Friday before last and so I, I've been catching up. I've been playing catch up a lot. I'm, I'm just not getting to feeling good yet.

When it came time to turn in his last regular essay, he had quit his job and brought in a rough draft to work on with a tutor. He said, "She's [Carol's] burying me. Hopefully, this will make a better impression on her. Hopefully, I'll show her." He did "show her." He received a B+, his highest grade of the semester.

Carol's course was designed to give students a great deal of individual attention from the tutors on their writing. As noted earlier, she relied on tutors to go over rough drafts of essays and to discuss revision strategies with students. The focal men, however, were rarely able to take full advantage of this opportunity because they did not bring rough drafts to class. Although these men did ask for my help outside the class, they did so with less regularity than the women. Carol realized that the male focal students did not do as much writing as most others in the classes. Like the men themselves, Carol understood their relative silence in writing in terms of time. She said of Federico:

If Federico had . . . [revised] he probably would have come out one of the strongest writers . . . that I'd ever seen in Appleton. . . . When he had the time, it would result in things like this [points to his best paper] and when he didn't, it would result in credit papers.

She also assumed that Amado did not have time to do his schoolwork either, stating, "He'd be a good student if he worked. I don't know what else was in his life that maybe kept him from it." She did not consider other factors such as past educational experiences as a possible cause for their failure to produce drafts.

The structure and sequence of the assignments surrounding each essay required that students have a completed draft, to one degree or another, for every class session. As the semester progressed and revisions became due, students who planned to revise for a higher grade had to work on two papers simultaneously. From their perspectives, Federico did not have sufficient time to devote to his writing and Amado did not have sufficient control of his writing to work within this rigorous framework. However, in Chapter Four, it was revealed that all of the focal students, male and female, led extremely busy lives and had numerous responsibilities that could conceivably interfere with the completion of their assignments. In addition, none had much experience writing. Yet, the women turned in rough drafts and revisions throughout the semester.

Voices in Assignment Interaction: Mexican American Focal Women

The women focal students, as noted earlier, were far more active in the interaction surrounding course assignments than the men. They received credit for turning in drafts and revisions and thereby, made their voices heard through their writing. Because they turned in most of their drafts and revisions, they did not need to explain, during tutorials, why essays were missing, as the men did. However, they too, discussed the personal hardships caused by the structure of interaction surrounding course assignments.

Isaura spoke a great deal about the sacrifices she made and the conflicts she felt between work, school, and family, especially with an infant son. Before the strawberry season began in late March, Isaura spoke of staying up until early in the morning to complete her assignments, often working in the bathroom to stay warm and to keep from disturbing her family. When she began picking strawberries six days a week in midsemester, completing her assignments became an even greater challenge.

> I think it is very hard to read and write and take care of the baby. Sometimes, after I come [home] from work, I have to cook, then bathe the baby, and at seven or seven-thirty I have time to read. And then, I read until ten or eleven and, ah, because I don't understand very well the reading, I have to go [over it] again and then write. . . . Since I start work, it's very difficult for me to learn. . . .

It's very hard for me to concentrate on the homework. . . . I feel very stressed. . . . I don't even have time to help my son to do his homework.

Like Isaura, Juanita was working full time. In addition, she was taking three other classes. She told me that all of her weekdays and evenings, except for Fridays, were spent in the classroom, either teaching as a migrant aide or taking classes. "On Fridays," she explained, "when I get home, I do cleaning and stuff, and then I do my homework. And then Saturdays and Sundays, I do a bunch of housework. And I do the wash." Like Isaura, she had little time for writing.

In addition to work and school, Mónica had taken responsibility of most of the household duties while her mother was recuperating from major surgery. In Chapter Four, Mónica spoke of having to make a commitment to the course, of having to meet with a tutor rather than visit her mother an extra hour in the hospital. What had started as a part time job at the local drug store, quickly became full time, in effect. Like the men, the women led extremely busy, often stressful lives, yet, unlike the men, they turned in drafts and revisions with regularity. One reason for this may be related to the social support they received that the men did not.

The women asked to meet with me outside of the class considerably more than the men. Mónica met with me eight times, Isaura six times, and Juanita three times. They also were able to work on their essays with the tutors in class because they regularly brought drafts when they were due. Furthermore, they encouraged each other to revise in informal discussions that provided peer support and perhaps even peer pressure to revise. In the following excerpt, Mónica, Juanita, and another woman sitting in the back of the classroom, Marisa, discussed revisions and encouraged each other to do them for better grades.

Mónica: You don't have to do it over?
Juanita: Um hm [no].
Mónica: You're doing it over?
Marisa: You're not going to do it over? No? Why not?
Juanita: ((It doesn't make any difference.))
Marisa: ( ) *ha hecho el otro*, huh? [did the other one, huh?]
Mónica: Uh huh [yes].
Marisa: You should try, just in case you–
Mónica: I did one already.
Marisa: You already missed one?

Mónica: I only have, *tengo [puro]* C's. [I have only C's.]
Marisa: Well, you're going to get a C in the class then.
Mónica: Unless I make [it up], and I can erase this one.

In this dialogue, Marisa encouraged Juanita and Mónica to revise their essays, suggesting that if they did not, their grades in the course would not improve.

These differing student responses to the course assignments were one of the sources of information that helped Carol to categorize students into re-entry men, re-entry women, babies, and those who have come to the States late in life. In this case, Carol saw the differences between the responses (or lack thereof) of the Mexican American men and the Mexican American women as part of a greater gender difference in the amount of course work completed by students that she had classified as re-entry men (such as Federico and Amado), re-entry women (such as Isaura), and babies (Mónica and Juanita) (as noted in Chapter Four). She knew that re-entry women were workhorses and even babies like Mónica and Juanita did their assignments. Re-entry men often "didn't have time to," in her opinion.

Although the women focal students appear to have been just as busy as the men, they nevertheless turned in more written assignments than the men. In comparison to the women, the men were silenced in interaction around course assignments. The teacher understood these differences in terms of the particular type she had assigned them, types that explained a student's response in terms of the students' current life situation rather than as a response to her course assignments or students' background educationally or linguistically.

STUDENT RESPONSE TO ASSIGNMENT CONTENT

Although the men and women differed in their responses to the structural constraints of writing assignments, particularly in the amount of writing produced for credit, they nevertheless shared similar strategies for producing writing in response to the content or topics of essay assignments. When students were not required to write about a particular text, but were given some freedom in providing content for the form Carol assigned, students nearly always chose topics that were related to their key themes. In other words, they chose to write about what they cared about, were concerned about, and were interested in. In Chapter Four, it was evident that students' key themes all reflected, in one way or another, their experiences as Mexican Americans in the Appleton area. I have called the assignments that allowed students to bring in content from their own experience "real" topics, "real" because the writers were allowed to define their own topics as real writers do, rather than accepting an imposed or academic topic for display to a teacher. However, when essay assignments provided both a required form and content and when interpreting readings was necessary for writing, students responded to them qualitatively differently than when assignments allowed for student choice in content. I have called these topics "academic." These assignments were the most decontextualized from the lives of students and the epitome of "academic" in their purposes.

Because focal students used their key themes when responding to real essay topics, they rarely had difficulty generating ideas or content for these essays. Examples of essay assignments that allowed for such responses include the turning point essay, which asked students to tell of a personal turning point in their lives and how it changed them; the interview essay, which allowed students to interview an older friend or family member; and the problem–solution essay, which asked students to write an argument about how to solve a particular problem of their choice. Parts of other essay topics also required real writing, such as the description of an experience students had had with the death of an animal in the animals essay.

Juanita's key theme, the education of Spanish-speaking students, was addressed in her turning point essay when she wrote about her desire to be a bilingual teacher:

> I feel that I could be a great teacher for migrant students, because I feel that I understand the problems that migrant students go through because, I was also a migrant student. . . . I think migrant students need more support and caring than other students, because these students go through a lot more than other students and also because I know their culture.

She chose the topic of bilingual education for her problem–solution paper, using information she had learned from her Chicano

Psychology and La Mujer classes to help strengthen her argument in favor of it. In her interview essay, she focused on her mother's upbringing in a small town in Mexico, lamenting particularly her mother's lack of educational opportunity there.

Real essay assignments gave Federico an opportunity to speak out for social justice, his key theme. For the problem–solution essay he wrote a bitter satire, in the style of Jonathan Swift's "Modest Proposal," taking on the ethos and voice of the Anglo American community that he felt was responsible for the lack of computers at the Appleton Center. He wrote, "Surely a teacher would be hard-pressed to explain computer jargon to someone accustomed to communicate in 'Mexican' rather than English." He later explained to me that he had heard the Spanish language referred to as "Mexican" many times in Appleton, once even at a city council meeting. He said, "It's derogatory . . . I feel it's sort of stereotypical. It hurts."

Amado also responded to real essay topics by writing about *his* key theme: religion to save Mexican American youth. His turning point essay focused on events leading up to and following his baptism five years earlier. In the interview essay, Amado wrote of an elderly church member whom he regularly visited, referring to her as a "benevolent spirit." And in his problem–solution paper, he wrote a letter to the board of directors of his church asking for funds for a basketball–volleyball court for the youth group. Significantly, this last essay, directly on his key theme, was the only one that he revised during the semester. It began:

Dear Brethren of the Church Board,

It is costing the church $50 to $60 to rent a gymnasium for our youth to have a recreation night once a month, and still we are not meeting our youth recreation demands. I'm aware of the fact that our church lacks such a facility of its own and that we are not able to convert our church's parking lot into a play area because of its limited use. Nevertheless, our youth need a weekly recreation night, not just once a month.

Mónica's key theme, maintenance of traditional Mexican American values, was seen in various ways in her essays on real topics. Her interview essay focused on the elderly next door neighbor whom she regularly visited. She introduced this essay in the following manner:

While sitting in Emma's living room, Emma looks over her wheel-chair and just out of nowhere says, "Are you taking anything?" I respond, "No," and she just kind of wonders, and says to me, "Yeah, right." If anyone else would ask me, "Are you taking anything?" I would get offended by their attitude, but not with Emma. I've known her for eight years, and she's had so much bad luck and a rough life.

Despite Emma's ill-treatment of Mónica, Mónica visited Emma regularly, helped her with her hair and her cat, and tried to be understanding toward the bitter, old woman.

Mónica also wrote graphically about preparations for a family feast, which included her father slaughtering a goat that she had made a pet.

He sent my brothers and me inside the house so we wouldn't see him when he killed it. But we could hear the goat scream as my father was killing it. In a few hours my brothers and I ran outside. We saw the poor goat hanging from the lemon tree. He was skinned and had an awful expression on his face, his tongue hanging completely out. He was sliced open from his neck down to his tummy. . . . We cried and cried, but there was nothing we could do anymore. The goat was dead.

Roast goat meals were a tradition among recent Mexican immigrants in the Appleton area. Although maintaining traditional values was sometimes challenging for Mónica, they were nevertheless, an important part of her life and were frequently reflected in her writing.

Isaura's essays focused on her key theme, the economic situation of Mexican Americans, by writing about her own economic situation in her turning point essay: "I still work in the fields and the work is not so bad because the wage is OK and we have good health insurance, but I hope I will have a different job in the future." In her problem–solution essay, she wrote of the shortage of affordable housing in the Appleton area that primarily affected the Mexican American community. In describing the plight of neighbors, she wrote:

Other families are living in garages, like Maria, Arturo, and their two children. This family just came from Mexico, and they can't find a house. Their relatives lent them a garage which is in bad condition: the wind comes in through the walls, water leaks from the roof, and they don't even have a place to put the clothes and food in.

Her animals essay described how poor her family had been when living in Mexico.

When both the form and content of essay assignments were controlled by the teacher, students had considerably more difficulty generating ideas and writing essays. Academic topics usually required not only that students write on a single topic, but also that they read and interpret at least one text. Typical academic topics were the compare–contrast essay of Douglass and Angelou, the compare–contrast final essay about the bombing of Japan, and the animals essay, which was mostly summary. Students devised strategies to respond to these topics, just as they devised strategies to respond to real topics—by selecting content in the area of their key theme. Federico tried to merge academic assignments with his key theme by changing the required focus of an essay. For example, the compare–contrast assignment asked students to:

> Write an essay in which you compare and contrast the children's struggle to learn. . . . In your conclusion, consider how Douglass, had he been present at Angelou's graduation, might have assessed the progress in education for African Americans in those hundred years separating his youth and Angelou's.

Federico wrote the following conclusion to his first draft of the essay:

> It is difficult for me to appreciate the black experience even though I have felt the sting of racism (although somewhat subtly). I, however, [would] like to acknowledge the huge contribution their culture and a great number of black individuals have provided this great country some white folks like to refer to as theirs.

> It is no mere coincidence that things have gotten better for a lot of us unfortunate enough to lack darkening pigmentation. The pitching in of a great deal of people from different ethnic groups, some Anglo Saxons among them, must also be acknowledged.

Federico concluded his comparison of Angelou and Douglass' situation by comparing it to his own:

> The reforms that continue to bring change about could not be possible without the cooperation of a lot of caring white folks. Even so, every time I come across another white person, I feel the necessity to look into their eyes and attitudes for signs of the Mistresses and Donleavys of this world.

In Angelou's story, Donleavy represented white society's prevention of educational, economic, and political progress by African

Americans. The Mistress served the same purpose in Douglass' essay. With these concluding comments, Federico moved his essay from the assigned focus, which had little meaning for him ("the black experience"), to one that reflected his concern with social justice in general and particularly for Mexican Americans like himself.

Federico brought this draft of the essay to class, where a tutor pointed out to him that he had not fulfilled the assignment as directed on the handout, particularly the directions for the conclusion regarding Douglass attending Angelou's graduation. He gratefully acknowledged the help and turned in his essay to Carol with the following conclusion replacing the preceding version.

> Angelou, like Douglass, felt the suffocating anguish of helplessness. She was facing the foe Douglass had faced one hundred years before. History was repeating itself once more. Douglass, had he been present, would have shed tears in anger against the condition whites imposed against blacks. He would have acknowledged the gains blacks had made, but would have decried the perpetuation of white supremacy forced upon blacks.

> Angelou, like Douglass, went on to become somebody despite the color of her skin and more importantly her gender. Today she is a landmark on the road towards equality. It's not easy to duplicate her experience within oneself. But every now and then, if one listens carefully, one can hear Mr. Donleavy chase another Negro around a corner, shouting angrily, "You are under arrest."

For this essay, Federico got his highest grade of the semester—and an end comment from the teacher that read: "This is a strange ending because you stop with Donleavy in an essay that focuses on the accomplishments of Douglass and Angelou." Federico chose that ending because what was important for Federico was the issue of justice and injustice, not the lives of Angelou and Douglass. Federico attempted to deal with the lack of meaning this academic assignment held for him by connecting it to his key theme: speaking out for social justice. In order to meet the requirements of academic discourse as envisioned by this teacher, however, he changed the ending where the tie to his key theme had been most apparent. This was not enough, however, to keep the teacher from commenting on how he had drifted from her assigned topic.

In order for students to write successful academic essays for English 10, they needed not only to write well, but also to read well and to interpret texts correctly. However, a number of students had difficulty with the material they were asked to read and interpret. Carol seemed unresponsive to this student concern.

Amado felt that the course readings were difficult to understand, and he asked the teacher unsuccessfully for help with them in class. During the animals essay unit, when students were supposed to summarize brief descriptions of dying animals written by Virginia Woolf, Isak Dinesen, and George Orwell, Amado suggested that the teacher put students in small groups so that they could talk about their interpretations of the essays. Carol gave this response.

> Carol: And all use the same ones [interpretations]? (Laugh)I don't want people to be influenced by other interpretations. The trouble with summarizing is that it requires interpreting the essays. And I don't want people to think that there is any one, right interpretation.
> Amado: I still don't have any idea what the essays are about.
> Carol: This is not a lit class and even if it were, it's not like I have one answer to it.

Carol then proceeded to tell students that any interpretation was valid as long as they could support it with evidence from the text. Other students admitted that they were having problems with the interpretations, too, but Carol still did not organize the class in discussion groups. Another student said, "I didn't get that much out of it [the reading for the animals essay], except the animals dying."

In our last tutorial, it became apparent that Amado was having difficulty fulfilling the final essay assignment—to compare and contrast three views of the atomic bombing of Japan in 1945— because he felt he had no background in this academic assignment, which asked students to "conclude by discussing what you have learned from reading about this historical event from these personal perspectives." Rather than attempt to discuss a topic he was unfamiliar with, he planned to simply avoid completing this part of the assignment. He said:

> I'm having trouble bringing forth from my own experience what I think about the bombings. Can I close with their summaries? That'd be great . . . I never heard about the bombing until I was at Portolá, probably.

In his final draft of this essay, he prefaced his conclusion by stating: "I have not yet reached my own moral conclusion toward the bombing because I feel that I need a better grasp of the subject."

Several other students made similar comments to me about this assignment, including Isaura and Mónica.

Not only was it difficult for students when essay topics required a certain amount of specific background knowledge, as in the essay about the bombing of Japan, but also when the readings themselves required this kind of knowledge for the most literal understanding of the text. Like Amado, Isaura also felt unable to come up with the interpretations of the readings that Carol expected. In her case, however, it was because of her difficulty comprehending the literal meaning of the text. In a tutorial, Isaura commented on a marginal note from Carol on her animals paper, which read, "How does the killing lead him to these realizations?" Then Isaura said, "I read it and I read it and couldn't get it." Isaura related this difficulty in "getting it" to difficulty in completing the writing assignments in a tutorial:

> I have known that I don't get many of the things that the writer want to say. . . . Maybe I got, I get one half, fifty percent, or something . . . and that's hard when Carol says write something (laughs). . . . What I'm going to write?

Later, she said that she had given up trying to interpret texts because she had received comments on her essays that suggested that she had misinterpreted the authors.

> I am afraid . . . to use interpretation because sometimes I don't do that, I don't ah say like what the writers ah . . . mean. . . . Like on the other essay I was reading last night . . . Carol told me [wrote in the margin], "Does she mean that?" . . . That's why I am afraid to, to put something. . . . I just left the Nakamura['s] feelings . . . I left them out.

The prevalent belief among students that they did not understand the text led them to avoid writing about the assigned topic. They adopted strategies such as leaving out discussions and interpretations of unfamiliar or difficult texts. Carol seemed oblivious to the fact that some of the skills she required were particularly challenging for people working in their second language and who had had little practice at such work in their earlier educational experiences. Although she required reading and interpretation, she did not feel obligated to teach them because English 10 was a composition course.

When students wrote about texts in response to academic essay topics, plagiarism and related "borrowing" activities occurred. Every semester, when the first academic essay was assigned, Carol gave a lecture warning against the evils of plagiarism, insisting that plagiarism was "a capital sin in schools and academic life." She told students they would need to learn paraphrasing, a "skill [that] will keep you going all through your college career."

Nevertheless, some students invariably had papers returned with comments in the margins such as "too close to the text." Federico had more than one paper like that. His compare–contrast of Douglass and Angelou had the most of these comments. Amado also had these comments on his compare–contrast essay. Other students lived in fear of such comments, so much so that how to avoid being accused of plagiarism became a frequent topic in tutorials. As Juanita asked me, regarding the essays to be summarized for the animals essay: "What if she [Carol] thinks I'm copying it off, it's like, what you saw, what you thought, what you liked, and you're putting it in here."

Juanita did not have a problem with plagiarism on that paper, but she did later in the semester on her problem–solution paper. She chose to write on her key theme, bilingual education. When I asked why she did not want my help, she said, "I figured it was something I knew a little about." She seemed pleased with the paper and proud of the fact that she was able to support her arguments with information she had gained in her Chicano Psychology and La Mujer classes, as well as her personal experiences as a migrant student and migrant aide.

The day the assignment was to be returned, graded, from the teacher, Carol told me that much of Juanita's essay appeared to be a "classic case of plagiarism" from some unknown source. Carol said, "She doesn't even understand the meaning of the words she used, like 'sagacity' and 'salient.'" Carol noted that Juanita had seemed "discouraged" to her and said, "I'm more worried about what led her to this than about the plagiarism itself."

Juanita received a "P" for plagiarized in the grade book for this assignment, and although she had the option to revise the essay, and told me and the teacher she would, she never did. In fact, she never revised another essay during the semester. She also refused to show me the essay when I asked to see it.

Students also used other methods of "borrowing" academic discourse, such as obtaining it from the lips of the teacher and the tutors. As I worked with students in tutorials, they frequently confessed that they had borrowed words and phrases from Carol as she spoke about a text or an author in class. Other students would try to get me to say something that they could use in their essays, often leading to stalemated tutorials; I tried not to say anything that would feed a line to students as they sat, pencil poised, patiently waiting for me to say something quotable. Isaura used both of these strategies regularly, as did Mónica, whom I frequently observed taking notes verbatim from Carol's lectures for this purpose. Once, Isaura was reading from a draft of her essay on the animals when she confessed:

> Isaura: ". . . From her experience she learned that when we want something we aren't to have, we can destroy the beauty of that thing."
> Kay: Um hm.
> Isaura: *That's Carol's words.* [emphasis added]
> Kay: (laughs) You did a great job with them. They sounded just like yours. (both laugh)
> Kay: (prompting) "From her experience she learns–"
> Isaura: Don't tell her.
> Kay: I won't; I wouldn't.
>
> [Later in the same tutorial:]
> Isaura: She's [Carol's] going to notice that these are her words.
> Kay: You think so? No she won't. It flows very beautifully from this.

Once, when I was trying to get Isaura to deepen her analysis of an essay by Orwell, she borrowed *my* words:

> Kay: Well, he killed the elephant to save face, right? To keep from being laughed at, so I think it was a combination of those things-
> Isaura: *Can I put 'to save face'?* [emphasis added]
> Kay: Um hm [yes].
> Isaura: (writing) to save . . . face . . . face or faces ?

Mónica learned to borrow the words of essay assignments. In the following excerpt, after a frustrating hour of tutoring in which she painstakingly worked on a summary of Dinesen's "The Iguana" for the animals essay, she looked again at the assignment sheet:

> Let me see, right here [on the handout] it says,"Essays by Orwell, Woolf, and Dinesen all use the death of a particular animal" so then, I'll just put that (laughs) . . . No wait, (starts writing) The essays . . . by Orwell, Woolf, and Dinesen, instead of "all use the death of a particular animal," [I'll write]

> "all have a death in their story" (laughs), yeah? (Continues writing) All have a death in their story.

Once after a tutorial with Amado, he asked if he could borrow the audiotape I had made of the tutorial to help him while he was writing his paper. He said, "I knew I was going to come here and all of these nice expressions, most of them were just going to go off into the air." Of course, I let him borrow it, because it was just as much his tape as it was mine.

Another strategy students developed in response to the requirements of academic discourse was "padding," or adding superfluous material or length to their essays. Each essay assignment had a required length, usually ranging from 750 to 1,000 words. This requirement caused concern for a number of students. Mónica's essays were handwritten, and she frequently joked about the advantages of writing every other line with large letters—"no more than four words per line"—to make the essay appear longer than it was. One time she told me she had planned to type her problem–solution essay, but decided not to because "it'd probably only cover half a page." Isaura expressed her concern regarding length in a tutorial.

> The first time that Carol says that we had to write seven hundred . . . words, I [thought] "Oh, my God, how I am going to write that much?" (laughs) I thought if [after] one page and a half I didn't know what to write, now . . . seven hundred to a thousand words, what could I say? The first essay was very difficult.

Federico showed the most concern of all the focal students about the length of his essays. In a tutorial, he recognized that the teacher wanted him to "knock it off and just state it in simple terms," but he said he could not because it would make him "look bad." When I asked why, he responded that if he stated it simply, the essay would be too short. He explained that from the assignment sheet, "the message you get, [is] make it big. I'd like to cut through and just lay it down in simple terms but then I'm afraid of just one or two pages, maybe two or three."

When students were faced with academic essay topics, they devised a number of strategies to approximate the academic discourse that Carol strived to develop in them, but at the same time they worked to give personal meaning to their writing. Students continued to use their key themes as a way of making their writing personally meaningful, and they resorted to plagiarism, padding, and avoiding or cutting subjects in order to present what they imagined would please Carol.

Nearly all of the focal students responded with dismay and concern when they received their graded essays. Some complained to me about them whereas, others accepted them stoically, like Amado who said, "If she writes all over it [his essay], I'll learn from it," and Isaura who commented, "Carol is very strict . . . but that's good." Federico usually responded to Carol's criticism by repeatedly stating, "She tore me up." As the semester wore on, he concluded, "She's burying me."

Juanita was the most vocal in her response to feedback and evaluation from Carol. Looking over her interview essay the night it was returned, she commented in amazement and horror, "She [Carol] looks at every little single word, every little single 'it' and 'oh' (clicks her tongue). . . . This is unbelievable, no. Could you imagine my next paper? Oh my God, (spare) me . . . everything's going to be wrong about this paper." After receiving her animals essay, she said, "I knew this paper was going to be like this (sighs). . . . I just want to throw this paper away." Of the class, she concluded, "It's like you have to write professionally, and I don't feel like I write professionally. . . . I know maybe someday I can, but I don't feel like it. . . . You know, it's like you have to do it so many times before you get it right and then you don't even get it right when you get it back." After receiving his essay, one student was observed wadding it up and "shooting" it into the wastepaper basket halfway across the room.

Although some students responded to the feedback and evaluation of their essays calmly, others appeared deeply troubled and hurt by it. As Juanita explained to me, "They [teachers] have to watch that [grading] because it's like a student, when he writes something, you don't go and mark it with red all over, because then he'll feel bad. . . . I understand, because I get the same thing."

In the interaction resulting from formal class assignments, Mexican American students did more revisions than their Anglo American counterparts. However, most of these revisions were completed by the Mexican American women; Mexican American men were comparatively silent in their interactions surrounding essay assignments. The Mexican American men explained their lack of revision in terms of the structure and sequencing of assignments. The structure of course assignments, in effect, silenced the Mexican American male focal students. Time—how much time they allocated to the class and how much time they had to complete assignments—was an important factor from their perspectives. Although the men often wrote rough drafts, these were not completed on the teacher's schedule. A lack of social support—from tutors in and out of class and from peers—also may have had an impact on the failure of the Mexican American focal men to have rough drafts and revisions. The women made more use of tutors in and out of class and had frequent discussions among themselves about revising. Although the women also had busy lives, they completed many more revisions, but not without complaining of how difficult it was for them to manage with all of the other responsibilities they had. The teacher was not surprised by either of these responses to her course assignments. She made sense of them based on her understandings of the differing types of students involved—re-entry men, re-entry women, babies, those who came to the States late in life—that were derived from gender, age, and language ability. The interaction of the students and course assignments served to both create and reinforce the teacher's initial impressions of these students.

The teacher's goal of teaching students academic discourse was evident in the focus on form in both the assignment and the evaluation of student essays. When students were allowed to tie the essay assignment to real topics—their key themes and personal goals, which were all related to the students' experiences as Mexican Americans—they did so consistently and had fewer problems initiating and developing ideas. In fact, real topics seemed to even encourage students to revise. Although Carol was aware that real topics made it easier for students to write—hence, the changes in her course syllabus to include an easier transition from personal to academic writing—she did not tolerate key themes or other real topics in many of the students' most important essays. To avoid being silenced, students used strategies such as plagiarizing and padding when they were faced with text-centered, academic essay topics.

The lack of uptake on students' key themes in Carol's response and evaluation, combined with her focus on form and her apparent lack of concern about students' difficulties with reading and interpreting assignments because of language differences—all resulting from her goal: to teach academic discourse—may have led to some of the students' hurt and frustrated responses to the teacher's evaluation of their writing. Here, the differing goals of the teacher and her students discussed in Chapter Four and, ultimately, the differing sources of those goals are apparent in the interaction between Carol and her students surrounding course assignments. Students learn from this "curriculum of directed instruction," as Erickson calls it, that their interests, concerns, and goals are not only different than the teacher's, but also less valued. Moreover, their small steps toward learning to be writers are not valued if they do match the teacher's timetable. The next chapter focuses on interactional differences in classroom talk, where silence, key themes, and differing goals reappear albeit in altered forms.

6

THE SOCIAL CONSTRUCTION OF SILENCE: CLASSROOM TALK

Use of a particular turn-allocation technique is neither random nor haphazard but reflects a strategic relationship between the teacher's and students' agendas and the practical classroom situation on a particular occasion.
—Mehan, 1978, p. 49

In Chapter Five, I showed that there were important differences across ethnicity and gender in the interaction around course assignments in English 10. The Mexican American students did more revisions than the Anglo American students and most of these revisions were completed by Mexican American women. The structure and content of the assignments had the effect of silencing the men's responses to the assignments. The timing and the focus on academic, rather than real topics that would allow them to write about their key themes, interfered with their production of drafts and revisions. In this chapter, however, an analysis of classroom talk reveals silence in a different form. In this situation the Mexican American women were silenced by the structure and content of interaction, whereas, the Mexican American men responded well to it. The timing of interaction and the emphasis on academic topics rather than real ones negatively affected the women's interaction in the classroom.

As the quotation by Mehan at the beginning of this chapter suggests, the structure of interaction—often IRE in this English 10 class—is reflective of whose agenda is being served. Also, variations in the interactional context—whole class discussions, one-to-one tutorials, or unofficial peer talk—lead to differing interaction patterns as the Mexican American focal women move from few opportunities to express themselves in whole class discussions to free reign in unofficial peer talk.

THE STRUCTURE OF WHOLE CLASS DISCUSSIONS

Interaction patterns during whole class discussions in English 10 varied according to ethnicity. Anglo American students participated in whole class discussions in much greater percentages than their numbers in the class would suggest. Using data from three typical class meetings yielding 310 exchanges, I found that although 55% of Carol's class was Mexican American and 45% was Anglo American during the semester in which taping was done, 81% of student initiations were made by Anglo American students. Only 19% of initiations were made by Mexican American students. This general trend held in all classes that I observed. Of the student responses to the teacher, 82% were made by Anglo American students and 18% were made by Mexican American students (see Table 4). Put another way, the Mexican American students initiated and responded to the teacher at approximately one third of the rate expected given their representation in the classroom, if gender and ethnicity had no effect on interaction. An analysis of gender differences within and across groups shows that the relative silence of Mexican Americans in whole class discussions was largely the result of silence on the part of the Mexican American women.

The Mexican American women represented a majority in the class (47% of all students), yet they contributed only 12.5% of the initiations and 8% of the responses. Expressed in interaction ratios, the Mexican American women contributed only one fourth of the expected initiations and one fifth of the expected responses (see initiation and response ratios Table 4). The Mexican American men (comprising only 8% of the class) initiated interactions at a rate much closer to that expected; they also contributed more responses than expected. So, although the Mexican Americans as a group appeared to speak relatively little in whole class discussions, the analysis by ethnicity alone masks the effect of gender on the interaction in the classroom.

Anglo American women also spoke relatively less than Anglo American men, but between the Anglo American men and the

Table 4
Whole Class Interaction by Ethnicity and Gender

	Mexican American TOTAL	Anglo American TOTAL	Mexican American Women	Mexican American Men	Anglo American Women	Anglo American Men
Representation of students in class (%)	55	45	47	8	32	13
Student initiations (%)	19	81	12.5	6.5	53	28
Student responses (%)	18	82	8	10	52	30
Student initiation ratio	0.35	1.80	0.26	0.83	1.65	2.15
Student response ratio	0.33	1.80	0.20	1.30	1.63	2.30

Note. Student initiation ratio =   the ratio of student initiations in comparison to representation.
　　　Student response ratio =   the ratio of student responses in comparison to representation.

Anglo American women the differences were not as great as between the Mexican Americans. The Anglo American men interacted only about 1.3 times more than the Anglo American women, whereas the Mexican American men initiated three times more interactions and responded six times more often than Mexican American women. Overall, males, regardless of ethnic background, interacted at rates higher than expected for their representation in the classroom. These figures indicate both ethnic differences and gender differences. The ethnic differences suggest an ethnic disadvantage in the Anglo American dominant culture and classroom, whereas, the gender differences reveal the prevalence of traditional gender roles in both ethnic groups but with greater effects for Mexican Americans suggesting a stronger patriarchal hierarchy among Mexican Americans than among Anglo Americans. Also, these data show that gender and ethnicity have a cumulative effect, creating a hierarchy with Mexican American women at the bottom and Anglo American men at the top of interaction frequency.

The remainder of this chapter qualitatively explores the situation yielding these quantitative results through an examination of the structure and content of classroom talk in whole class discussions, one-to-one tutorials, and unofficial peer talk. In particular, it will examine the interaction of the focal students and the teacher from their differing perspectives in an attempt to understand and interpret the interactional patterns observed in the classroom discourse.

The characteristics of interaction in Carol's class played an important role in the relative silence of Mexican American women during whole class discussions. As discussed in Chapter One, the Initiation-Response-Evaluation interaction sequence (or IRE) is common in most classrooms, and Carol's class was no exception to this rule. Of the 310 exchanges analyzed during typical whole class discussions in Carol's class, 79% of the exchanges in the class were teacher-initiated and 57% were based on the IRE format. Twenty-one percent of the exchanges were initiated by students. The control of classroom talk by the teacher during these whole class discussions naturally limited the amount of talk that students in the class could accomplish. In the following example of typical discourse from Carol's class, the IRE sequence is evident, as well as another characteristic of the talk in this classroom: the minilecture. Found in other classrooms as well (Hull, Rose, Fraser, Castellano, 1991), the minilecture was usually added onto evaluations of student responses after a series of IRE episodes on a single topic. It was used to tie the questions and answers that immediately preceded it to the larger point of the lesson. It also served structurally to interrupt the flow of teacher-student interaction and revert attention to the teacher. The long turns at the beginning and end of the following transcript are examples of such minilectures from this class.

Teacher: Focus, organization, details, right? That's what they're [the tutors] going to be looking for. . . . Let's take an essay which you're all familiar with, the Maya Angelou essay on graduation and talk about each one of those three things . . . . Of the three things, let's take details [writes the word "details" on the board]. Would you say that she gives a lot of specific details? To describe? What are some things you remember? Specific details?

Susan: The yellow dress.

Teacher: Even something like the yellow dress. That's a really good example. What is she trying to show by telling you about the yellow dress?

Susan: The pains that ((they went to)). How important it was to have every single-

Teacher: Yeah, right, that graduation was so important that everything that was connected to it was somehow special. . . . As soon as I said details, someone said, "yellow dress." Maybe some of you could go even further. Yellow dress. . .?

Susan: The daisies, the embroidered daisies on the dress . . . and the lace.

Federico: Grandmother ((made it.))

Teacher: Yellow dress with embroidered daisies. I don't know if she tells you the kind of lace. I don't know if she tells you the kind of material it is. See the difference between my grandmother made me a dress or my grandmother took spec-. Look, look at the degrees. My grandmother took special pains because that day was so important. This one is abstract. My grandmother made me a dress for my graduation because it was such a special day. My grandmother made me a yellow dress for graduation. My grandmother made me a yellow dress with lace and embroidered daisies. See the degree? From one pole, from the abstract to the concrete? And the reason specific details are so important is for just the reason that you hear. As soon as I said to you tell me something from the story that you remember. The reader retains those images, specific words like that, concrete terms, concrete references like that make the reader remember your story. In a way that you wouldn't remember if she had just said, "Oh everyone took great pains." What else do you remember that shows the community taking pains like this or members of her family?

Through the pervasive use of teacher-initiated questions ("Would you say that she gives a lot of specific details?" "What is she trying to show by telling you about the yellow dress?") and evaluated responses ("Even something like the yellow dress. That's a really good example." "Yeah, right, that graduation was so important. . . ."), the teacher maintained control of the floor, speaking, on the average, twice for every student turn.

Because the teacher had control of the floor, the IRE structure also served to help the teacher maintain control of the content. Therefore, subjects that the teacher deemed important were the focus of attention while topics of interest and concern to the students were not given attention, unless they happened to coincide with the teacher's (Fraser, 1990). The focus of nearly all of the interaction in this class was either on the text, *Fields of Writing*, the organization of student writing, or *English Workbook* assignments. Students generally were not asked to relate their personal experiences to these topics. For example, in the preceding excerpt students were asked to discuss the text *qua* text, completely decontextualized from their own experience. They were to simply describe the text and what the text was supposed to do, not to discuss their responses to it. In the preceding minilecture, the teacher focused student attention on the abstract or concrete nature of the language in the text (concepts discussed in a previous lesson) and how concrete details would be important in their next essay assignment, tying the reading to their course work, but not to their personal experiences. Moreover, questions asked about the text were primarily literal, such as "What are some things you can remember?" and "What else do you remember that shows the community taking pains like this or members of her family?" Questions such as these often took the form of "known information questions"— that is, when a teacher asks a question that he or she already knows the answer to—such as "What is she trying to show by telling you about the yellow dress?"(Cazden, 1988; Mehan, 1979). In this way, the teacher maintained control by maintaining academic authority. Through the evaluation of questions to which she knew the answer, the teacher remained the source of knowledge, and student knowledge based on their own experience of the world and previous education was not acknowledged or valued.

Although the rules of participation during the whole class discussions in Carol's class generally required that the teacher provide an evaluation of student responses, this evaluation did not necessarily come after each student spoke; it was often postponed for a few turns. In addition, the teacher rarely called on students (unless they raised their hands), and raising one's hand and waiting to be called upon was unusual in this class. Instead, students just spoke out in response to a teacher initiation, often at the same time. At least two students (one of them the focal student Amado) independently characterized the fast-paced interaction in Carol's classes as "rolling." The following example illustrates these interactional structures. The subject of this lesson was an *English Workbook* exercise about abstract and concrete language.

Teacher: Did you do okay with Exercise 23? That part of-
  Stevie: - I didn't understand about "word."
Teacher: The word "word." Concrete or abstract?
     |Amy: Concrete.
     |Stevie: You can see it.
     |John: Abstract.
     |Marisa: Abstract.
  Stevie: Words that are spoken words, wh-, word-
  Beatriz: - Yeah, spoken word or?
Teacher: Wh-, what's the definition of a concrete word?
  Stevie: See it.
Teacher: You can hear it, see it, smell it, touch it, taste it.

In this excerpt, students Amy, Stevie, John, and Marisa all spoke out simultaneously to answer the teacher's question making for a fast pace that required students to jump into the interaction quickly and fairly loudly if they were to be heard. No one raised a hand. Little was done in this class to protect a student's turn if another started to interpret or speak simultaneously. Students had to fend for themselves interactionally in the whole class discussions.

The interactional structures and the restrictions on content that I have described are important for understanding how the Mexican American women were silenced during whole class discussions. In the next section, I describe the ways students attempted to break the silence imposed by these constraints. The importance of the structure and timing of interaction, social support for interaction, real versus academic discourse, and attempts to make personal connections through key themes (all seen in

Chapter Five) reappear in the interaction of focal students during whole class discussions.

The Silence of Mexican American Focal Women

As the numbers presented in the beginning of this chapter suggest, the classroom discourse of the Mexican American focal women in whole class discussions was characterized by pervasive silence. As in the previous chapter, the term "silence" is used relatively here. Although the women did speak, it was so little compared to their numbers in the classroom, that the effect was virtual silence. Each of the focal women—Isaura, Mónica, and Juanita—volunteered to speak only twice the entire semester, whereas, one male Mexican American focal student took as many as 20 turns in a single class session. In this section, I analyze the various strategies the women used to break the silence resulting from constraints on the structure of interaction in whole class discussions and the official language of the classroom. I also discuss the role played by social support in their attempts.

The combination of classroom interaction, tightly controlled by the teacher, and fast-paced interaction between the students and the teacher—the "rolling" effect described earlier in the chapter—played an important part in the silence of the Mexican focal American women. In order to find an opening during these "rolling" exchanges, the women waited until interaction slowed. On each occasion when the women spoke, the teacher had just completed a minilecture. These short monologues served to slow the fast pace of interaction between the students and the teacher, thereby allowing the women to find openings for interaction. The following example is from the first of the two whole class discussions during the semester, in which Isaura volunteered to speak. The episode followed a rather lengthy minilecture; the teacher discussed the importance of students using concrete language in their essays. I provide only the end of the minilecture here because it was so long.

Teacher: . . .We need details. It's just like at the bottom of [Lesson] 32 when they give you the sentences and ask you to elaborate. Alright. Let's take a break. How 'bout, ah, any other questions? Did I miss anyone?
    Isaura: How 'bout labor?
Teacher: Pardon?
    Isaura: Labor.
Teacher: L-a-b-e-l? [spells out word] What do you think?

|John: No
|Amy: No, Labor, O-R
Teacher: Labor. L-a-b-o-r. [spells out word] What do you think?
Amy: Abstract.
Cynthia: I don't know.
Teacher: Make it concrete. Make labor concrete.
Stevie: Physical labor.
Teacher: Well, physical labor's still abstract. . . .

[Guessing by various students continues for several pages of transcript until the teacher finally says:]

Teacher: Pounding nails. Carpentry is abstract. Pounding nails is concrete. Alright. Ten minutes, ah, come right back at twenty-five of.

In this exchange, Isaura chose to talk only after the teacher had given a rather lengthy minilecture and specifically asked for student input. The same strategies can be found in her only other attempt to speak in whole class discussions one month later.

When Isaura spoke again in class, the structure and content of the resulting discourse bore an uncanny resemblance to her earlier experience in whole class discussion. In this exchange, the class was again reviewing an *English Workbook* assignment, this time an etymological exercise on the word *chocolate*. The class had already determined that chocolate came to the Spanish language from an Aztec word. The teacher then conducted a minilecture on how an Aztec word would become part of the Spanish language by reviewing the history Mexican colonization. Again, I will provide only the conclusion of this minilecture:

Teacher: . . . They land and they say,"This is ours, I claim this in the name of King Ferdinand of Spain." So Mexico becomes a Spanish colony, and along with the, the beverage they take back the name, only . . . made, made Spanish. What, how do you spell this in Spanish, chocolate?
Isaura: C-H-O-
Teacher: Say is, C-H, C-H (Starts writing it on board)
Isaura: C-O
Teacher: No "H"? (Erases "H")
Isaura: Yes,
Students: C-H-O
Teacher: C-H-O-
Maria: C-O-L-O-T-E, like that [sic].

> Teacher: And how do you pronounce it?
> Class (in unison): Chocolate.
> Teacher: Chocolate, right.

As with her first attempt to speak, Isaura volunteered in class. Again, she was misunderstood by the teacher and unable to finish making her point, even though this time she chose a topic that she was more knowledgeable of than the teacher—the Spanish language. In both cases, the slowing of interaction during the minilecture and specific elicitations by the teacher appear to have provided Isaura, a relatively unpracticed speaker of English, the time she needed to produce her responses. She once explained to me in a tutorial that she tended to "think in Spanish," which caused a time lag because she had to "translate in[to] English. . . . and all that grammar."

Although Mónica and Juanita also spoke after minilectures, the relatively long stretches of discourse to which they responded were not always the teacher's. Mónica spoke not only after a teacher minilecture, but also after a guest speaker from the local University of California campus spoke for an extended period. (Again, in the interest of space, I have abbreviated the extended talk of the advisor.)

> UC Advisor: . . . Let me just stop here. I want to see if any of you have questions that I can answer about UC or I can answer questions about ((a lot of the other UC campuses)) Does anybody have any? I've answered all the questions? How'd I do that?
> Mónica: Doesn't financial aid give you a certain time, you know. . .?

This interaction was one of the two times Mónica spoke in class during this semester. As with Isaura, she chose an opportunity when the pace of interaction had been slowed by a minilecture and the person in control of the interaction had specifically asked for input from the class.

Likewise, Juanita spoke only twice during the semester: once after a teacher minilecture and once after a stretch of discourse by a fellow student. In the excerpt that follows, she disagreed with a long statement by a student about Spanish-speaking students and bilingual education.

> Lucy: If they're, I see the need to have the, the equipment there to help them, but if they're born here in Appleton, and that's you know, or they're born here in America, or wherever, then and they've gone through the school system since kindergarten, that by the time they reach junior high, they should

be able to at least, you know, do their school work in English. The thousands of dollars that are spent on textbooks alone, to have English and Spanish versions. . . .

Juanita: But then how could they be considered bilingual if they don't know their own language?

In all cases but one, the Mexican American focal women only spoke when the teacher had opened the floor to students with an elicitation in the form of a question. The elicitations, like the minilectures, effectively slowed the fast-paced interaction described at the beginning of this chapter, allowing the women to find openings when they could interact in whole class discussions.

Another characteristic of the exchanges in the previous section is the presence of interruptions. Each time Isaura was interrupted and misinterpreted in the interactions, she did not speak again during the episode. Apparently, well-meaning students jumped into the interactions in an attempt to help the teacher understand what Isaura had said. Isaura did not take part in the guessing that ensued after her original question regarding the word *labor*. In her last turn, she repeated the word *labor* in an effort to make the teacher understand her. When the teacher did not understand Isaura a second time, other students spoke up, clearly with the good intention of clarifying the misunderstanding, but again, they took over the interaction and Isaura was silenced.

Although Isaura was not allowed to finish her question, both Mónica and Juanita, who were also interrupted as they spoke in class, maintained their turns by reciprocating interruptions. In the following example, Mónica repeatedly used this interactional strategy, speaking up throughout the teacher's attempts to answer her. The interaction occurred when the teacher was outlining the organizational options for the final exam essay on the chalkboard. The students were to summarize and compare three essays. Mónica raised her hand.

> Teacher: Mónica?
> Mónica: Do we give our own personal opinion after-
> Teacher (emphatically): Yes
> Mónica: each-
> Teacher: That's why-
> Mónica: After-
> Teacher: That's why what I was saying before-
> Mónica: But after each one?
> Teacher: Now this part, this part is, this part is summary (refers to board).
> Mónica (under breath): Uh huh.

> Teacher: This is just factual (refers to one part of board). This (refers to other part of board) is your personal opinion.
>
> Mónica: So then after each one of them?
>
> Teacher: Well, that, that, that depends, um, the, the assignment says um, (reads from handout) "Consider the way each person felt about . . . conclude-"
>
> Mónica (softly) : So it would be-?
>
> Teacher: -by discussing what you have learned by reading this historical, ah, about this historical event from these personal perspectives, so I'm-
>
> Mónica (under her breath): Umm-
>
> Teacher: -mostly bringing in your personal view-
>
> Mónica (softly): -at the end.
>
> Teacher: -at, at the, as, as a conclusion. However, if you think Lawrence is a hooligan, or you know, a nonsympathetic wretch who doesn't appreciate suffering, don't hesitate to put it in as you go along. Don't be afraid to use "I" all the way through the paper.
>
> Students: (laugh)
>
> Teacher: You know, you don't have to wait to the end to bring your view in.

Although it took her four turns to complete her question, Mónica persevered, interrupting the teacher as the teacher had interrupted her. Even after she completed her question, she continued to break into the teacher's answer, asking for clarification over a series of several turns ("So then after each of them?" "So it would be?"). Even after this struggle, Mónica did not get the information that she sought during the episode. After a few moments, she leaned over to me and asked, "So are we suppose' to give our personal view in the middle or after all three summaries?"

Similarly, when Mónica asked the visiting advisor from UC about financial aid, she was interrupted.

> Mónica: Doesn't financial aid give you to a certain time, you know, financial aid-
>
> UC Advisor: The deadline to apply?
>
> Mónica: Yeah.
>
> UC Advisor: You know-
>
> Mónica: -Not to apply, but, you know, certain time, they give you money a certain time.

like three years or so, (pause) you know what I mean?

UC Advisor: I'm not sure if I know what you're asking. When you apply for financial aid they give you the money you need each quarter. Quarter by quarter. If you do get loans, which is what, um, um, they were talking about earlier. If you get loans, you usually have time after you've graduated to pay that back, but you don't start paying it back until a year after you've graduated.

Kay (whispers to Mónica): Does that answer your question?

Mónica (whispers to Kay): Somebody told me financial aid only gives you three years. (Pause) I guess not.

PCC Advisor: On the Cal Grant, I received a Cal Grant when I went to school and they told me that I would have it for four years if my grade point average stayed a 2.5. I applied every year and what they wanted to see was that my grades were still good and that my financial, ah, situation hadn't changed. But they did promise me four years. . . .

Mónica (whispers to Kay): Uh huh, see.

Both times Mónica spoke in whole class discussions, whether to the UC advisor or the teacher, her questions were interrupted ("Do we give our own personal opinion after—", and "Doesn't financial aid give you to a certain time, you know, financial aid—, ") and then misinterpreted. The UC advisor assumed, before Mónica finished her question, that she was asking about application deadlines. Even when Mónica corrected the advisor's misinterpretation, the advisor continued to provide the wrong information to Mónica. Only when a second person, the counselor at PCC, spoke up did Mónica get her information. Likewise, the teacher did not allow Mónica to finish asking her question about the essay organization before she started answering. When Mónica tried to get a clarification of the teacher's answer, she still did not get an acceptable response. In neither case did she receive the information she had attempted to gain. Only through the intervention of others, did Monica's questions get answered.

Juanita, too, was interrupted during her interactions. She also persevered in a description of her elementary school experiences and even more so in making points about bilingual education and discrimination.

Juanita: But, bilingual classes are being taught in English and Spanish-

|Lucy: They should be, they should be in both lan-
    guages.
|Teacher: Hence the term, huh?
Juanita: -So the, the kids are learning both.

In this interaction, Juanita and Lucy had been disagreeing on
the relative merits of bilingual education. Both Lucy and the
teacher interrupted Juanita before she finished making her point
that students were not only taught in Spanish, but also in English
in bilingual education classes. She waited the two turns and eventually finished her point despite the interruptions.

On the rare occasions when the Mexican American focal
women took part in whole class discussions, they were invariably interrupted and often misinterpreted. Those women who
had been raised in the United States and who were confident in
their English fought to keep the floor when they were interrupted, with varying degrees of success. Isaura, who was in this
class to improve her English speaking skills, did not attempt to
maintain the floor when her classmates interrupted her. The
structure of interaction in this context prevented her from being
heard.

Mónica and Juanita chose to speak when there were clear
sources of support for their interaction in the classroom, that is,
when something or someone encouraged them to interact. Both
times Mónica interacted in whole class discussions, she received
direct encouragement from her tutor—me. Before Mónica asked
her question of the UC advisor, she leaned over and whispered to
me, "I thought they only give you a certain time, three years or
something." I replied, "I can't remember. I think it's changed since
. . . ."

Meanwhile, the UC advisor was saying:

> UC Advisor: . . . There is financial aid available. We
>   really want you to go on, to try to continue
>   your education, to graduate, to get a
>   diploma, take it home, show your family
>   what you did. Um, OK?

During this, Mónica leaned over to me:

Mónica (whispers to me): Should I ask her?
            Kay: Yeah.
        Mónica: Should I ask about time?
            Kay: That's good.

Only after I had given her my support did Mónica ask:

> Mónica: Doesn't financial aid give you to a certain
> time, you know, financial aid?

When Mónica spoke up to ask about the final essay organization she first leaned over to me and asked, *sotto voce*, "Do we give our personal view after each essay or after all three?" I answered that I was not sure and encouraged her to ask the teacher. Mónica responded, "OK, I'm going to." From the back row, she bravely raised her hand and asked, "Do we give our own personal opinion after-?"

Mónica did not make it a habit to ask me such questions during whole class discussions, but in both cases when Mónica spoke up in class, she had asked me to answer her question first, one-to-one. Only when I could not answer her question did she consider asking the question aloud. Even then, before she raised her hand each time, she seemed to need encouragement. The first time she spoke up, she asked me if she "should" first and the second time, when I did not know the answer, I encouraged her to ask. This apparent need of encouragement was not surprising considering what she said at the beginning of Chapter One about why she did not interact more during class discussions:

> Mónica: You know, sometimes I feel like speaking out. Because, you
> know, I know things that I can say, but then I'm all like,
> nahh, they don't want to hear it (laughs).
> Kay: I think they do. . . .
> Mónica: 'Cause you know, that was one of my fears, speaking out in
> classes. I've always been bad, until I know the whole class,
> then I feel free, a little. You know, I don't say anything. That
> was my fear always in high school. Then when I took the
> introduction into business and the supervision [in college],
> that was my fear too.

Ironically, Mónica made this comment just a few weeks before the end of the course after commenting on how unusual it was for Juanita to have talked in the previous class session. Although Mónica felt that she should have talked more in class, she also felt that the class was not interested in her ideas. Furthermore, she felt that she did not know the class well enough. Because the structure of interaction in the class allowed for official interaction to occur only in the form of whole class discussion, which focused on teacher–student question and answer, or one-to-one tutorials, there were few opportunities for students to get to know each other and feel comfortable with each other. Students sat in rows facing the front of the classroom the entire semester. The fact that Mónica was interrupted and misinterpreted when she tried to talk would certainly serve to reinforce her belief that people were not listening. Furthermore, the counselor's comment,"I'm not sure I know what you mean," was not an attempt to elicit a more thorough statement of the question. Instead, it had the effect of being a disparaging statement, suggesting Mónica was unable to clearly articulate a question.

Juanita's decision to talk for the first time in class appears to have been supported by an interaction between the teacher and Juanita that occurred earlier in the same whole class session. Carol was explaining to the class the importance of making the focus (or thesis) of their essays clear when she called on Juanita to share her introduction, which stated the focus of her essay. This interaction became a positive, affirming moment.

Teacher: Um, Juanita, do you have your paper handy? Read your, read the, read your draft, it's good. Read the opening. This is someone who is announcing ahead of time what she's going to do in her paper, OK?

Juanita (reads her essay): Frederick Douglass, who lived in the South is more ((discriminated against)) than Maya Angelou who lived in the South during the 1940s when segregation laws were strictly reinforced [sic]. Both write about the struggles they encounter and eventually overcome in order to get an education. Frederick Douglass' struggle to learn, to learn has it much more difficult than Maya Angelou, but both are limit, limited in what they can do with their education and both mention how they perceive their limits in society.

Teacher: OK, she says (starts writing on chalkboard) Douglass, how'd you put it? Had it harder? What was the? Did you use the word harder or?

Juanita: Douglass, um, struggle to learn is much more difficult.

Teacher: OK, struggle is much more difficult, much harder, much more difficult, and then she put but both face limitations. (The word "focus" is written on the board.) This is a really good example of a crystal clear focus.

Other Student: Um hm.

Teacher: And she said it in her first paragraph. Now what the reader is going to look for, what any of you would look for as you read that essay is does she show this? She's got two

things, two main things she's got to show,
she's got to show their facing limitations
imposed on them by society, and won't you
admit these are different, one's a slave,
one's in segregated society. And she has to
show this, that he had it much harder in
struggling against these limitations. Wh
what facts could you use to prove this?
That he had it harder, that it was harder
for him to struggle against?

The positive feedback from Carol in front of the class was particularly important, if not somewhat contradictory, considering that
the teacher had just accused her of plagiarism during the tutorial
segment of this very class. Moreover, Juanita was already somewhat suspicious of the English department at PCC after her experiences in English 5 and her difficulty getting placed in English 10.
Juanita also thought of Carol as "kinda mean" after she had asked
Carol if she could leave class early one evening because she was
feeling ill. Carol advised her against it because she was going to
explain the new essay assignment. Juanita left anyway.

At the same time, Carol felt that Juanita was "angry" and "bitter" about her past educational experiences and that Juanita
believed "there's a conspiracy against her here at Portolá." Given
Carol and Juanita's strained relationship, the public praise of
Juanita's introduction may have provided Juanita with the kind of
approval and self-esteem (remember that she, like Isaura, said
that she lacked it) to speak up later in the class session.

Isaura's experience suggests how interaction that might have provided a positive experience and created a supportive environment,
became, as the teacher later characterized it, "a mistake." The final
time Isaura spoke in class, she did not volunteer. Rather the teacher
asked her to read from her essay that had just been graded and
returned. It was about a month after the last time she had volunteered. The teacher had been asking students with good animals
essays to read their final sections aloud. After each, she asked the
class to comment by asking questions such as, "What details do you
remember?" or " How did that work?" After each reading, she had
taken four or five student comments. Three essays had already been
read when Carol asked Isaura to read the section of her animals
essay, in which she described her mother killing a chicken in Mexico
so the family could eat. Because of her accent and because she was
self-conscious and spoke softly, it was difficult for me and for students near me to understand Isaura. The following is what she read,

taken from her essay, not the audiotape, because recording quality was poor due to Isaura's quiet voice:

> Like Virginia Woolf, I too witnessed the death of an animal. I was twelve years old and I lived in Mexico when one cold morning my mother told me to catch a chicken from the corral. She pointed to the chicken I was supposed to catch. It was the fattest. As I was opening the small door from the corral, the chicken flew away. I run after her until the chicken got under the bushes and there I caught her. My mom took the chicken by the neck and twisted it around for about two minutes and then she pulled the neck apart from the chicken. Instantly the blood came down to the floor. And for awhile she held the chicken against the floor so that its flutter didn't splatter the blood everywhere. The chicken moved her legs vainly as she wanted to retain her life. But it was shaking. Its flutter became weak, and at last she relaxed. The struggle was over the chicken was dead.

When Isaura finished reading the essay, there was a moment of awkward silence that Carol quickly moved to fill:

> She's making a connection to what Woolf said about the struggle of the moth. It's still trying to struggle to retain its life, she says, even though it's had its neck broken. Really, um, makes you wonder what we do to animals, doesn't it? Now in this case it wasn't for the thrill of watching something die, or to save face, or to get something pretty, it was necessary to do this for the sake of the survival of her family, that's why she was doing it. Umm, but it doesn't make the killing any less hard to imagine. That's a really good description.

Unlike her response to the other essays that had been read in class, Carol did not ask students to list the details they had heard or how they worked, nor did she open the floor for discussion of Isaura's essay. Instead, she repeated the gist of Isaura's story, something she had not done with the other students. She then took it upon herself to point out what was interesting about the story. She used this approach because she assumed that students had had difficulty hearing and/or understanding Isaura because of her accent.

In an interview later, Carol discussed Isaura's classroom discourse in general, and this incident specifically, saying that Isaura spoke "very softly" and had "an accent as well." She continued:

> I know she's really hard to understand. When she would talk in class sometimes people would strain to . . . try and hear her. . . . One reason I asked her to read her paper is 'cause I wanted people to see . . . because a person speaks in this way, don't judge them as not intelligent or not good in their writing . . . that was my purpose for having

her read one thing, was to show this class this is somebody who's really smart and a really good writer and uh, I know that you've heard her before and maybe you don't think she's a very good student, but she is.

This quotation reveals that Carol's purpose in having Isaura read was based on the assumption that the class had judged Isaura negatively based on her oral skills (as Carol once had, when she categorized her as someone who had "come to the States late in life"). She hoped that after the class heard some of Isaura's writing, they would begin to judge her positively, as Carol now did. But reflecting on the success of her attempt, Carol commented:

I don't know if they had it [a copy of the Isaura's essay] in front of them. If they didn't, I made a bad mistake, 'cause what I should have done, and I don't think I did this, is um, have what she was reading in front of them to look at. . . . If I had her just read, it probably made it worse, not better, 'cause supposedly this was good, but they [the class] didn't understand it.

Carol realized, upon reflection, that her well-intentioned effort may have left a negative impression on the class rather than the positive one she intended.

As for Isaura, there was no indication that Carol's public praise of her work raised the low self-esteem she described herself as having in Chapter Four. Even after she learned that she had an A- in the course, she insisted that she was "the lowest of everybody" in the class. She assessed herself not just on the basis of her writing, as Carol did, but on her speaking too. She did not attempt to speak again in whole class discussions after this incident.

Social support (or the lack thereof) appears to have been an important factor in the interaction of the Mexican American women in whole class interaction, but support such as that shown Mónica and Juanita was rare in this class, particularly during whole class discussions. Based on her interviews and interaction in the classroom, it seems Carol assumed that the silence of some women was inevitable. She did not consider it important for students to talk in class nor did she give grades for class participation. She did not attempt to alter the situation, although she was aware of it. In Chapter One, I presented Carol's perspective on student silence:

It's one thing for a student not to speak, it's another for them to be tuned out, or not to care, or to feel it's not relevant. . . . I mean you, you can read so much on their faces. . . . There are the folks who never speak but you know are there. . . . Sometimes when people don't speak it worries me, and sometimes it doesn't worry me at all, just 'cause, you know that they don't, they're among those people who don't speak in class, and they're shy for whatever reason.

These three women employed interactional strategies, such as speaking after minilectures and elicitations, to attempt to overcome the silence imposed on them in whole class discussions by the particular structure and content of this classroom. In the next section, I present the strategies employed by the men in whole class discussion and point out the differences and similarities in the interaction of the Mexican American men and women in the classroom.

The Voices of Mexican American Focal Men

Unlike the Mexican American focal women, the interaction of the Mexican American focal men in whole class discussions was characterized by more talk than would be expected, considering their scarcity in numbers. Although they faced the same limited interaction structure as a result of the IRE format, they employed differing strategies for interacting within that structure. The men initiated requests, made comments, and sometimes even disagreed with or challenged statements made by the teacher. In this section, I describe how Amado and Federico negotiated the structure of whole class discussions.

Amado and Federico asked questions in whole class discussions to initiate talk about particular essay assignments or to ask for more general course information. Typically, questions from Amado asked Carol about the content of an upcoming essay, "But what if you just focus on their goal? One similarity?" Or a more general question of this nature asked, "What's our final exam gonna be like?"

Questions were also used to clarify points in class discussion. For example, when Carol was discussing abstract and concrete words, Federico asked for a clarification:

    Federico: You say it's subjective?
        Carol: Yeah, it's very subjective.
    Federico: It's not objective?
        Carol: Yeah, it's not objective.

Unlike the women, who generally waited for a teacher-initiated question to speak up or for interaction to be slowed by a minilecture, the men broke the steady IRE, teacher-controlled pattern of whole class discussions, creating their own openings by initiating requests for information.

Federico and Amado also initiated by making unsolicited comments during whole class discussions. These comments generally were a recognition of problems in their writing or comments about writing in general. For example, when Carol was discussing the proper development of the interview essay, she made the point that one should not put too much detail into the essay:

> Carol: The motto for this paper should be "Don't write a book."
> Amado: I have a tendency to do the opposite: I generalize.
> Carol: The second motto for this paper is "The reader does not know my grandmother [the subject of many interview papers]."

On another occasion, when Carol was describing an essay assignment, Federico spoke up, flatly stating, "I can tell lousy writing from nine feet." And after a pause, concluded, "I guess that's a thing to avoid, huh?" Carol agreed with him and the discussion moved to how to distinguish "lousy" writing from that that was not. The men often spoke up like this, making their presence in the classroom known. Although their requests for information and off-hand comments interrupted the smooth flow of interaction in the classroom, Carol did not seem bothered by it. On the contrary, the interaction style of the focal men served to establish a rapport between these students and the teacher, a point I will develop in more detail later.

Sometimes Federico and Amado asked questions and made comments that seemed opposed to the teacher's stated opinion. In the following transcript, Federico openly disagreed with the teacher's description of one aspect of the writing process:

> Carol: You know how if you've ever kept a journal or a diary and you want to remember something that happened to you, you just jot down phrases really quickly, and as soon as you read those phrases, the whole memory of the experience can come back to you . . . everything comes back to you, all the details come back to you-
> Federico: [If] you're writing a certain thing, "Oh, wait a minute, that didn't happen that way."
> Carol (summing up): -or you remember more sometimes.
> Federico: Yeah.
> Carol: Yeah.
> Federico: But they don't suddenly come rushing in.
> Carol: I see.
> Federico: I'm not flooded with them.

> Carol: Yeah, everyone is different in that way, how their memories work, and how their imaginations work. Um, did some of you have that experience that you were writing about a time and you remembered a lot of details about those experiences? Yeah? Did some, did some of you go through that?
>
> Stevie: Yeah, I remembered a lot.
>
> Teacher: Yeah, people are different in the way their memories work, and their imagination. For an experience to work, though, on paper, you need to have enough details so that your reader will be able to understand the experience that you went through. If you put it down in just a very sketchy way, I'm not saying you've got to remember every single detail, but you have to remember enough so that they have a context to understand the experience.

Similarly, Amado's questions sometimes showed that he openly disagreed with something the teacher had said. After Carol provided an outline for the animals essay that specifically called for presenting summaries first, Amado asked, "We don't necessarily have to start with our summary, do we? I wanted the introduction to have interweaving." Carol responded to Amado by stating that she could not provide a formula like a math teacher. She said that Amado's decision would have to depend on what he was trying to prove. In this case, as in many others, Carol's assertions were often softened and qualified as a result of the disagreeing statements made by the Mexican American men. This interaction strategy further heightened the profile of the Mexican American men in class and contributed to Carol's positive evaluation of re-entry men.

Although there were no obvious signs of social support for the men as there were for the women, the teacher did not appear to respond negatively to Federico or Amado's interaction strategies. Although the interruption of an IRE-patterned classroom often receives a negative response if a teacher does not expect it (Hull, Rose, Fraser, & Castellano, 1991), Carol did expect such interaction from re-entry men and found it normal. Considering how she characterized re-entry men, this interaction style, in both content and form, seemed to leave a good impression on Carol. Of Amado, Carol said:

> Amado, I thought in the first weeks, um, was going to be a really good addition to the class. Because he's so outgoing. . . . He was the only one I had ever seen in all the years I've done the interview

actually stand up. He actually stood up and faced the class. . . . And he also spoke a lot in the first weeks. He had questions, he had answers, he had comments, he talked a lot to the people around him. He was very outgoing. Um, so I guess it appeared to me that his main strength would be his, um, willingness to participate in the class.

And, as noted in Chapter 4, Federico left a good impression, much as Amado had. Carol stated:

There's, there's a confidence about him. Again, as a thinker and as just a human being. He's not, he doesn't seem cowed, or um, afraid of the experience of returning to school. He's not um, you know, he's mastered a lot of things in his life.

The men's use of a variety of interactional strategies—requests, comments, even challenges—led the teacher to judge them favorably. Evidently, these challenges and comments, particularly in a predominantly IRE interactional pattern, reveal a confidence and courage that impressed Carol. Moreover, the frequent talk of these men in whole class discussions served to build a rapport between themselves and Carol that the Mexican American focal women did not develop. In interviews, Carol admitted knowing little about Mónica and Juanita, hardly being able to distinguish between the two. She once admitted that she had not gotten to know Juanita as she had the men, stating:

I didn't get to know her [Juanita] well enough, as I got to know Federico and Amado. . . . You can't miss people like that [Federico and Amado]. These students have an expertise that, you know, it's more than just writing papers, it helps to gauge their future academic success.

Although she said she did not grade based on classroom talk, she responded positively to it and each positive interaction with the men provided a context and support for future positive interactions between the teacher and the focal men.

THE CONTENT OF WHOLE CLASS DISCUSSIONS

Although the men interacted more during whole class discussions than the women, they, like the women, preferred to discuss topics in ways that were real rather than academic, the preferred mode of the teacher. Focal students, male and female, asked questions that they did not have answers to—questions about how to complete an assignment, what was on the final exam, what a concept meant. Mónica's questions were qualitatively different than the type of known information questions initiated by the teacher. Mónica asked real questions about how to get financial aid and how to organize the final essay. When Isaura asked, "How 'bout 'labor'?" she had a real question about whether that word was considered abstract or concrete by the teacher.

Likewise, the questions that the women responded to were in all cases, real questions as opposed to academic, or known information questions. When Isaura asked about the word *labor*, the teacher had asked if students had any more questions. When she gave her spelling of chocolate, the teacher had asked how to spell it; it was clear from Carol's response that she truly did not know how to spell *chocolate* in Spanish. Similarly, Juanita's initial response in class came after a real question about whether students had felt discrimination in their educational careers, a question that the teacher could not possibly know the answer to. Mónica's first response came after the counselor asked if there were any more questions, another real question.

The men and women all preferred to talk about subjects that were related to their key themes or to related topics to their key themes through their talk. As I explained earlier, however, the teacher rarely asked students to relate their personal experiences in whole class discussions. Instead her focus was on the text and writing assignments, which, as seen in Chapters Four and Five, supported her goal for the class: teaching academic discourse. Those rare occasions when the topics under discussion were related to students' various key themes were often the times the focal students chose to speak.

Amado frequently responded during whole class discussions in ways that revealed his key theme: religion to save Mexican American youth. On the first night of class during introductions, Amado took on his role as spiritual leader after a particularly poignant introduction of a student who was coming back to school to make a better life for herself; he magnanimously commented: "Isn't it wonderful that we're here to solve society's problems rather than becoming them?"

He frequently responded to readings by focusing on their religious aspects, however obscure. For example, when students were discussing contrasting renditions of the bombings at Hiroshima and Nagasaki, Amado raised his hand in class and commented, "I was surprised at the chaplain's praying over a bombing mission. What kind of prayer would you say over a bombing mission?" even though the chaplain was a minor character. Later, he noted that another character took part in religious protests against the bombings.

Federico also responded when his key theme was raised. He became particularly involved in the whole class discussions of Douglass and Angelou and of George Orwell's essay "Shooting an Elephant," all readings focused on social justice—his key theme. Because these lessons tended to take a fairly strict IRE format, most of his turns were simply responses to rather literal questions about the text, such as:

> Teacher: What actually happens? What specifically happens?
> Federico: Falling on their faces.

In the discussion of Orwell's essay, after much dialogue, again, on "what happens" in the text, Federico initiated a turn, making the point that imperialism, as described in the essay, "is against human nature." He tried to take the discussion of Angelou's essay further than the teacher when he asked, "Why does she [wish them dead]? Because of her dying optimism?" This question reminds me of Federico's own optimism as a young soldier, an optimism that died upon his return to the injustices of Appleton. When the teacher asked if Donleavy was intentionally hurtful to Angelou and others, Federico made the point that Donleavy was a victim of his own environment and upbringing and would not recognize what he said as insulting, a clear parallel to comments he had made about the people in Appleton who, he wrote, showed in their "eyes" and "attitudes" that they were "Mistresses" and "Donleavys."

Key themes were particularly effective in eliciting talk from the focal women, especially Juanita. As noted earlier, Carol rarely asked questions that allowed students to talk about their key themes, but when students were preparing their Douglass–Angelou comparisons, Carol began a broad discussion about societal issues, relating the situations of Douglass and Angelou to the present. Carol's initiating question was "Are there impediments to learning still around in society today? Do you feel that they exist in education?" These questions led students to talk about their observations, but not about their personal experiences. Finally, Carol asked a question that elicited Juanita's first voluntary comment in class after months of silence, a question that allowed Juanita to talk about her key theme: the education of Spanish-speaking students.

> Carol: Did any of you ever feel in your let's say elementary or high school education that there was any

discrimination or obstacles of this sort facing you because you belonged to a specific racial group or ethnic group or even gender group? That maybe, you know, no one can say to you,"You can't go to school," 'cause you in fact got to go to school, until a certain age, but maybe more subtle forms of discrimination? (Juanita raises hand.) Juanita?

Juanita: Um, yeah, I went to Shoreline Elementary School, and that's like, there's hardly any-

Others student: Mostly white, huh?

Juanita: Yeah, mostly white.

Carol: Oh, it is?

Juanita: And when I went, well now there's more Hispanic students going, but when I went there was only like five or ten. It wasn't like a lot.

Carol: In the entire school?

Juanita: In the entire school. And I did, I felt that towards students, they would call me Mexican and all that stuff like that, and also, um, I was, see I remember this, um, you know, you get your spoon in your lunch, at the lunches and all the kids were blowing um, they were popping the, like, um-

Other student: The little bag that it comes in.

Juanita: Uh huh, the little bag.

Carol: Oh, yeah, yeah, yeah.

Juanita: And they were popping it and the teacher only got mad at me, and she sent me out and she, and she told me to throw [out] my lunch and I wasn't the only one doing it, and I, and I remember that and she, had me sit outside on the and it was really hot and I remember that we had a migrant aide during that time and she said "Why are you out here in the sun when it's really hot?"

Carol: Um hm.

Juanita: I go, well I told her what had happened and she went to go talk to the teacher about it and she changed me to a different place, but she still had me there.

Carol: Hm, hm.

Juanita: It's like a lot of, um, stuff that I remember from the teachers.

Carol: How 'bout academically? Did you ever feel like, or any of you, that, that you were told which, like if you're a man and you want to get into nursing or you're a woman and you wanted to be a lawyer, or because of your ethnic group that you were subtly reminded that that wasn't really your place, that's not what you're supposed to be doing?

Later in the class, the discussion turned to the use of English and Spanish in the education of local youth. This topic was also central to Juanita's key theme and again, she got involved in the interaction. In the first exchange, she related an aspect of her own experience, which, as noted in Chapter Four, was the impetus for her decision to pursue a bilingual teaching credential. The second episode was even more directly on point—a discussion of the merits of bilingual education. The topics of the day's discussion contributed to Juanita's decision to take part. Although Douglass and Angelou had been the topics of class discussions for weeks, the educational experiences of the Mexican American students in the class and the topic of bilingual education had never arisen. Because of the type of questions characteristically asked, most were either about the text or about assignments, rarely about student experiences. As it was, the students, not the teacher, raised and developed the topic of bilingual education this day.

As Chapter Five suggested, none of the personal topics that were allowed in this unusual class discussion (including bilingual education) were expected, encouraged, or even desired in students' academic writing; on the contrary, they were discouraged. Despite this class discussion, the Douglass and Angelou essay topic remained a strict compare–contrast of Douglass and Angelou's educational experiences, with no reference to the students' experiences. In the discussion of the students' written work, we saw how the teacher did little to respond or encourage students to develop the personal or real content of their essays. Similarly, there was little "uptake" (Nystrand & Gamoran, 1991) on student talk about personal experience in the classroom, even when elicited by the teacher. Juanita's heart-rending story of abuse and neglect in the elementary school was met with no response from the teacher except "Hm, hm" and a swift change of the subject—"How 'bout academically?"—implying that the content of her story had been either unimportant or inappropriate. Carol's response later in the lesson to the disagreement between students on the topic of bilingual education was to provide a few platitudes, such as, "It'd be nice if we could all be bilingual . . . ," as if she were hesitant to delve too deeply into educational discrimination and bilingual education, although they were real issues in these students' lives and topics of heated debate in the community.

Both male and female Mexican American focal students preferred to talk in class when the content of the discussions allowed for them to raise some aspect of their key themes in their talk. The lack of real questions and subjects in the discourse of whole class discussions made it difficult for students to make the personal connection necessary for meaningful interaction.

ONE-TO-ONE TUTORIALS

Focal students interacted with me in one-to-one tutorials almost every week as a part of regular class activities. I also saw focal students in one-to-one tutorials outside of class, but less often and, as mentioned earlier, with differing frequency. During these one-to-one tutorials, students not only asked for and received help with their writing, but they also revealed their concerns about writing and their key themes. Unlike whole class discussions, students controlled the interaction in one-to-one tutorials unless they relinquished it by making requests of the tutor that allowed for academic or known information questions. Because the tutorial sessions had significantly less IRE interaction, there were more opportunities for students' agendas to be heard. In addition to a change from IRE to IRIR, there was also a significant change in the number of participants in the interaction—from over 30 students, three tutors and one teacher as auditors to only one auditor with less power than the teacher alone. Talk in whole class discussions is almost performance-like because of the audience and evaluation aspects; in tutorials those factors are absent, leading to more natural conversational structure and content.

Although Mexican American focal women appeared virtually silent during whole class interaction, they were not silent during other types of interaction in the class. In Chapter Five, I showed that their voices were heard through their writing. In one-to-one tutorials, they also made themselves heard, using strategies such as initiating requests, making comments, and challenging the tutor—the same types of strategies the Mexican American focal men used in whole class discussion. The changes in the interactional context from whole class discussion to one-to-one tutorials had an important impact on the women's interactional patterns.

Mexican American Focal Women: Breaking Silence

The women frequently initiated in tutorials, asking for advice on writing assignments, for clarification of concepts, and for information about the course. Requests for advice on writing assignments took two forms: general requests for help and more specific questions. The women commonly invited me to respond generally to their essays with statements such as Mónica's: "Read it and tell me if it's OK," or the slightly less direct question form used by Juanita: "But I mean, does it sound right?" More specific questions on particular essays were those like Isaura's initiation: "He didn't want to kill the Indians, but I don't know how to put that," or Mónica's question about the animals summaries: "So, um, like right here I would write about, that's what I don't know, how to start this."

The women, particularly Isaura, frequently asked about concepts such as abstract versus concrete words and figurative versus literal language. If the women did not feel a question had been answered adequately or they still did not understand a concept, they would doggedly repeat their questions, bringing the dialogue back around to a topic again and again. Isaura provided a classic example of this when she wanted a definition of the word *persona*, which Carol asked students to define in preparation for a discussion of Swift's "A Modest Proposal." Isaura had written down the two definitions of *persona* in her Spanish/English dictionary, but wanted to know which one was the one Carol wanted.

    Isaura: (points to her homework) Which one of these?
       Kay: OK, "character" (starts reading the definitions)
    Isaura: "One's personality as seen through others?"
       Kay: Um hm, um hm.
    Isaura: Which one is the . . . ?
       Kay: Either, well, they're both correct. Um, which one does she want you to think of ? It's probably close to this one . . . because she'll say Swift takes on a particular persona in this piece.
    Isaura: Like a particular character, or?

We continued to discuss the two definitions and went on to definitions of other words that she had questions about (*satire* and *irony*), but again she returned to the question of persona, asking "So the persona, I'm not clear about this." Juanita used a similar strategy when we discussed the organization of one of her essays, repeatedly asking me, "But where do I put this?" as I tried to encourage her to figure that out on her own.

The women also asked for information about the course and school in tutorials. Isaura asked a number of questions about the AA Degree and how to proceed through the English sequence during these one-to-one tutorials.

Early in the semester, when Juanita was having understandable difficulties memorizing the rules of comma usage, she wanted to know about the final exam, asking:

Juanita: But we are going to have a final, huh?
Kay: We are going to have a final, but it's not going to be on the *English Workbook*, it's going to be a paper.
Juanita: On what?
Kay: Ah, she [Carol] hasn't decided yet probably. But it's not going to be in-class either, it's a take home. I mean, it's just another paper.
Juanita: Oh.
Kay: You have two weeks to write it.
Juanita: Here I am worrying about the
Juanita: Here I am worrying about the-
Kay: Yeah, but the point is, you're going to have two weeks to write it, OK. So you're going to have some commas probably in that paper, it's true. But you'll have your book with you, you can look them up. Right?
Juanita: You can't get help on that last, last paper.
Kay: Yeah, you can.
Juanita: You can?
Kay: Probably, yeah. She has let people in the past.
Juanita: Was it like a hard paper for everybody or?
Kay: It's not impossible; it's just average.
Juanita: It's just like any paper?
Kay: Yeah, it's just another paper.
Juanita: (sighs) (laughs)
Kay: Feel better? Sort of?
Juanita: Yes.

The women asked a variety of questions in one-to-one interaction. In fact, they asked so many questions that they seemed to be making up for their lack of questioning in whole class discussions. Numerous questions during each tutorial pertained specifically to the content covered in the previous whole class discussion, showing that indeed, the Mexican American focal women had questions to ask and things to say during whole class discussions, but the interactional context prevented them from being heard. Like the focal men's requests in whole class discussion, the women asked questions in tutorial interaction about specific assignments, concepts discussed in the course, and general course information. The women got their questions answered, but only because there was a change in the interactional context.

Like the men during whole class interaction, the Mexican American focal women frequently made comments about them-

selves generally and as writers specifically during one-to-one tutorials. For example, after a long tutorial session, Isaura commented,
"You know how I feel sometimes when I write? I feel like I am ridicu-
lous." In one-to-one tutorials, the women also pointed out the problems in their essays without being prompted to do so. A typical
instance of this occurred when Juanita pointed out a problem in
the essay we were going over together:

> Juanita: See right here also. I'm starting to say, "I worked."
>   Kay: Yeah.
> Juanita: That doesn't sound right to the whole thing, does it?
>   Kay: It seems like it's out of place, you're right, you're right.
> Juanita: Yeah.
>   Kay: Now I wonder if, um,
> Juanita: Like I should start it with something else, or?

And in a tutorial with Isaura, I had just completed reading over
her latest draft when she said:

> Isaura: I didn't mention what Carol says here.
>   Kay: Uh oh.
> Isaura: Um, (referring to handout) "their attitude to the [bombing]."
>   Kay: Yeah, yeah.
> Isaura: Because I didn't understand it, ah.
>   Kay: Attitude (laughs), I know, um,
> Isaura: Do you think that would be OK, or?
>   Kay: It's, it's really good [referring to her essay].
> Isaura: Or do I have to include it?

The problem Isaura points out here is one that leads her to
"avoid academic discourse," one of the strategies for writing
described in the previous chapter.

The women in one-to-one interaction initiated not only to ask a
variety of questions, but also to make general comments. Like
their question-asking, this strategy also is reminiscent of the
strategies used by the men in whole class interaction.

The women frequently disagreed with me as we discussed how
their essays might be improved, with such comments as "Well,
didn't I write before how I felt?" In the following excerpt, I had just
suggested to Juanita that she summarize her points at the end of
an essay we were working on:

> Juanita: And that's what you want me to put down in the bottom?
>   Wouldn't that be kind of strange though?
>   Kay: I don't know, well, I don't know. Why do you think it would
>   be strange?
>   If you don't want to, you don't have to.

Juanita: Well, no, because I already think that I wrote here, up in the top why, the reasons that I think I would be good, because I explained right here. Why would I have to write it down here again?

In one-to-one tutorials, the same women who were virtually silent in whole class discussions, and who responded only to elicitations in that interactional context, were found to initiate requests and comments, even challenging the authority of the tutor. Of course, the authority of the teacher and the authority of the tutor (especially one who sat in the back of the class with the "babies") are different, as is the rhetorical power of a challenge in front of the class and one in private one-to-one interaction. Unfortunately, the teacher, who responded favorably to these interactional strategies from the men in whole class discussions, was unaware that the women used them regularly in one-to-one interaction.

Mexican American Focal Men: Sustaining Voice

The structure and content of the interaction of Mexican American male focal students in one-to-one tutorials was much like that of the Mexican American focal women in the same interactional context and reminiscent as well of the interaction of Mexican American men in whole class discussions.

Like the women in one-to-one tutorials, the men asked for global responses to their essays. For example, Federico formally began one of our tutorial sessions by asking me to read a draft of his compare–contrast essay, stating, "I'd appreciate your comments." This strategy was also used after a session, in which revision occurred. Amado closed a tutorial by asking me to re-read his newly revised essay: "I'm going to ask you the last favor. And that is that you go over it again, that you read it again, and place this [a revised section of the essay] here; and see how it makes it."

The Mexican American men also asked for specific advice about certain aspects of essays that they were working on. For example, Amado was concerned about the title of his last essay for the course ("What actually happened at Hiroshima and Nagasaki") and asked, "The title, did you think that was a long title?" The men also made requests for clarification of concepts discussed in class. For example, Federico asked a question to better understand the compare-contrast assignment: "She [the teacher] wants you to write about them [Douglass and Angelou]?"

The Mexican American men also initiated to make a variety of comments and observations, most of them about themselves and their writing. For example, Amado explained how he did not want to spend too much time on the final exam essay, stating, "And you know, being the last essay, you just want to push it out of the way, and you don't really want to put a lot of effort into it, you know," whereas Federico offered his "It's just a stop-gap" comment during a tutorial.

Like the women, the men also indicated flaws that they perceived in their essays. For example, Federico noted of his animals essay, "I wrote short summaries on them. Perhaps I should elaborate more." And Amado recognized that his essay digressed, warning me: "That's what I meant to tell you, Kay . . . I got off the subject, OK."

The comments made by the men in one-to-one interaction were similar to the comments they made in whole class interaction. In both contexts, the men spoke about themselves and their writing. In the one-to-one interaction, however, they were able to talk more about both of these subjects, but they took advantage of the opportunity less often than the women as noted in Chapter Five.

Like the women, the men also disagreed with me, defending their essays against the onslaughts of the tutor. Federico was particularly vocal in his response to my criticisms

> Kay: This is a compare-contrast essay.
> Federico: Right.
> Kay: That's the big thing, OK?
> Federico: I felt I was doing that in, in the argument.
> Kay: Ahh-
> Federico: -But only by implication.

Challenges made by the men in one-to-one interaction, as with the women, were primarily defenses of student writing against tutor or teacher comments. They continued, however, to be received positively by the authority being challenged, as the behavior in both the men and the women was similar to that observed in advanced composition students at major four-year universities (Fraser, 1990).

In-class, one-to-one tutorial sessions were mandatory and thereby positively sanctioned. So, both male and female students received social support to participate in this type of interaction. If students did not have drafts, however, the tutorials might be less beneficial. The nature of one-to-one interaction, as opposed to 30 to 1 as in the whole class discussions, also suggests support for greater interaction on the part of the student, despite teacher and tutor tendencies to appropriate control of the interaction. With only one other person in the conversation, students were guaranteed an interested audience. Voluntary tutorials with me outside of class provided yet additional opportunities to receive social support, something that the women took more advantage of than the men.

The men and women shared similar strategies for responding to the content of one-to-one tutorial interaction. Because the students were generally in greater control of tutorial sessions, academic or known information questions were reduced. However, students occasionally turned the session over to the tutor by requesting information and in such moments, academic questioning did occur. For example, once after Mónica gave me the floor by asking a question about her essay, as tutor I asked a test-like academic question, a known information question of sorts.

> Mónica: But how would I start, like, writing this, like?
> Kay: OK, let's imagine that you were asked to do a summary of just this one piece, what would you start with . . . ? What would you start with in your summary?

Of course, I had an idea of how a summary should start, but I wanted to know if Monica did. I did not realize then, however, that she would not have asked me a question to which she knew the answer. She, like the other students, only asked real questions. Later in the interaction, when it became apparent that Monica truly did not know the standard summary introduction (including title of the piece to be summarized and full name of author), she got the real answer to her real question. Whether students asked general or specific questions, all student questions were real, unlike the tutor's.

The extent to which the tutor assumed control of the interaction varied with each focal student. Some students did not tolerate such known information questions, turning them back on the tutor. For example, when Amado asked if the title of his essay was too long, the tutor responded, "How long do you think a title should be?"— another academic question. Amado repeated his request, "I don't know, you tell me. I don't have enough experience."

During these tutorials, I learned much about the students' personal histories, past educational experiences, and key themes. The bulk of this information is in Chapter Four, statements such as Isaura's, "I would like to work in another thing, but I don't know where to look for work, I don't know what I want, I don't know who can help me." Many of the comments in one-to-one tutorials were of this nature. Students repeatedly made connections between their key themes and the work they were doing for English 10 in an effort to bring meaning to their writing.

For example, my first tutorial session with Juanita involved working on her turning point essay in which she described her fear of returning to school. In preparation for revising the essay, she talked about her life as a migrant student, her current feelings of inadequacy as a student and as a writer, her desire to become a bilingual teacher, and the problems she found with the bilingual teachers at the school where she worked as a migrant aide. All of these topics were related to and came to define her key theme.

Federico usually spent most of our tutorial time talking about various aspects of his key theme: speaking out for social justice. Usually, this talk was directly related to the coursework we were covering in the tutorials—or at least it would start out that way. One tutorial began with a discussion of the lack of computer classes available at the Appleton Center, the topic of his problem–solution essay. Federico linked the lack of computers to the fact that most of the students at the Center were in his words, "Hispanic." He continued to talk about the injustices suffered by Mexican Americans in the community, linking the lack of voter turnout to the fact that many Mexican Americans, in his opinion, were not United States citizens. He blamed the complicated application process for dissuading many from applying. However, he had a solution to the problem.

> I think just a person being here five or ten years, whatever the time limit, should be enough. Have them mail a letter, "Would you like to become a citizen?" Just like American Express.

Although support for taking part in such interactions was built into the course curriculum, when students had the opportunity to see a tutor outside of the classroom, the women focal students chose to take part in one-to-one tutorials more than the men. In these tutorials, the women interacted much as the men did in whole class interaction, initiating a variety of interactions. With the change in the interaction from a fast-paced IRE pattern to a slower IRIR pattern, the women had time to formulate their questions, to ask them, and to get the information that they were not getting from class. They also were much less likely to be interrupted by either a classmate or the tutor. The IRIR pattern allowed the women to choose their own topics and the one-to-one situation provided plenty of social support for their talk. They could be certain their auditor was always interested. Despite the changed structure of interaction in one-to-one tutorials, there were still occasions when the interaction would revert to the academic questioning found in whole class discussions. During unofficial peer talk with these same women, however, such questioning completely vanished and students explored together the real problems of writing.

UNOFFICIAL PEER INTERACTION

During in-class tutorial times, the teacher strongly discouraged talk among the students. She did so with speeches such as this one given when she prepared students for their first tutoring session:

> Now the way this is gonna work is this. Think of this as a kind of workshop. They're [the tutors] going to be coming around and the room might get a little noisy, but we prefer that you don't talk to one another 'cause it's going to be so noisy with just the tutors talking to students, so there'll be a kind of rumble throughout the room, um, we'll try to keep it to a minimum, though.

In describing another class to me, Carol praised the students' silence, saying, "You should hear how quiet it is in there. It's really amazing. Maybe that's another reason why the students are doing better. Maybe there is really a lot more time to devote to the work because they can't monkey around."

Although Carol strictly forbade it, some students frequently chatted during tutorial time while they waited for a tutor to reach them. This unofficial peer interaction allowed students to get information about the class that they did not get during whole class discussions or tutorials. It was also an opportunity to discuss strategies for success in the course, such as revision, and to compare grades and essays. Finally, the women used it as an opportunity to discuss topics of personal interest and to show group solidarity through choice of topic and language. This interaction often occurred in Spanish.

The following discussion, in English, was held informally during one-to-one tutorial time. It shows the kind of talk and the kind of learning that occurred with neither a teacher nor tutor actively involved. Although I was present during the interaction, I was primarily an auditor rather than an active participant.

> Mónica: You know, you know what I didn't do on mine? I didn't describe.
> Marisa: That's what I forgot, too.
> Kay: Oooh.
> Marisa: But I was going to turn it in like that and when she returns it to us, I'm going to re-submit it.
> Mónica: So then, there's no way-
> Juanita: Re-submit, re-submit (Juanita laughs).

Kay: That sounds very professional, doesn't it? Yes, I'm listening.

Marisa: Well, I'm going to turn it in again (laughs).

Mónica: Mine, like there's no way, you know, like I can put it in here, like maybe like, um . . .

Juanita: Well, mine has a part-

Marisa: At the beginning?

Juanita: At the beginning.

Marisa: Or at the end?

Juanita: ( ) at the beginning because it would be more -

Marisa: Appropriate.

Kay: So people could get a mental picture.

Juanita: Yeah.

The women were able to identify problems and solve them together, without any help from experts. In addition, they took part in a full range of interactional moves, asking questions, answering them, displaying an expertise in writing that was rarely revealed in either of the other interactional contexts. Because Carol seldom saw students in one-to-one interaction or unofficial peer interaction, her estimation of their abilities was limited to her observations of their interaction in whole class discussions and with course assignments. Had Carol heard and understood what occurred during this unofficial peer talk, she might have changed her opinion of Juanita and Mónica as near "babies" who "monkeyed around." Instead, she might have considered them as intelligent, capable, young women who were using class time well, rather than wasting it. The men did not take part in such unofficial peer talk. This may be part of the reason they did not produce as many drafts and revisions as the women. The peer interaction encouraged the women to write by creating peer pressure. The men did not have that extra motivating force. In the next section, I describe how the interaction of the men and women appeared to affect Carol's decisions with reference to their placement in English 15.

CLASSROOM INTERACTION AND RECOMMENDATIONS TO ENGLISH 15

In Chapter Four, I presented Carol's method of classifying students vis à vis the skills she felt were necessary for success in English 15. These informal classifications were based, first, on how students wrote on the in-class assessment during the first class meeting and then on how they interacted in whole class discussions. Her opinions were revised, if necessary, after she read students' responses to biweekly essay assignments. By the end of the course, Carol had completed making her judgments of students, including their final grades and her recommendations for future courses in English. Recommendations for future courses were presented to students in conference with the teacher on a form they were to submit with their registration the following semester.

Both Amado and Federico received B-s in English 10. Carol had had high hopes for Amado early on because of his classroom talk, but these were dashed by his lack of production in writing. She described him as a student who gave a very good first impression, but who was little more than a "real good salesman," who sold himself to the teacher "'cause he's so charming" and who knew "how to behave appropriately in any given circumstance," but who didn't do "as much work" and was ultimately a "disappointment." Of Amado, she said:

> I think he did one revision . . . just this pattern, or lack of pattern of revision. I mean, he never did anything that, that it was possible to do.

Similarly, Carol had been impressed by Federico's interaction during whole class discussions and on his first formal essay. However, as with Amado, these interactions led to expectations that were not fulfilled.

> With Federico, I always felt that his confidence [in the classroom]— that's why I expected more of him as a writer. The surface told me that he was a very able writer and thinker and student, and when he didn't perform, it used to make me mad at him. Just like with Amado. The same response to Amado.

At the end of the semester, Carol said of Federico, "There's another student who I'd say stood perfectly still" (an indirect reference to Amado), a "typical re-entry male." Carol said she was disappointed in his progress and "sad that he didn't do better."

Federico and Amado were both recommended to English 15, despite Carol's disappointment with their written performance. She presented her rationale for sending the men on as follows:

> I don't worry so much about students like Federico, that's why I feel like maybe, although he didn't have a very successful 10 course, I'd throw him into 15 and let him make his way, 'cause I think he could. Um, um, Amado was like that. You know. Amado is the same kind of re-entry guy.

The women generally earned course grades equal to or better than the male focal students in English 10, but only one of them was recommended to English 15 and that was done with some hesitation. Although Isaura was ultimately recommended to 15, Carol revealed some second thoughts about doing so, despite giving her an A- as her final grade in the course. On the evening she was to give Isaura her recommendation, she asked me what I thought of Isaura's work, knowing that I had tutored her extensively. I told Carol that I thought Isaura was a "strong writer," and Carol responded:

> I do too and I hate to see her . . . I thought about it a lot and I think she's going to find it a strain. . . . Maybe I'll just warn [her]. Sometimes when I do that, the folks who've thought about it, they decide to wait.

Carol's ambivalence about promoting Isaura may well have been conveyed to Isaura in Carol's "warning" to her. Carol told Isaura:

> For the most part, the assignments are more difficult. . . . You know the one you did tonight on Douglass and Angelou? . . . That's *your* last paper. In my 15 class, that's the first one. So you can see it's. . . . There'd be reading and the usual writing. Um, so it would be very like you're used to here. And you've, you've worked really hard in this class. You wouldn't have it a lot easier.

Isaura did decide to wait. During the year following this course, she did not take any English classes at the community college.

Mónica earned the same grade as Amado and Federico, a B-. Unlike the men, however, she was not recommended for English 15. Instead, Carol suggested that she take another course at the same level as English 10. With Juanita, Mónica had been labeled a near "baby" because she talked or "monkeyed around" during tutorial time when students were supposed to be silently working. Carol was unaware that while the "babies" were talking, they supported and perhaps even pressured each other into revising, taking this opportunity to interact because opportunities to talk in whole class discussion had been denied them. In fact, Carol rarely interacted with Mónica at all, except through written essays and feedback on essays. As I mentioned earlier, Carol had difficulty distinguishing her from Juanita and the other young Mexican American women in the back of the class.

Juanita received a B in English 10, but unlike the men who received lower grades—B-'s—she was *not* recommended to English

15. Instead, Carol recommended that she take another English 10 level course. Juanita immediately recognized that there was "something wrong with this" evaluation and decided she would "challenge" English 15, as she had challenged English 10, rather than repeat the same level of English. To do that she would sign up for English 15 without a recommendation, take the in-class assessment on the first night of class and risk being asked to move to a lower level of English if she failed it.

During an interview, Carol reflected on Juanita as a student in her class:

> She did really well on the final. . . . It was her best grade of the semester. In any case, um, I saw her as a B-/C+ student, and I always send those students to English 10 [again].

Although Juanita's work improved during the semester, culminating in her highest grade of the semester on the final and earning her a "solid B" in the course, the teacher never stopped seeing her as a B-/C+ student and therefore recommended that she take English 10 again. The men, however, both earned B-s in the course, rather than "solid Bs," yet she recommended that they go on to English 15.

Carol's recommendations of Juanita and the focal men appear inconsistent with her general policy regarding recommendations to English 15. In interviews, Carol explained how she made her decisions about recommendations as:

> Anyone who's a solid "B," I figure they can make it in English 15. . . . B-/C+ student who never gets higher than a B, I say, you know, English 10 level is a better place.

Apparently, letter grades on student papers were not the sole basis of teacher recommendations in Carol's class. The differences in how she viewed students as a result of their initial interactions in classroom talk and later, their interaction surrounding course assignments—as re-entry men, re-entry women, babies, or those who've come to the States late in life—appear to have influenced her recommendations as well. Although the re-entry men and women, deemed hard workers in Carol's eyes, were recommended to English 15, the two almost babies (Mónica and Juanita) were not recommended to go on. Furthermore, Carol's recommendation of Isaura was less than enthusiastic, but, it may be recalled, Carol had been unsure initially whether to classify Isaura as one who came to the States late in life or a re-entry woman. Apparently, this ambivalence still affected Carol's decision about Isaura.

From this examination of the interactional differences between Anglo American and Mexican American students and between male and female students, we continue to learn more about the sources of silence among Mexican American students. Indeed, Mexican American students in this class did talk less than their Anglo American counterparts in whole class discussions, but what at first appeared to be differences resulting from ethnicity alone were in fact the result of a combination of factors: ethnicity, gender, and language proficiency.

Although the Mexican American men initiated requests, made comments, and even challenged the teacher during whole class discussions, the women were effectively silenced, speaking only in response to elicitations by the teacher that requested real rather than academic responses or asked specifically about their key themes (unless directly encouraged to initiate by an authority, as in the case of Mónica). The silence of the Mexican American women was also related, in part, to the structure of whole class interaction, specifically, the fast pace and propensity for overlap and interruption found in this classroom. These characteristics of talk in the classroom prevented the focal women from interacting, particularly Isaura who was less proficient in her English speaking. The women used a variety of strategies to attempt to break the silence. The women preferred to speak only after teacher turns that effectively slowed the pace of interaction. Once they had the floor, the women maintained it only by warding off interruptions, some more successfully than others. Words of encouragement or praise appeared to provide direct support for the interaction of the women in whole class discussions.

Other aspects of the interaction also led to silence on the part of the focal women, including the teacher misunderstanding or misinterpreting what was said (both Mónica and Isaura experienced this), a lack of uptake on topics that revealed students' key themes (Juanita's long discourse on elementary school was barely remarked on), and the fact that the women were already unsure of their abilities as students, describing themselves as having "low self-esteem" and directly expressing their fear of speaking in class.

In other interactional contexts, however, the Mexican American women were not silenced and interacted as fully as the men had in whole class discussions. In one-to-one tutorials, both men and women initiated to make requests, statements, and occasionally challenges. Unofficial peer talk also provided support for interaction through social relationships. Although the focal women had to break the teacher's rule about silence in order to interact during class, when they did so, it often led to initiations and responses about real topics related to the course work at hand. In addition, students moved between raising and answering questions easily, revealing academic knowledge that they had been prevented from displaying in whole class discussions. The fact that these conversations often took place in Spanish reveals the importance of L1 for building social support and for developing knowledge. Yet, the teacher did not see the performance of these women in one-to-one tutorials and unofficial peer talk. Moreover, she insisted to me that Spanish was never spoken in her classroom. She only saw these students' writing and their limited interaction in whole class discussions. Using this information, the teacher determined final grades and course recommendations much to the detriment of the women. In the end, none of the women were encouraged to go on to the next level of English, although they had received grades the same as or higher than the men.

Many of the themes that became apparent in the classroom talk of Mexican American students reflect those themes found in their interaction around course assignments in Chapter Five, but with the gender patterns reversed: The women were relatively silent in classroom talk, the men were silent in response to course assignments. In both classroom talk and course assignments, the structure of interaction, whether it was the timing of talk or the timing of assigned revisions and rough drafts, proved problematic to one of the groups. In both contexts, social support played an important role for students who were active participants. In their talk, as in their writing, students showed a preference for interaction that allowed for the expression of key themes in the response to real, as opposed to academic, elicitations, although they were rarely provided "uptake" on such themes. In Chapter Seven, I explore the significance of these findings in greater detail as I discuss their relationship to previous research in related areas.

7
"LISTEN TO THE SILENCES"

Listen to the silences, the unasked questions, the blanks. Listen to
the small, soft voices, often courageously trying to speak up.
—Rich, 1979, p. 243

Listening to silences can be just as instructive as listening to voices,
maybe more so. As Adrienne Rich suggests, unasked questions and
blanks can speak volumes. I designed this study to examine questions of ethnicity and gender in classroom interaction in an attempt
to better understand how Mexican American college students and
their teacher negotiate the literacy learning necessary for success
in a basic writing course. What I found was a silence that shouted
for my attention. Although most studies of Mexican American classroom interaction have focused on either the teacher's treatment of
students (differential treatment) or the differences in interaction
between student homes and the school (cultural mismatch) as
explanations for interactional differences, I attempted to understand the silence of Mexican American students by looking at the
sociocultural and educational context of the classroom (both
diachronically and synchronically), the personal histories and educational experiences of the students and the teacher, and the interaction in the classroom in an attempt to consider a broader range
of influences on their interaction. In the end, I found that numerous factors led to the silence observed in this classroom, not just
the interaction style of the home or that of the teacher.

The students in this study lived and worked in a community,
like many across the United States, in which minorities, in this
case Mexican Americans, have been silenced for generations—
politically, economically, culturally, and linguistically. Schools in
such communities, as institutions of socialization into the local
culture, teach silencing from generation to generation. Students

191

are silenced by a lack of access to equal educational experiences as a result of segregation and a lack of bilingual instruction. In attending these schools and in their lives as members of such communities, minority students experience many moments that teach them they are expected to remain silent and they are not expected to excel. When faced with such situations, many students drop out of school or fail to continue beyond the diploma or high school equivalency exam. The students in this study were exceptional because they persevered despite numerous negative educational experiences. These negative experiences can lead to low self-esteem, but they also lead to developing strategies for coping with these negative experiences.

The situation in which one lives and spends time naturally affects one's perspectives and interests. As a result of their experiences, the students in this study were interested in improving their lives and the lives of other Mexican Americans. The teacher, removed from the lives and school experiences of these students, concerned herself primarily with school, giving little consideration to how school might be made meaningful for students. Although students were highly motivated to attend school and persevered against great odds, they did not participate at a level one would expect, given their great motivation and sacrifice. They did not participate largely because the content of school was not related to what was important in their lives—what I have called their key themes.

Moreover, the teacher—well-meaning, well-educated, and very experienced—seemed unaware of how the structure of interaction in her classroom excluded students by silencing them. She did not consider voice important for them. She used gender and language categories to explain the success and failure of students, but did not examine how her own classroom might have been a contributing factor to such successes and failures. In the end, the Mexican American students contributed far less than the Anglo American students in whole class discussions and course writing assignments. Moreover, there were striking differences in the type and amount of interaction based on gender.

In drawing conclusions from this study, there is a danger of making generalizations about cultural groups (ethnic- or gender-based) that lead to the creation of stereotypes that may govern a teacher's decision-making process and result in behavior that is essentially no different than prejudice. Although it is important to be aware of cultural differences in the classroom, one must not let this awareness interfere with attempts to discover the educational needs of each and every individual in the classroom. This study describes the interaction of a number of quite different individuals in response to a similar classroom, educational, and sociocultural context. Although the ability to generalize the findings of any study as small as this is limited to similar situations, other studies of Mexican American students' classroom interaction and studies of gender differences in classroom interaction coincide with the findings of this study.

My findings present numerous challenges to teachers of Mexican American adults. They suggest the need for teachers to depart from traditional teaching practices and the educational philosophies that they represent, practices and theories, by which many were not only trained but also raised. If such an endeavor is to be successful, constant and considerable reflection are required of the teacher, as is the ability (and willingness) to be both flexible and creative.

SILENCE IN THE MULTICULTURAL CLASSROOM

The Mexican American students were silenced through an interplay of factors: ethnicity, gender, linguistic barriers, the structure and content of the course, and the social and educational context of the community. This silencing interfered with Mexican American students' access to the same educational benefits as their Anglo American counterparts. In general, the Mexican American students—male and female—interacted less frequently than the Anglo American students. The Mexican American men were silenced in written interaction, and the women were silenced in classroom talk. Although both the Mexican American and Anglo American women were relatively silent during whole class discussions compared with the men of their particular ethnic group, there was a greater discrepancy between the interaction of the Mexican American men and women than between Anglo American men and women. Moreover, the Anglo American women, although less verbal than the Anglo American men, were still more talkative than the Mexican American men or women, thereby creating an ethnic and gender hierarchy of interaction in the classroom.

Previous research on gender and classroom interaction among Anglo American and Anglo British girls has also found silence to be a repeated theme. For the most part, Anglo girls have been found to respond with more silence than Anglo boys in the classroom (Eccles & Blumenfeld, 1985; Stanley, 1986; Swann, 1988; Whyte, 1984). Like Swann who found that British 9–11 year-old-boys "chipped in" more often than girls in class discussion, this study revealed that both Anglo American men and Mexican

American men initiated more than the Mexican American women in class discussions. Like the findings of Eccles and Blumenfeld (1985), the boys received more interaction from the teacher.

However, such studies do not explain the ethnic hierarchy found in this classroom or more specifically, why there is such a great difference in the classroom talk of Mexican American men and women. The fact that the Mexican American women speak the least of both Mexican Americans and of women could be a result of the double minority syndrome, an explanation that maintains that women of color are doubly affected (negatively) by virtue of their gender and ethnicity. Although there have not been any studies specifically on the interaction of Mexican American adult women in the classroom prior to this one, Nieto-Gómez (1973) suggests "the quiet Chicana" is a typical response to the conflict between the Chicana student's "traditional role in relation to men" and the role of the "independently minded student" (p. 49). Mirandé and Enríquez (1979) discuss the cultural conflict between the expectations of the home and the expectations of the school, noting, "To the extent that they [Chicanas] conform to these expectations [those of the school] by becoming assertive, competitive, and self-reliant, they deviate from their own cultural expectations"(pp. 132–133). Undoubtedly, the hierarchy within the Mexican American culture has an influence on classroom interaction. It may make the Mexican American women more vulnerable to negative experiences outside the home because their self-esteem has already been damaged. Alone it does not create the patterns of silence and voice described in this book. In fact, family played an important role in providing moral support to the focal women in this study. The Mexican American culture is not solely responsible for the patterns of silence and voice described in this book. In addition to interaction in the home and cultural socialization as factors in students' interaction, past educational experiences, the content and structure of the classes in which they are currently enrolled, and linguistic barriers also play a role.

Furthermore, unlike studies that argue that silence is a successful strategy for the women (Stanley, 1986; Swann, 1988) or that young women are unwilling to participate (Whyte, 1984), this study reveals that Mexican American women were actively developing strategies to break the silence, such as finding openings and warding off interruptions, but they were eventually silenced by the content and structure of whole class interaction.

This study provides a good reason for us to wonder to what extent the interactional differences that were found to be ethnically based in previous research were in fact rooted in gender difference, as they were in this study. It is worth repeating Swacker's (1975) warning that "any sociolinguistic research which does not, at least, specifically give consideration to the sex of the informant might well be of questionable validity" (p. 82). Research that examines classroom interaction across both gender and ethnicity is needed, because previous studies that did not examine gender may provide only half of the story.

The difference in the interaction of the genders across ethnicity in this study is reminiscent of the work of Grant (1985) who found differences in the interaction of young girls and boys across ethnicity and gender in classroom interaction. However, she found that the girls and their teacher interacted *more* than the boys rather than less, as in this study. This finding suggests that girls start out talking more then gradually become silent because gender and ethnic differences are learned, not innate. Socialization that leads to these differences begins early, becoming more fully developed and refined with age, as the work of Edelsky (1977) and Whiting and Edwards (1973) shows. This study highlights the role that the classroom can play in the socialization process through the structure and content of interaction.

The findings of this study also suggest the need to compare the responses discovered here of Mexican American focal students in differing interactional contexts with those of adult students of other ethnicities in an attempt to better understand how interaction is enacted for Mexican American students as well as for students of other ethnicities. It would be interesting to learn if members of other ethnicities respond to similar interactional structures and content with silence and to learn how gender plays a role in any interactional differences discovered. Do differing groups employ different interactional strategies or similar ones in differing amounts? Do students of other ethnicities try to break silence? There is also the need to examine adult gender differences among other ethnic groups. As noted earlier, most gender-related research has been conducted with middle-class Anglo American and British participants.

Structure of Interaction

The structure of interaction in both the course assignment and classroom talk had a silencing effect on Mexican American students. The male Mexican American focal students responded with silence to the structure of interaction surrounding the assignments, that is, the timing and sequence of assignments and revisions during the semester. The female Mexican American focal students responded with silence to the structure of class-room talk, particularly the fast pace of interaction and frequent interruptions by both the teacher and other students, factors that could influence the interaction of women with low self-esteem, particularly non-native speakers of English. In other interactional contexts, however, specifically one-to-one tutorials and unofficial peer talk, the Mexican American focal women were not silent. Instead, they asked questions, made comments, and challenged authority just like the other students in the class, including the Mexican American males.

Previous studies, primarily from the differential treatment per-spective, have also found limited classroom interaction among Mexican American students as compared to their Anglo American counterparts. Like the report of the U.S. Commission on Civil Rights (1973), this study found that Mexican American students initiate and respond less during classroom discussions than Anglo American students. And the rolling interaction style, documented in Carol's college level class, bears a remarkable resemblance to the interaction described in Parsons' 1965 study of the K–8 school in the town of Guadalupe. He found that the teachers asked gen-eral questions to which the Anglo American students responded by shouting out the answers. The Mexican American students, how-ever, did not participate in these activities.

Interactions similar to those found among Mexican American males in this study have also been documented. In Grant's 1985 study of ethnic and gender differences in classroom interaction, both black and white males challenged the teacher in whole class interaction, as much as they did in this study. Females in Grant's study were not found to challenge the teacher, nor did the focal women in this study. By looking at other interactional contexts, however, the present study reveals that Mexican American females *do* challenge, just like the males in whole class interaction. Although there is a qualitative difference between challenging a teacher in front of the class and challenging a tutor privately, both suggest a student's confidence in her knowledge of the subject and in her ability to make a point effectively.

Other studies have also documented differences in Mexican American student interaction patterns depending on the inter-locutors. Students have been found to be silent in whole class dis-cussions but quite interactive in other contexts. Like "Veronica" in the 1981 study by Carrasco, Vera, and Cazden and "Lupita" in

Carrasco (1981), the Mexican American women in English 10 were seen as unresponsive during whole class interaction, but when working in other contexts, particularly with peers, they revealed many more cognitive and language-based skills. In all three studies, the teacher underestimated the students' abilities because of their lack of interaction in the whole class context. As in the case of "Lupita," who was nearly retained a year as a result of a misassessment, Carol's assessment of the Mexican American women affected their academic progress. Both Juanita and Mónica were prevented from moving on to English 15 as a result of Carol's recommendations.

Although this study shows that mismatch between home and school is not the sole source of interactional difference between Mexican American students and their teachers, findings of many mismatch studies suggest that the fast-paced, even competitive nature of the interaction in the classroom may have been at odds with the kind of interaction typically found in Mexican American homes. Adding credence to this finding, is the fact that students seemed quite comfortable in other interactional contexts where the participant structures varied from that found in whole class discussions. The differences in interaction as a result of changes in context that were observed in this study suggest the need to observe students in a variety of classes with a variety of teachers. One wonders: how does interaction occur in other classroom contexts and how do Mexican American students and their other teachers interact?

The lack of interaction with course assignments by Mexican American focal men and the teacher's response to it is reminiscent of studies such as those by Parsons (1965) and the U.S. Commission on Civil Rights (1973) that document teacher perceptions of Mexican American students as putting forth "less effort" or doing less work in school. Such teacher perceptions fail to reveal a consideration of classroom factors, such as the structure of interaction surrounding course assignments, that may contribute to a lack of participation by Mexican American students, especially those with little experience writing in school.

The experiences of students like Amado and Federico also raise questions about process-oriented classrooms (Applebee, 1986; Dyson, 1992). This study found conflicts between the teacher's conception of process as revealed in the structure of assignments and the students' experience of it. There is a continuing need to question how process-oriented theories of teaching writing, the constraints of the classroom, and student writing practice interact in order to further our knowledge of how best to teach composition in the classroom. As Dyson and Freedman (1991) note:

> If the subprocesses of writing are recursive, any classroom structures that demand that all students plan, write, and revise on cue or in that order are likely to run into difficulty. Writers need flexibility, and they need time to allow the subprocesses to cycle back on each other. (p. 760)

In interaction surrounding course assignments, there is a need to imagine alternative methods of reconciling the administrative constraint of evaluating student writing with the unpredictable nature of the writing process, particularly if a teacher professes a process approach. One way that teachers could avoid creating a context that leads to silence on the part of some students would be to have a portfolio assessment in which students work at their own pace to perfect their assignments, with grades being postponed until the end of the semester. In this way, evaluation and feedback would not become confused either, as is often the case.

Social Support

The silencing of Mexican American focal students in this study was ameliorated by various types of social support, including praise and encouragement from the teacher. Mexican American focal students *did* interact when they received social support from the teacher, tutors, or peers. When the teacher praised a student or the tutor suggested talking, students spoke up. When students encouraged each other to interact, as when the women encouraged revising, they were more likely to do so. The men seemed to find support for their talk in whole class interaction from previous successful interactions in similar situations. A rapport was developed between the teacher and the male students that supported further interaction in the same context. Contexts in which students received "uptake," or an interested response, also provided support for interaction.

The Mexican American focal women rarely found support for whole class interaction. Instead, they were interrupted when they attempted to speak (remember Mónica and Isaura), or the topics they raised received little attention, as in Juanita's story of her elementary school experience. Because the men rarely had rough drafts in class, they missed out on the social support for writing available in one-to-one tutorials that they badly needed. Moreover, they rarely took advantage of tutorials outside of class.

As in this study, the importance of social support in the interaction of Mexican American students has been found in other research, primarily that of successful classroom environments for Hispanic students. Ammon (1985) found that a successful classroom environment for bilingual Spanish/English third graders was, among other things, a comfortable environment where students could move about freely and speak in both of their languages without fear of reprisals. Likewise, García, et al. (unpublished manuscript) found that informal classroom environments, in which an almost "familial" relationship existed between the students and teacher, were those in which Latino students were most successful.

Community presents itself, for a variety of reasons, as an appropriate metaphor for the ideal classroom context for students such as those described this study. First of all, it would be appropriate to create a sense of community in the classroom to provide social support for interaction—both classroom talk and course assignments. Such a community would provide an open atmosphere where interaction is structured more like a conversation than an oral exam and where teachers, tutors, and students show interest in what others have to say by following up on it, by asking questions, and by providing other forms of "uptake."

This sense of community ideally would provide students an opportunity to get to know one another and to feel comfortable together so that women, such as Mónica, who felt uncomfortable speaking up until she felt she knew everyone, could feel more at ease in front of the group and take part in interaction more readily. It would also legitimize the type of unofficial interaction that the women in this study engaged in only at the risk of negative sanctions (such as the label *baby*).

Moreover, findings of much of the mismatch research suggest that this environment would more closely resemble the cooperative environment found in Mexican American homes and would provide for a nonthreatening situation in which students could explore new ideas. The use of peer groups and collaborative learning techniques would also mitigate the sense of competition in the classroom that indirectly threatens students and interferes with learning, while enabling students to have more control over the learning situation.

Talk in such a classroom community would be organized to ensure that both Mexican American men and women are included in classroom interaction by providing for a variety of interactional contexts. As noted in Chapter One, the preeminence of social interaction in the learning process is emphasized by Vygotsky

(1978) when he writes, "Human learning presupposes a specific social nature" (p. 88). In this study, if the women had not had alternative contexts for interaction such as one-to-one tutorials and written assignments, it is unclear how some of their questions and ideas would have been articulated. If the men had not been able to interact in whole class discussions, they would not have had an opportunity to express themselves as fully. Although the lessons of this study suggest the need to provide a variety of interactional contexts for students, they do so with the caveat that in no context should silence be considered normal or acceptable, considering what is known about the process of learning.

Britton (1990) argues for the need to allow expressive talk into classroom discussions, talk such as that seen among students outside of the classroom, talk that is "self-presenting and self-revealing" (p. 105). He further notes that "our knowledge of the world is inextricably bound up with the way we feel about the world" (p. 105). He warns, however, that encouraging such discourse requires more than simply removing existing constraints on the structure of interaction in the classroom; it also requires that teachers earn the "trust" of their students (p. 125). He concludes that teachers need to be "flexible" in planning their curriculum, allowing for "negotiation" and "input" from students (p. 127).

The classroom in this study did not provide for any official peer interaction, yet the talk of the women during unofficial peer exchanges revealed the educational value of such interactions, even when they are unplanned by the teacher. Moreover, students like Amado specifically requested opportunities to work with their peers. The appropriateness of such structures in the classroom are suggested by other studies of Mexican American classroom interaction and by the Vygotskian conception that learning can be supported by capable peers.

The role of unofficial peer groups in providing social support for classroom writing and talk among adult students has rarely been studied, yet it became an important factor in student interaction in this study. Questions that this study raised include: How do adults negotiate the creation of peer groups, how do they work to support interaction, and are there gender differences in the uses of these groups? This study also raises questions about the types of interaction that are appropriate in the classroom. In this study, as in others previously cited, interaction that did not fully benefit a good number of students (as evidenced by their silence) was pursued, despite the teacher's knowledge that not all students were responding. Why do teachers continue to value interaction that does not serve the needs of all students, and how do we train teachers in other modes of interaction that will benefit a more diverse student body? These are questions that rarely have been explored yet, they are of considerable concern, particularly when well-informed, well-educated, well-intended, and highly experienced teachers such as Carol continue to pursue methods that poorly serve a number of their students.

Second Language Support

In all interactional contexts, it is important for the teacher to be aware of the special needs of second language speakers and writers. Time, in particular, is of importance to both groups. This study revealed how second language speakers, especially the less self-assured and less-experienced, needed time to prepare what they wished to say aloud. Teachers need to help students gain and keep opportunities to speak, rather than interrupting or letting students interrupt.

In-class writing assignments are also situations in which students who have a first language other than English may suffer, often without a teacher's full awareness. Isaura and Amado both spoke of the difficulties of in-class writing assignments, and the teachers' evaluations of Isaura and Federico changed from negative when she saw their in-class assessments to positive after she saw revisions of them. Translation, grammar, and spelling all take time and effort that is difficult for monolingual teachers to appreciate. Unless it is a teacher's intention to punish students for being non-native speakers and writers of English, he or she must allow for the time these students need to produce English.

A classroom, whether mainstream, ESL, or bilingual, should be accepting and encouraging of all forms of English and Spanish and of code switching. Mexican American students in this class often used Spanish to talk with one another and apparently did not feel hesitant to use it in front of and with their tutor as well. They did not, however, feel they were allowed to use it in more formal classroom contexts or in their writing, and they made certain that the teacher never heard them speak Spanish. Previous research on classrooms with successful Mexican American students found that teachers allowed bilingual students to use both of their languages as they pleased, supporting the use of L1, as well as L2, in the process (Ammon, 1985; Reyes, 1991; Reyes & Laliberty, 1992). Students who are not supported in their use of

L1 show difficulties both academically and behaviorally from very early in their school careers (Laosa, 1977; Trueba, 1983).

The teacher's use of a two-tiered grading system in this study (letter grades for most students, CR grades for recent immigrants) revealed her recognition that evaluation needs to be sensitive to the particular situation of individual students. However, rather than relegating students to repeating a course when they have just begun it, as the CR system did, teachers (and administrators) need to think about alternative methods of assessing all students. These methods not only need to recognize the educational histories of students and their goals, they also need to be sensitive to students' abilities in more than one language. Previous research has shown how easy it is to misassess L2 students if one does not consider their language backgrounds (Carrasco, 1981; Carrasco, Vera & Cazden, 1981; Díaz, Moll, & Mehan, 1986).

Content of Interaction

The Mexican American students' lack of interaction was also influenced by the teacher's preference for academic topics rather real topics in oral and written interaction. Mexican American focal students attempted to voice their key themes in both their writing and talk, but in various ways these efforts were silenced. Students responded with relative silence to both types of classroom interaction studied—course assignments and classroom talk—when the topics were academic. Whenever students were allowed to write about a real topic, they usually wrote about their key themes, but the teacher's goal was for students to acquire academic discourse, and she used topics unrelated to students' interests to accomplish this. The teacher also silenced students indirectly by failing to provide "uptake" when students raised their key themes in essays or class discussion.

As discussed in Chapter Four, students' key themes were intimately tied to their experiences as Mexican Americans in the community of Appleton. The preference of focal students to use key themes in their talk and their writing is corroborated by previous research on successful classrooms for Mexican American students. Other studies have also found that Mexican American students do better when allowed to write about their interests rather than about topics of little relevance to their lives. The students in the study reported by Trueba (1987) and Díaz, Moll, and Mehan (1986) found that successful classes allowed students to have lessons on topics of interest to them and of importance to their community. Similarly, Moll (1988) found that successful teachers of Hispanic students draw upon students' experiences to help them understand their lessons. Ammon (1985) found that successful teachers of Mexican American writers allowed students to write on topics of interest to the students. Unlike the teacher in this study, the teacher in the Ammon study seemed genuinely interested in what students wrote about and showed this interest and concern to the students.

The teacher in this study, Carol, was most interested in preparing students for the next level of English, English 15. She felt obligated to the students and the school to teach students what she knew, from her experience (primarily on the main campus), they would need. Carol was "bureaucratically constrained" (Cicourel & Mehan, 1985) by a course sequence that made her class, English 10, a prerequisite for English 15. Moreover, she felt her professional reputation was at stake. If the students she recommended to English 15 did not perform well at that level, other instructors in the department would think poorly of her teaching. The teacher's reasons for pursuing her curriculum as she did are certainly understandable, leaving the question of how the teacher's goals and the students' might both be met in a single course worth considering.

Although the teacher's goal for her students was that they learn academic discourse in order to prepare for the next level of English, the students viewed such learning as instrumental to other goals, most of them having to do with their positions as Mexican Americans in the community. The perceived needs of her students, the administration, and other teachers kept Carol from pursuing the students' interests as did her own sense of what was appropriate classroom content. However, learning academic discourse is not prevented by allowing student interests—their real topics and key themes—to drive the class assignments. Rather, such student involvement would enhance their learning. Barnes (1990) explains the situation as follows, "The [students] want to understand—not in order to complete a school task or to get a grade—but to pursue a purpose of their own" (p. 46). The example of Federico's rough draft for the Douglass/Angelou compare–contrast essay comes to mind as an example of how student goals and interests and the teacher's might be successfully combined in a lesson. Instead of a basic compare–contrast essay with a thesis provided by the teacher, the assignment could have been a compare–contrast essay for the purpose of providing grist for

Federico's argument about continuing educational discrimination against people of color. To go a step further, the teacher could have suggested other readings related to the educational situation today, perhaps related to the education of Mexican Americans rather than African Americans. Such a change in the assignment would teach the same academic skills, as well as the ability to create an original thesis and the ability to write from an argumentative rather than an expository stance. Allowing students to read and write about topics of interest and concern to them does not jeopardize the learning of academic abilities, rather it enhances them by providing motivation. Along these lines, Vygotsky (1978) suggests that "teaching should be organized in such a way that reading and writing are necessary for something. . . . Writing must be relevant to life . . . and meaningful" (pp. 117–118).

Furthermore, because students bring some background knowledge to such activities, they are better able to work with the material because they have a foundation on which to build. Britton (1990) explains that "learners must bring with them whatever they already know and believe and attempt to re-interpret that in the light of [new] evidence offered. . . . Engagement, then, is a process of knowing, a process in which meaning is negotiated by constructing a version of the unfamiliar from the raw material of the familiar" (pp. 107–108). Had the final essay exam in this class been on a topic in which students had some background knowledge and interest rather than on the bombing of Japan, there might not have been the abysmal results Carol reported. Students would have been better able to successfully complete the readings and ultimately arrive at opinions about the readings.

Here again, *community* provides an ideal metaphor for an appropriate classroom environment. A community shares common concerns and works toward solving or forwarding them. The focal students shared a common interest in the situation of Mexican Americans in the community, and Anglo American students also showed an interest in community affairs, although from a different perspective. Topics with this focus could have provided interesting and meaningful content for the learning of academic skills that the teacher considered important. Moreover, Isaura's goal of improving her spoken English could have easily been met in a class focusing on academic writing, if the teacher had provided a variety of interaction situations that allowed for student talk. The goals of teachers and students can coexist and ultimately be achieved, but only if teacher and students recognize both sets of goals as legitimate and important to making learning meaningful in the classroom. This study reveals a need to further evaluate the qualitative differences in student responses when they are allowed, even encouraged, to connect the content of the course under study to issues of personal interest and importance to them, their key themes.

This study also raises questions about the common notion that academic writing is somehow more advanced than the types of writing that would have been classified as real in this study, such as narrative or personal writing. Furthermore, there is a need to examine the assumption that the best way to improve as a writer is to become a more academic writer with a more expository style. The students in this class were found to rely on "padding," "plagiarizing," and "avoidance" strategies when faced with academic writing tasks. Any high school or college level instructor knows that these strategies can be found across a broad range of students. Therefore, there is a need to better understand how these strategies work—or don't work—to further students' writing abilities. Are they a necessary part of "inventing the university" (Bartholomae, 1985) or do they suggest a more fundamental flaw in our assumptions about how writing should be taught and learned?

Social and Educational Context

The silencing of Mexican Americans in the community and schools of Appleton created a context that allowed the interaction in Carol's classroom to seem normal to her and to her students. For generations, Mexican Americans had been denied participation in political, economic, social, and educational opportunities in the community. The situation of Appleton is not an isolated case. What happened there has happened throughout communities in California and the Southwest (Acuña, 1988; Weinberg, 1977; Wollenberg, 1976). Similar patterns exist for other minorities in the United States as well. A recent example can be found in my current hometown—Durham, North Carolina. The African American community has a history of being disenfranchised—politically, through Jim Crow laws and before that through slavery—and educationally, through segregation and unequal schooling and before that through slavery. Economically, the town thrived on tobacco processing plants rather than frozen food, but as with Mexican Americans in Appleton, the workers with the dirtiest and lowest paying jobs in the plants were African Americans.

Schools that were once *de jure* segregated remain de facto segregated after the unification of two districts. Recently, district officials recommended a desegregation plan that, like the Appleton plan, used two zones and attempted racial balance only within the zones rather than attempting racial balance throughout the district. Predictably, an Anglo American parent organization has now filed suit against the district to prevent the enactment of even this modest, and likely ineffective, desegregation plan.

SILENCE, EDUCATIONAL ACCESS, AND MINORITY ACHIEVEMENT

As outlined in Chapter One, a theoretical assumption of this study is that learning occurs through social interaction. With this perspective, if social interaction does not occur or is limited, then learning is limited or does not occur. When students are put in contexts that lead to silence, they continue to be denied educational equality. Therefore, when the Mexican American focal students were put in educational contexts that led them to respond with silence, their learning was not promoted. Even when they attempted to interact, students failed to receive the help they asked for or needed. For example, when Mónica asked a question about the organization of the final essay, she was interrupted by the teacher and never received a clear response. Similarly, Isaura was interrupted when she asked if the word *labor* was an abstract or concrete word and never received a clear answer. The schedule of drafts and revisions prevented the Mexican American men from receiving the benefits of feedback on early drafts of essays and higher grades as a result of their revisions.

Students also had their educational access limited because the teacher evaluated their ability and progress in the composition course not only on their written work, but also on their verbal interaction in the classroom. This method of evaluation was seen both in Carol's classification of students early in the semester and in her final grades and recommendation at the end of the semester. The tendency for teachers to judge students based on their classroom talk has been noted in other studies as well (Cazden, John, & Hymes, 1972; Hull, Rose, Fraser, & Castellano, 1991; Michaels, 1981). Teachers' judgments of students based on talk is biased in favor of those who interact most similarly to the teacher's preferred mode of interaction, in this case as in most, IRE. The IRE mode, as I noted in Chapter One, predominates in mainstream, middle-class homes, leaving students with different interaction patterns or backgrounds at a distinct disadvantage in terms of current and future educational access.

Furthermore, the use of the IRE pattern, which relies on known information questions and evaluation of students' responses, reveals an underlying philosophy of education that assumes students are empty vessels to be filled with knowledge from an authority (the teacher or the text) that they will regurgitate unchanged for evaluation during whole class discussion. This epistemology does not coincide, however, with theories of how people make new knowledge their own: by making it meaningful to their lives. Barnes (1990) has written that such interaction "ignores what the students already know . . . [which] is the most important element in learning, since new knowledge is built upon the reconstruction of the old" (p. 43). Likewise, Freire (1970) has called this approach to education the "banking" model of education and critiqued it because it "negates education and knowledge as processes of inquiry" (p. 58).

Although most of the focal students were first generation immigrants, because they had spent the majority of their lives in the United States and attended U.S. schools almost exclusively, they had taken on many of the attributes of "caste-like" minorities, as defined by Ogbu and Matute-Bianchi (1986), including the formation of "a sense of peoplehood or collective social identity in opposition to the collective social identity of the dominant group" (p. 94). This sense of collective social identity was evident in the focal students' talk and in their writing about the Mexican American experience in the Appleton area, particularly in their desires to help other Mexican Americans in their fight against educational, political, and economic oppression. However, their opposition was not evident in their interaction in English 10, despite their negative educational experiences past and present.

Students attended school voluntarily. In fact, they were paying for it. They attended regularly, and, in the case of the focal students, they sought outside help. Although, undeniably, students had been ill-treated in their past experiences in school and continued to show signs of ill-feeling and even distrust as a result, this did not prevent them from completing the course, nor did it lead them to act in open hostility toward it. Moreover, the tenacity of some of these students must be taken into account—like Amado, who had taken seven semesters of English to reach the basic writing level, Isaura who stayed up until 2 a.m. to complete her assignments, and Juanita who felt wronged by many of her educational encounters, but continued doggedly to pursue her goal of becoming a bilingual teacher.

Although silence has been interpreted by some researchers as a political response of resistance to the hegemonic educational system (Fine, 1991; Walsh, 1991), there was little evidence in this study to indicate that the silence of these students or students like these was an attempt to resist the education that they were making so many sacrifices to obtain. The classroom data reveal that students tried to interact, but were silenced by the structure and content of interaction. Isaura and Mónica's attempts to interact were thwarted by interruptions. Juanita did not talk because she found the content unengaging. She was quite willing to interact when the subject was pertinent to her interests. Similarly, although the structure of course assignments proved problematic for the men, they also attempted to interact, although sometimes they were not heard because of the way that interaction was structured around assignments. Also, student silence changed with changes in the interactional context, further suggesting that theirs was not an oppositional response. For example, the women who were thwarted in their attempts to interact during whole class discussion interacted quite willingly in one-to-one tutorial sessions. Likewise, although the men's revisions were not heard in the context of course assignment interaction, they did revise, nonetheless.

Rather than expressing opposition to the dominant society in school, these students found schooling instrumental to the expression of their opposition in other contexts, such as the workplace. As noted in Chapter Four, when Juanita was asked why she continued with school in the face of so many negative experiences, she replied:

> I know that I need this English class for what I want to do. And I know that I need to improve, and I know that I have to, you know, keep going and not give up because then that will be the end of it . . . if I think that way. I think that you have to think positive, not negative, and if there's someone that wants to put me down, well fine, that person has a problem.

She needed the class in order to reach her goal of becoming a bilingual teacher, which was first, a response to her own experiences as a bilingual Mexican American student but ultimately, a response to the situation of other bilingual Mexican Americans in similar situations.

The students' personal experiences and educational histories were affected by the history of social, political, and educational silencing described in Chapter Three. They were affected by economic injustices, educational injustices, and political injustices that stemmed from generations of such interaction between Anglo American and Mexican Americans in California. Despite these facts, they did not oppose or resist education self-destructively, in the manner described by resistance theorists (Giroux, 1983; Willis, 1977), rather they embraced it as a way to constructively respond to their oppression and to support their work within the system to change the situation of Mexican Americans. The students were not passive victims in the classroom or outside of it. In both contexts, they actively sought to break the silence that generations of Mexican Americans before them had failed to escape. Certain assumptions about the meaning of silence to women and ethnic minorities in the classroom must be reconsidered.

In writing about the classroom silence of women and other traditionally oppressed groups, Adrienne Rich (1979) implores her readers to "listen to the silences, the unasked questions, the blanks" (p. 243). As teachers and researchers, we should accept Rich's challenge. We should notice silences in the classroom, in whatever form they may take, we should attempt to understand the various contexts that create these silences and their meanings to the silenced, and ultimately, we should refuse to accept silence as the status quo.

APPENDIX A

TRANSCRIPTION CONVENTIONS

( )	Unintelligible on tape.
((word))	Educated guess at what was said.
(laughs)	Nonverbal cues and action.
[ ]	Information added by researcher to help the reader interpret the transcript, translations.
Student: But- Teacher: -Yes	Interruptions.
|Amy: |Stevie:	Simultaneous talk.
. . .	Text removed for ease of reading.

APPENDIX B

Name_____Assignment_____
0–Unacceptable 1–Poor 2–Weak 3–Average 4–Good 5–Excellent

RHETORIC
Well–defined thesis
  and clear plan
  of development   0   1   2   3   4   5
Organization; solid
  supporting evidence;
  maintaining focus   0   1   2   3   4   5
                                      ____ x 5 = ____
                                      Subtotal

LANGUAGE
Style; individuality;
  readability   0   1   2   3   4   5
Word choice   0   1   2   3   4   5
                                      ____ x 3 = ____
                                      Subtotal

EDITING
Grammar; sentence
  structure, usage   0   1   2   3   4   5
Punctuation   0   1   2   3   4   5
Spelling   0   1   2   3   4   5
Form and Appearance 0   1   2   3   4   5
                                      ____ x 1 = ____
                                      Subtotal

Comments

REFERENCES

Acuña, R. (1988). *Occupied America: A history of Chicanos.* (3rd ed.). New York: Harper & Row.

Aguirre, A., Jr. & Martinez, R. (1993). *Chicanos in higher education: Issues and dilemmas for the 21st century.* ASHE–ERIC Higher Education Report No. 3. Washington, DC: The George Washington University, School of Education and Human Development.

Alvarado, E. (1990a, March 12). A bigger [Portolá] in the year 2000. *[Appleton Daily News],* p. 11.

Alvarado, E. (1990b, May 10). Complaints surface about downtown festival. *[Appleton Daily News],* pp. 1, 9.

Alvarado, E. (1990c, May 24). Task force calls for new desegregation plan. *[Appleton Daily News],* p. 9.

Ammon, P. (1985). Helping children to write in English as a second language. Some observations and some hypotheses. In S. W. Freedman (Ed.), *The acquisition of written language: Revision and response* (pp. 65–84). Norwood, NJ: Ablex.

Applebee, A. (1986). Problems in process approaches: Toward a reconceptualization of process instruction. In A. R. Petrosky, & D. Bartholomae (Eds.), *The teaching of writing* (pp. 95–113). Chicago, IL: National Society for the Study of Education.

[Appleton] Valley Chamber of Commerce. (1991, September), [Appleton] community economic profile. Appleton, CA: Author. p. 5.

Ball, K, (1989, May 18). Task force on school desegregation set up. *Appleton Daily News,* p. 9.

Barnes, D. (1990). Oral language and learning. In S. Hynds & D. L. Rubin (Eds.), *Perspectives on talk and learning* (pp. 41–54). Urbana, IL: National Council of Teachers of English.

Bartholomae, D. (1985). Inventing the university. In M. Rose (Ed.), *When a writer can't write* (pp. 134–165). New York: Guilford Press.

Bartholomae, D. & Petrosky, A. (Eds.). (1986). *Facts, artifacts and counterfacts: Theory and method for a reading and writing course.* Portsmouth, NH: Boynton/Cook.

Brazil, E. (1990, October 28). "Apple City" is wave of the future. *San Francisco Examiner,* pp. B–1, B–3.

Britton, J. (1990). Talking to learn. In D. Barnes, J. Britton, & M. Torbe (Eds.), *Language, the learner, and the school* (pp. 91–130). Portsmouth, NH: Boynton/Cook.

Brophy, J. & Good, T. (1974). *Teacher–students relationships: Causes and consequences.* New York: Holt, Rinehart and Winston.

Brown, G. H., Rosen, N. L., Hill, S. T., & Olivas, M. A. (1980). *The condition of education for Hispanic Americans.* Washington, DC: National Center for Education Statistics.

Bruner, J. (1990). *Acts of meaning.* Cambridge, MA: Harvard University Press.

Camarillo, A. (1979). *Chicanos in a changing society.* Cambridge, MA: Harvard University Press.

Camarillo, A. (1984). *Chicanos in California: A history of Mexican Americans in California.* San Francisco: Boyd & Fraser.

Carrasco, R. L. (1981). Expanded awareness of students performance: A case study in applied ethnographic monitoring in the bilingual classroom. In H. T. Trueba, G. P. Guthrie, & K. H. Au (Eds.), *Culture and the bilingual classroom* (pp. 153–177). Rowley, MA: Newbury House.

Carrasco, R. L., Vera, A., & Cazden, C. B. (1981). Aspects of bilingual students' communicative competence in the classroom: A case study. In R. P. Durán (Ed.), *Latino language and communicative behavior* (pp. 237–249). Norwood, NJ: Ablex.

Carter, D. & Wilson, R. (1993). *Minorities in higher education, 1992. Eleventh annual status report.* Washington, DC: American Council on Education (ERIC Document Reproduction Service No. ED 363 250).

Carter, T. P. & Segura, R. D. (1979). *Mexican Americans in school: A decade of change.* New York: College Entrance Examination Board.

Casso, H. J. (1975). Higher education and the Mexican American. In G. Tyler, (Ed.), *Mexican Americans tomorrow: Educational and economic perspectives* (pp. 137–163). Albuquerque, NM: University of New Mexico Press.

Cazden, C. (1973). Problems for education: Language as curriculum content and learning environment. In E. Haugen & L. Bloomfield (Eds.), *Language as a human problem* (pp. 137–150). New York: W.W. Norton & Co.

Cazden, C. B. (1988). *Classroom discourse: The language of teaching and learning.* Portsmouth, NH: Heinemann.

Cazden, C. B., John, V., & Hymes, D. (Eds.). (1972/1985). *Functions of language in the classroom.* Prospect Heights, IL: Waveland.

Census committee says city faces undercount. (1990, July 11). *[Appleton Daily News]*, p. 13.

Cepeda, R. (1986). Significance of transfer for Blacks and Hispanics. *California Community College News, 3*(2), 4–6.

Cervantes, C. (1991, Jan. 4). Love it or leave it. [Letter to the editor]. *[Appleton Daily News]*, p. 24.

Chacón, M., Cohen, E. G., Camarena, M., Gonzalez, J., & Strover, S. (1982). *Chicanas in postsecondary education.* Palo Alto, CA: Center for Research on Women, Stanford University.

Chacón, M. A., Cohen, E. G., & Strover, S. (1986). Chicanas and Chicanos: Barriers to progress in higher education. In M. A. Olivas

(Ed.), *Latino college students* (pp. 296–324). New York: Teachers College Press.

Cicourel, A. & Mehan, H. (1985). Universal development, stratifying practices, and status attainment. In D. J. Treiman & R. V. Robinson (Eds.), *Research in social stratification and mobility, Vol. 4* (pp. 3–27). Greenwich, CT: JAI Press.

Cinco de Mayo has become big event. (1991, May 7). [*Appleton Daily News*], p. 24.

Coates, J. (1986). *Women, men, and language: A sociolinguistic account of sex differences in language.* London: Longman.

Cummins, J. (1986). Empowering minority students: A framework for intervention. *Harvard Educational Review, 56,* 18–36.

Davies, L. (1983). Gender, resistance and power. In S. Walker & L. Barton, (Eds.), *Gender, class and education* (pp. 39–52). London: Falmer.

Delgado–Gaitan, C. (1987). Traditions and transitions in the learning process of Mexican children: An ethnographic view. In G. Spindler & E. Spindler (Eds.), *Interpretive ethnography of education at home and abroad* (pp. 333–359). Hillsdale, NJ: Erlbaum.

de los Santos, A. G., Jr. (1984). The connection between postsecondary programs for Hispanics and elementary and secondary schools. In S. H. Aldophus (Ed.), *Equality postponed: Continuing barriers to higher education in the 1980's* (pp. 68–84). New York: College Entrance Examination Board.

Dewey, J. (1916/1944). *Democracy and education.* New York: The Free Press/Macmillan Publishing.

Digest of education statistics, 1994. Washington, DC: U.S. Department of Education, National Center for Education Statistics.

Dixon, B. L. (1988). *Success of Hispanic students in English classes.* Rancho Santiago, CA: Rancho Santiago Community College District.

Díaz, S., Moll, L. C., & Mehan, H. (1986). Sociocultural resources in instruction: A context specific approach. In California State Department of Education (Ed.), *Beyond language: Social and cultural factors in schooling language minority students* (pp. 187–230). Los Angeles: Evaluation, Dissemination and Assessment Center, California State University, Los Angeles.

Donato, R. (1987). *In struggle: Mexican Americans in the [Appleton] Valley schools, 1900–1979.* Unpublished doctoral dissertation, Stanford University, Palo Alto, CA.

Dumont, R. (1972). Learning English and how to be silent: Studies in Sioux and Cherokee classrooms. In C. B. Cazden, V. P. John, & D. Hymes (Eds.), *Functions of language in the classroom* (pp. 344–369). Prospect Heights, IL: Waveland.

Dunn, G. (1989). *Santa Cruz is in the heart.* Capitola, CA: Capitola Book Co.

Dyson, A. H. (1992). The case of the singing scientist: A performance perspective on the "stages" of school literacy. *Written Communication*, *9*(1), 3–47.

Dyson, A. H. & Freedman, S. W. (1991). Writing. In J. Flood, J. Jensen, D. Lapp, & J. Squire (Eds.), *Handbook of research on teaching the language arts* (pp. 754–774). New York: MacMillan.

Eccles, J. S. & Blumenfeld, P. (1985). Classroom experiences and student gender: Are there differences and do they matter? In L. C. Wilkinson & C. B. Marrett (Eds.), *Gender influences in classroom interaction* (pp. 79–114). Orlando, FL: Academic Press.

Edelsky, C. (1977). Acquisition of an aspect of communicative competence: Learning what it means to talk like a lady. In S. Ervin–Tripp, & C. Mitchell-Kernan (Eds.), *Child discourse* (pp. 225–243). New York: Academic Press.

Elsasser, N., & John–Steiner, V. P. (1977). An interactionist approach to advancing literacy. *Harvard Educational Review, 47*(3), 355–369.

English Department handbook. (1991, Fall). Portolà Community College.

Erickson, F. (1982). Taught cognitive learning in its immediate environments: A neglected topic in the anthropology of education. *Anthropology and Education Quarterly, 8*, 149–180.

Erickson, F. (1987). Transformation and school success: The politics and culture of educational achievement. *Anthropology and Education Quarterly, 18*, 335–383.

Fillmore, L. W. (1982). Instructional language as linguistic input: Second language learning in classrooms. In L. C. Wilkinson (Ed.), *Communicating in the classroom* (pp. 283–296). New York: Academic Press.

Fine, M. (1989). Silencing and nurturing voice in an improbable context: Urban adolescents in public school. In H. A. Giroux & P. L. McLaren (Eds.), *Critical pedagogy, the state, and cultural struggle* (pp. 152–173). Albany, NY: State University of New York Press.

Fine, M. (1991). *Framing drop–outs: Notes on the politics of an urban high school.* Albany, NY: State University of New York Press.

Fingeret, A. (1989). The social and historical context of participatory literacy education. In A. Fingeret & R. Jurmo (Eds.), *Participatory literacy education.* San Francisco: Jossey-Bass.

Fink, A. (1982). *Monterey County: The dramatic story of its past.* Santa Cruz, CA: Western Tanager Press/Valley Publishers.

Fishman, P. M. (1983). Interaction: The work women do. In B. Thorne, C. Kramarae, & N. Henley (Eds.), *Language, gender & society* (pp. 89–101). New York: Newbury House.

Fraser, K.L. (1990). *The rhetoric of Rhetoric 10: Classroom and conference interaction in a college composition course.* Unpublished manuscript. University of California at Berkeley, Graduate School of Education.

Freire, P. (1970). *Pedagogy of the oppressed.* New York: The Seabury Press.

Galaviz, F. & McGrath, P. (unpublished manuscript). *Puente Project: Building bridges.* Unpublished manuscript. Chabot Community College, Hayward, CA.

Gallagher, P. (1989, Fall). A pocket history of [Portolá] College. *Student guide,* p. 68.

García, E. E. (1983). *Early childhood bilingualism: With special reference to the Mexican–American child.* Albuquerque, NM: University of New Mexico Press.

García, E. E. & Carrasco, R. L. (1981). An analysis of bilingual mother–child discourse. In R. P. Durán (Ed.), *Latino language and communicative behavior* (pp. 257–270). Norwood, NJ: Ablex.

García, E. E., Flores, B., Moll, L. C., Prieto, A., & Zucker, S. (unpublished manuscript). *Effective schools for Hispanics.* Unpublished manuscript.

Gearing, F. & Epstein, P. (1982). Learning to wait: An ethnographic probe into the operations of an item of the hidden curriculum. In G. Spindler (Ed.), *Doing the ethnography of schooling: Educational anthropology in action* (pp. 240–267). New York: Holt, Rinehart and Winston.

Gilligan, C. (1982). *In a different voice: Psychological theory and women's development.* Cambridge, MA: Harvard University Press.

Giroux, H. A. (1983). Theories of reproduction and resistance in the new sociology of education: A critical analysis. *Harvard Educational Review, 53,* 257–293.

Gomez, et al. v. The City of [Appleton], 88 C.D.O.S. 5379.

Goodenough, W. (1971). *Culture, language and society.* Reading, MA: Addison-Wesley.

Goodwin, M. H. (1980). Directive–response speech sequences in girls' and boys' task activities. In S. McConnell–Ginet, R. Borker, & N. Furman (Eds.), *Women and language in literature and society* (pp. 157–173). New York: Praeger.

Goodwin, M. H. (1990a). *He said–She said: Talk as social organization among Black children.* Bloomington, IN: Indiana University Press.

Goodwin, M. H. (1990b). Tactical uses of stories: Participation frameworks within girls' and boys' disputes. *Discourse Processes, 13,* 33–71.

Grant, L. (1985). Race–gender status, classroom interaction, and children's socialization in elementary school. In L. C. Wilkinson & C. B. Marrett (Eds.), *Gender influences in classroom interaction* (pp. 57–77). Orlando, FL: Academic Press.

Griswold del Castillo, R. (1990). *The Treaty of Guadalupe Hidalgo: A legacy of conflict.* Norman, OK: The University of Oklahoma Press.

Gumbiner, J., Knight, G. P., & Kagan, S. (1981). Relations of classroom structures and teacher behaviors to social orientation, self–esteem, and classroom climate among Anglo American and Mexican American children. *Hispanic Journal of the Behavioral Sciences, 3,* 19–40.

Gumperz, J. J. & Hernández–Chavez, E. (1972/1985). Bilingualism, bidialectalism, and classroom interaction. In C. Cazden, V. P. John, &

D. Hymes (Eds.), *Functions of language in the classroom* (pp. 84–107). Prospect Heights, IL: Waveland.

Gutierrez, K. D. (1992). A comparison of instructional contexts in writing process classrooms with Latino children. *Education and Urban Society, 24,* 244–262.

Hakuta, K. (1986). *Mirror of language: The debate on bilingualism.* New York: Basic Books.

Heath, S. B. (1983). *Ways with words.* Cambridge: Cambridge University Press.

Heckman, S. (1990, May 4). Excitement builds for Cinco de Mayo. *[Appleton Daily News],* pp. 1, 9.

Heizer, R. F. & Almquist, A. F. (1971). *The other Californians: Prejudice and discrimination under Spain, Mexico, and the United States to 1920.* Berkeley, CA: University of California Press.

Hendrick, I. G. (1977). *The education of non–whites in California, 1849–1970.* San Francisco: R & E Research Associates, Inc.

hooks, b. (1989). Talking back: Thinking feminist, thinking black. Boston: South End Press.

Hudson, J. (1988, September 9). Hispanic counselor helps others beat odds. *[Appleton Daily News],* p. 4.

Hull, G. & Greenleaf, C. (1990, June). *You got to wisen up: The remedial composition class as gatekeeper.* Paper presented at the Young Rhetorician's Conference, Monterey, CA.

Hull, G., Rose, M., Fraser, K. L., & Castellano, M. (1991). Remediation as social construct: Perspectives from an analysis of classroom discourse. *College Composition and Communication, 42*(3), 299–329.

Hymes, D. H. (1972). Models of the interaction of language and social life. In J. J. Gumperz & D. Hymes (Eds.), *Directions in sociolinguistics* (pp. 35–71). New York: Holt, Rinehart & Winston.

Hymes, D. H. (1974). *Foundations in sociolinguistics: An ethnographic approach.* Philadephia: University of Pennsylvania Press.

Johnson, B. (1988a, June 13). School rules debated: Bilingual class assignments. *San Jose Mercury News,* p. 1B.

Johnson, B. (1988b, August 3). *San Jose Mercury News,* p. 10.

Johnson, B. (1988c, September 1). Voting for a change. *The Sun,* pp. 12, 13.

Johnson, B. (1989a, April 24). Bilingual plan is adopted: [Appleton] trustees accept proposal. *San Jose Mercury News,* pp. 1B, 4B.

Johnson, B. (1989b, April 28). Segregation is under review by [Appleton] area schools. *San Jose Mercury News,* pp. 1B, 2B.

Johnson, B. (1990, May 30). Integration efforts questions: [Appleton] schools remain segregated. *San Jose Mercury News,* pp. 1B, 2B.

Jordan, C. (1985). Translating culture: From ethnographic information to educational program. *Anthropology and Education Quarterly, 16,* 105–123.

Keller, G. D. & Van Hooft, K. S. (1982). A chronology of bilingualism and bilingual education in the United States. In J. A. Fishman & G. D.

Keller (Eds.), *Bilingual education for Hispanic students in the United States* (pp. 3–19). New York: Teachers College Press.

Kitts, A. (1990). Student airs grievances to board. *[Portolá College Press]*, pp. 1, 3.

Knowles, M. (1973/1978). *The adult learner: A neglected species.* (2nd ed.). Houston, TX: Gulf.

Koch, M. (1973). *Santa Cruz County: Parade of the past.* Fresno, CA: Valley Publishers.

Koss, J. (1989, January 11). Election suit protest. *[Appleton Daily News]*, p. 1.

Krashen, S. D. (1976). Formal and informal linguistic environments in language acquisition and language learning. *TESOL Quarterly, 10,* 157–168.

Labov, W. (1972). *Language in the inner city: Studies in the Black English Vernacular.* Philadelphia: University of Pennsylvania Press.

Lakoff, R. (1975). *Language and woman's place.* New York: Harper & Row.

Laosa, L. M. (1977). Inequality in the classroom: Observational research on teacher–student interactions. *Aztlán: The International Journal of Chicano Studies Research, 8,* 51–67.

Laosa, L. M. (1981). Maternal behavior: Sociocultural diversity in modes of family interaction. In R. W. Henderson (Ed.), *Parent–child interaction: Theory, research, and prospects* (pp. 125–167). New York: Academic Press.

Laosa, L. M. (1982). School, occupation, culture and family: The impact of parental schooling on the parent–child relationship. *Journal of Educational Psychology, 74,* 791–827.

Last desegregation hearing tonight. (1990, February 13). *[Appleton Daily News]*, p. 9.

Lave, J. (1988, May). *The culture of acquisition and the practice of understanding.* (IRL Report #88–0007), Palo Alto, CA: Institute for Research on Learning.

LeCompte, M. D. (1981). The Procrustean bed: Public schools, management systems, and minority students. In H. T. Trueba, G. P. Guthrie, & K. H. Au (Eds.), *Culture and the bilingual classroom* (pp. 178–195). Rowley, MA: Newbury House.

Lewis, B. (1976/1986). *[Appleton]: Memories that linger.* Volume I. Santa Cruz, CA: Otter B Books.

Lewis, B. (1980). *[Appleton]: Memories that linger.* Volume II. Santa Cruz, CA: Valley Publishers.

Lydon, S. (1989, December 26). How history was made in the 1980's. *[Appleton Daily News]*, p. 13.

Lydon, S. (1980). Introduction. In L. Rowland, *Santa Cruz: The early years* (pp. xi–xvi). Santa Cruz, CA: Paper Vision.

Lydon, S. (1985). *Chinese gold: The Chinese in the Monterey Bay region.* Capitola, CA: Capitola Book Company.

Madrid, A. (1986). Foreward. In M. A. Olivas (Ed.), *Latino college students* (pp. ix–xvii). New York: Teachers College Press.

Malmin, J. P. (1982). *Corralitos*. Self-published.

Maltz, D. N. & Borker, R. A. (1982). A cultural approach to male–female communication. In J. J. Gumperz (Ed.), *Language and social identity* (pp. 196–216). Cambridge: Cambridge University Press.

Manuel, H. T. (1965). *Spanish–speaking children of the Southwest: Their education and public welfare*. Austin, TX: University of Texas Press.

McClure, E. (1978). Teacher and pupil questions and responses and the Mexican–American child. *The Bilingual Review: La Revista Bilingüe, 5* (1&2), 40–44.

McDermott, R. P. & Gospodinoff, K. (1981). Social contexts for ethnic borders and school failure. In H. T. Trueba, G. P. Guthrie, & K. H–P. Au (Eds.), *Culture and the bilingual classroom: Studies in classroom ethnography* (pp. 212–230). Rowley, MA: Newbury House.

McGowan, R. J. & Johnson, D. L. (1984). The mother–child relationship and other antecedents of academic performance: A causal analysis. *Hispanic Journal of Behavioral Sciences, 6*, 205–224.

McLaughlin, B. (1985). *Second–language acquisition in childhood: Vol. 2. School–age children*. (2nd ed.). Hillsdale, NJ: Erlbaum.

McWilliams, C. (1948/1968). *North from Mexico: The Spanish–speaking people of the United States*. New York: Greenwood.

Mehan, H. (1978). Structuring school structure. *Harvard Educational Review, 48*(1), 32–64.

Mehan, H. (1979). *Learning lessons*. Cambridge: Cambridge University Press.

Meier, K. J. & Stewart, J., Jr. (1991). *The politics of Hispanic education: Un paso pa'lante y dos pa'tras*. Albany, NY: State University of New York Press.

Michaels, S. (1981). "Sharing time": Children's narrative styles and differential access to literacy. *Language in Society, 10*, 423–442.

Miller, S. (1982). Classical practice and contemporary basics. In J. J. Murphy (Ed.), *The rhetorical tradition and modern writing*. New York: Modern Language Association.

Mirandé, A. & Enríquez, E. (1979). *La Chicana: The Mexican American woman*. Chicago: University of Chicago Press.

Moffett, J. (1981/1988). *Coming on center: Essays in English education*. Portsmouth, NH: Boynton/Cook.

Moll, L. C. (1988). Some key issues in teaching Latino students. *Language Arts, 65*, 465–472.

Moran, C. (1990, May 19). Bilingual ed works. [Letter to the Editor]. *[Appleton Daily News]*, p. 13.

Morse, L. W. & Handley, H. M. (1985). Listening to adolescents: Gender differences in science classroom interaction. In L. C. Wilkinson & C. B. Marrett (Eds.), *Gender influences in classroom interaction* (pp. 37–56). Orlando, FL: Academic Press.

Mylar, I. L. (1929/1970). *Early days at the Mission San Juan Bautista*. Fresno, CA: Valley Publishers.

National dropout statistics field test. (1992). Statistical Analysis Report. Washington, DC: American Institutes for Research. (ERIC Document Reproduction Service No. ED 341 723)

Nichols, P. C. (1980). Women in their speech communities. In S. McConnell-Ginet, R. Borker, & N. Furman (Eds.), *Women and language in literature and society* (pp. 140–149). New York: Praeger.

Nichols, P. C. (1983). Linguistic options and choices for Black women in the rural South. In B. Thorne, C. Kramarae, & N. Henley (Eds.), *Language, gender and society* (pp. 54–68). New York: Newbury House.

Nieto–Gómez, A. (1973, Spring). The Chicana perspective for education. *Encuentro Femenil,* pp. 34–61.

Nystrand, M. & Gamoran, A. (1991). Instructional discourse, student engagement, and literature achievement. *Research in the Teaching of English, 25*(3), 261–290.

Office of Institutional Research. (1990-1991). *[Portolà] College fact book.* [Shoreline] CA: [Portolà] Community College.

Office of Student Research. (1983). *Background data for discussion of retention of underrepresented minority students.* Berkeley, CA: Office of Student Research.

Ogbu, J.U. (1978). *Minority education and caste.* New York: Academic Press.

Ogbu, J.U. (1982). Socialization: A cultural ecological approach. In K. Borman (Ed.), *The socialization of children in a changing society* (pp. 253–267). Hillsdale, NJ: Erlbaum.

Ogbu, J.U., & Matute–Bianchi, M. E. (1986). Understanding sociocultural factors: Knowledge, identity, and school adjustment. In California Department of Education (Ed.), *Beyond language: Social and cultural factors in schooling language minority students* (pp. 73–142). Los Angeles: Evaluation, Dissemination and Assessment Center, California State University, Los Angeles.

Ortiz, F.I. (1977). Bilingual education program practices and their effect upon students' performance and self–identity. *Aztlán: International Journal of Chicano Studies Research, 8,* 157–174.

Ortiz, F.I. (1988). Hispanic–American children's experiences in classrooms: A comparison between Hispanic and non–Hispanic children. In L. Weis (Ed.), *Class, race, and gender in American education* (pp. 63–86). New York: State University of New York Press.

Orum, L.S. (1986). *The education of Hispanics: Status and implications.* Washington, DC: National Council of La Raza.

Parmeter, S–H. (1990). A test of cultural literacy. *Central California Writing Project Newsletter, 3*(4), 3–5.

Parsons, T.W., Jr. (1965). *Ethnic cleavage in a California school.* Unpublished doctoral dissertation, Stanford University, Palo Alto, CA.

Philips, S.U. (1972/1985). Participant structures and communicative competence: Warm Springs children in community and classroom. In C.

B. Cazden, V. P. John, & D. Hymes (Eds.), *Functions of language in the classroom* (pp. 370–394). Prospect Heights, IL: Waveland.

Pitt, L. (1966). *The decline of the Californios: A social history of the Spanish–speaking Californians, 1846–1890.* Berkeley, CA: University of California Press.

Portolà College Governing Board meeting minutes. (1987, March 2).

Portolà picked to launch new program. (1990, August 17). [*Appleton Daily News*], p. 15.

Preliminary planning report for an [Appleton] Center. (1987, April 6). Office of the President. [Portolà] Community College. [Shoreline], CA. 9 pp.

Professional Development Program, University of California, Berkeley (1990). [*Minority placement and achievement statistics: Subject A*]. Unpublished raw data.

Proud winners. (1991, March 25). [*Appleton Daily News*], p. 11.

Quarnstrom, L. (1990, December 10). Rubbing elbows? No, not exactly. *San Jose Mercury News*, p. 1B.

Revised Minutes of the Off-Campus Ad Hoc Committee. (1991, April 1) [Portolà] Community College.

Reyes, M. de la Luz (1991). A process approach to literacy using dialogue journals and literature logs with second language learners. *Research in the Teaching of English, 25*, 291–313.

Reyes, M. de la Luz & Laliberty, E. A. (1992). A teacher's "Pied Piper" effect on young authors. *Education and Urban Society, 24*, 263–278.

Reynolds, A. (1933). *The education of Spanish–speaking children in five Southwestern states.* Office of Education Bulletin 1933, No. 11. Washington, DC: U.S. Department of the Interior.

Rich, A. (1979). *On lies, secrets, and silence: Selected prose 1966–1978.* New York: W.W. Norton & Co.

Rodríguez, R.G. (1991). [*Portolá*] *College Fact Book, 1990–1991.* [Portolá], CA: [Portolá] College Office of Institutional Research.

Rodríguez-Brown, F. & Elías-Olivares, L. (1983). Linguistic repetoires, communicative competence and the Hispanic child. In C. Rivera (Ed.), *An ethnographic/socio-linguistic approach to language proficiency assessment* (pp. 27-41). Clevedon, England: Multilingual Matters.

Romo, R. (1983). *East Lost Angeles: History of a barrio.* Austin, TX: University of Texas Press.

Rosenthal, R. & Jacobson, L. (1968). *Pygmalion in the classroom: Teacher expectations and pupils' intellectual development.* New York: Holt, Rinehart and Winston.

Sacks, H., Schegloff, E. A., & Jefferson, G. (1974). A simplest systematics for the organization of turn–taking in conversation. *Language, 50*, 696–735.

Sánchez, R. (1983). *Chicano discourse: Socio–historic perspectives.* Rowley, MA: Newbury House.

Santa Cruz County's logging. (1990, July 16). *San Jose Mercury News*, p. 6A.

Sapiens, A. (1982). The use of Spanish and English in a high school bilingual civics class. In J. Amastae & L. Elías–Olivares (Eds.), *Spanish in the United States: Sociolinguistic aspects* (pp. 386–412). Cambridge: Cambridge University Press.

Schumann, J. H. (1978). The acculturation model for second language acquisition. In R. Gingrass (Ed.), *Second language acquisition and foreign language teaching*. Washington, DC: Center for Applied Linguistics.

Serbin, L. A., O'Leary, K. D., Kent, R. N., & Tonick, I. L. (1973). A comparison of teacher response to the preacademic and problem behavior of boys and girls. *Child Development, 44*, 796–804.

Shaughnessy, M. (1977). *Errors and expectations*. New York: Oxford University Press.

Sheldon, A. (1990). Pickle fights: Gendered talk in preschool disputes. *Discourse Processes, 13*, 5–31.

Shuy, R. (1969, February). *Sex as a factor in sociolinguistic research*. Paper presented at the Anthropological Society of Washington, Washington, DC. (ERIC Document Reproduction Service No. ED 027 522)

Silver, J. (1989). *[Appleton] on strike*. [Film]. [Appleton], CA: Migrant Media Education Project.

Skutnabb–Kangas, T. (1981). *Bilingualism or not: The education of minorities*. Clevedon, England: Multilingual Matters.

Soifer, R., Irwin, M., Crumrine, B., Honzaki, E., Simmons, B., & Young, D. (1990). *The complete theory–to–practice handbook of adult literacy: Curriculum design and teaching approaches*. New York: Teachers College Press.

Spender, D. (1982/1989). *Invisible women: The schooling scandal*. London: The Women's Press.

Stanley, J. (1986). Sex and the quiet schoolgirl. *British Journal of Sociology of Education, 7*(3), 275–286.

Stanworth, M. (1983). *Gender and schooling: A study of sexual divisions in the classroom*. London: Hutchinson & Co. Ltd.

Starkey, T. (1978, September). The López family. In *[Appleton]: "I would have told it if I had a chance/Si tuviera chansa, lo habría dicho." A collection of oral histories of ethnic people*. [Appleton], CA.

Steward, M. & Steward, D. (1973). The observation of Anglo–, Mexican–, and Chinese–American mothers teaching their young sons. *Child Development, 44*, 329–337.

Swacker, M. (1975). The sex of the speaker as a sociolinguistic variable. In B. Thorne & N. Henley (Eds.), *Language and sex: Difference and dominance* (pp. 76–83). Rowley, MA: Newbury House.

Swann, J. (1988). Talk control: an illustration from the classroom of problems analysing male dominance in conversation. In J. Coates & D. Cameron, (Eds.), *Women in their speech communities: New perspectives on language and sex* (pp. 122–140). New York: Longman.

Tannen, D. (1982). Ethnic style in male–female conversation. In J. J. Gumperz (Ed.), *Language and social identity* (pp. 217–231). Cambridge: Cambridge University Press.

Tannen, D. (1990a). Gender differences in topical coherence: Creating involvement in best friends' talk. *Discourse Processes, 13,* 73–90.

Tannen, D. (1990b). *You just don't understand: Women and men in conversation.* New York: Ballantine Books.

The Condition of education, 1992. (1992). Washington, DC: U.S. Department of Education, National Center for Education Statistics.

Thompson, G. (1987). *University of California at Berkeley retention update.* Berkeley, CA: Office of Student Research.

Tixler y Vigil, Y. & Elsasser, N. (1976). The effects of the ethnicity of the interviewer on conversation: A study of Chicana women. In B. L. Dubois & I. Crouch (Eds.), *Papers in Southwest English IV: Proceedings of the conference on the sociology of the language of American women* (pp. 161–170). San Antonio, TX: Trinity University.

To everybody. (1990, May 5). *[Appleton Daily News],* p. 12.

Townsend, D. R. & Zamora, G. L. (1975). Differing interaction patterns in bilingual classrooms. *Contemporary Education, 46*(3), 196–202.

Trevino, L. (1988a, August 16). [Shoreline] High prepares for student transfers. *[Appleton Daily News],* p. 13.

Trevino, L. (1988b, August 25). School board stuggles with bilingual plan. *[Appleton Daily News],* p. 11.

Trevino, L. (1988c, October 27). Bilingual sessions dragging. *[Appleton Daily News],* p. 11.

Trevino, L. (1990, May 7). A weekend to celebrate. *[Appleton Daily News],* pp. 1, 9.

Trueba, H. T. (1983). Adjustment problems of Mexican and Mexican-American students: An anthropological study. *Learning Disability Quarterly, 6,* 395–404.

Trueba, H. T. (1987). Organizing classroom instruction in specific sociocultural contexts: Teaching Mexican youth to write in English. In S. R. Goldman, & H.T. Trueba (Eds.), *Becoming literate in English as a second language* (pp. 235–252). Norwood, NJ: Ablex.

U.S. Commission on Civil Rights. (1973). *Teachers and students: Differences in teacher interaction with Mexican American and Anglo students. Report V: Mexican American Education Study.* Washington, DC: U.S. Government Printing Office.

Valdés, G. (1988). The language situation of Mexican Americans. In S. L. McKay & S. C. Wong (Eds.), *Language diversity: Problem or resource?* (pp. 111–139). New York: Newbury House.

Valdés–Fallis, G. (1978). *Code switching and the classroom teacher.* (Language in Education: Theory and Practice No. 4). Arlington, VA: Center for Applied Linguistics.

Vásquez, O. (1993). A look at language as a resource: Lessons from *la clase mágica.* In M. B. Arias & U. Casanova (Eds.), *Bilingual education: Politics, practice and research* (pp. 199–224). Ninety–second

Yearbook of the National Society for the Study of Education, Pt. II. Chicago: University of Chicago Press.

Vygotsky, L. (1978). *Mind in society: The development of higher psychological processes.* Cambridge, MA: Harvard University Press.

Wagner, V. (1989, August 17). The learning curve: Latinos and higher education. *The Sun,* p. 11.

Walsh, C. (1991). *Pedagogy and the struggle for voice.* New York: Bergin & Garvey.

Weber, D. J. (Ed.). (1973). *Foreigners in their native land: Historical roots of the Mexican Americans.* Albuquerque, NM: University of New Mexico Press.

Weinberg, M. (1977). *A chance to learn: A history of race and education in the United States.* Cambridge: Cambridge University Press.

Weinstein, R. S. (1986). *The teaching of reading and children's awareness of teacher expecations (pp. 233-252).* In T. E. Raphael (Ed.), *The contexts of school based literacy.* New York: Random House.

Wells, G. (1981) *Learning through interaction: The study of language development.* Cambridge: Cambridge University Press.

Wells, G. (1985). Preschool literacy–related activities and success in school. In D. R. Olson, N. Torrance, & A. Hildyard (Eds.), *Literacy, language, and learning* (pp. 229–255). Cambridge: Cambridge University Press.

Wertsch, J. V., Minick, N., & Arns, F. J. (1985). The creation of context in joint problem–solving. In B. Rogoff & J. Lave (Eds.), *Everyday cognition* (pp. 151–171). Cambridge, MA: Harvard University Press.

West, C. & Zimmerman, D. H. (1983). Small insults: A study of interruptions in cross–sex conversations between unacquainted persons. In B. Thorne, C. Kramarae, & N. Henley (Eds.), *Language, gender and society* (pp. 103–117). New York: Newbury House.

West, C. & Zimmerman, D. H. (1991). Doing gender. In J. Lorber & S. A. Farrell (Eds.), *The social construction of gender* (pp. 13–37). Newbury Park, CA: Sage Publications.

[White Pine Review] wins literary honor. (1990, January 18). *[Appleton Daily News],* p. 10.

Whiting, B. & Edwards, C. P. (1973). A cross–cultural analysis of sex differences in the behavior of children aged three through eleven. *The Journal of Social Psychology, 91,* 171–188.

Whittle, R. (1990, December 28). More like Mexico. [Letter to the Editor] *[Appleton Daily News],* p. 24.

Whyte, J. (1984). Observing sex stereotypes and interactions in the school lab and workshop. *Educational Review, 36*(1), 75–86.

Wilcox, K. (1982). Differential socialization in the classroom: Implications for equal opportunity. In G. Spindler (Ed.), *Doing the ethnography of schooling: Educational anthropology in action* (pp. 268–309). New York: Holt, Rinehart and Winston.

Willis, P. (1977). *Learning to labor.* New York: Columbia University Press.

Wollenberg, C. M. (1976). *All deliberate speed: Segregation and exclusion in California schools, 1855–1975.* Berkeley, CA: University of California Press.

Yetter, L. (1988, August 29). English-only left out. [Letter to the editor] *[Appleton Daily News]*, p. 24.

Zabin, C. (1991, March 4). Latinos now 61 percent of population. *[Appleton Daily News]*, pp. 1, 9.

Zimmerman, D. H., & West, C. (1975). Sex roles, interruptions, and silences in conversation. In B. Thorne & N. Henley (Eds.), *Language and sex: Difference and dominance* (pp. 105–129). Rowley, MA: Newbury House.

Zinn, M. B. (1979). Field research in minority communities: Ethical, methodological, and political observations by an insider. *Social Problems, 27*(2), 209–219.

AUTHOR INDEX

A

Acuña, R. 51, 53, 54, 55, 56, 69, 70, 71, 205, 211
Aguirre, A. Jr. 4, 211
Almquist, A. F. 52, 216
Alvarado, E. 60, 76, 211
Ammon, P. 12, 18, 199, 201, 203, 211
Applebee, A. 197, 211
Arns, F. J. 7, 223

B

Ball, K. 76, 211
Barnes, D. 8, 203, 207, 211
Bartholomae, D. 123, 205, 211
Blumenfeld, P. 23, 193, 194, 214
Borker, R. A. 21, 218
Brazil, E. 31, 58, 211
Britton, J. 10, 200, 204, 211
Brophy, J. 11, 14, 211
Brown, G. H. 4, 212
Bruner, J. 29, 212

C

Camarena, M. 4, 212
Camarillo, A. 65, 212
Carrasco, R. L. 10, 17, 19, 20, 196, 197, 202, 212, 215
Carter, D. 4, 212
Carter, T. P. 4, 5, 212
Casso, H. J. 72, 212
Castellano, M. 11, 152, 170, 206, 216

Cazden, C. B. 5, 7, 10, 20, 154, 196, 202, 206, 212
Cepeda, R. 72, 212
Cervantes, C. 61, 212
Chacón, M. 4, 212
Cicourel, A. 5, 203, 213
Coates, J. 14, 22, 213
Cohen, E. G. 212
Crumrine, B. 10, 221
Cummins, J. 9, 213

D

Davies, L. 23, 213
Delgado-Gaitan, C. 12, 213
de los Santos, A. G. Jr. 5, 213
Dewey, J. 10, 213
Díaz, S. 12, 20, 202, 213
Dixon, B. L. 5, 213
Donato, R. 73n, 74, 75, 77, 78, 79, 213
Dumont, R. 1, 213
Dunn, G. 56, 213
Dyson, A. H. 197, 198, 214

E

Eccles, J. S. 23, 193, 194, 214
Edelsky, C. 21, 195, 214
Edwards, C. P. 21, 195, 223
Elías-Olivares, L. 18, 220
Elsasser, N. 7, 41, 214, 222
Enríquez, E. 194, 218
Epstein, P. 14, 215
Erickson, F. 13, 26, 121, 214

SUBJECT INDEX